SECRETS OF THE
NORTH ATLANTIC ISLANDS

THE LOSS OF THE STEAMER "HOME" AT OCRACOKE ISLAND

SECRETS OF THE
NORTH ATLANTIC ISLANDS

EDWARD ROWE SNOW

DODD, MEAD AND COMPANY · NEW YORK · 1950

PRINTED IN THE UNITED STATES OF AMERICA
BY THE CORNWALL PRESS, INC., CORNWALL, N.Y.

INTRODUCTION

From time immemorial, islands have held a magic fascination for the human race. The most commonplace island has some legend connected with it, stimulating schoolboys to explore it with the thrilling possibility of smugglers' caves and buried loot. In the midst of a nerve-wracked world, how many adults do not find themselves now and then dreaming of a beautiful island—preferably in the tropics—where none of the hectic rush or dull routine of modern civilized life intrudes? To many of us, an island has become a body of land surrounded by adventure, romance, mystery and excitement. In all of literature, what stories rouse one's sense of adventure like *Treasure Island* and *Robinson Crusoe?*

Having more than my share of the universal interest in islands, twelve years ago I decided that some day I would visit at least an outstanding few of the more than one thousand islands which lie in the Atlantic off the North American continent. Many, like Manhattan, are both famous and mysterious. Others, like Richmond's Island, were once the scenes of exciting events and have now fallen into all but local obscurity. But, whether well known or little known, the islands I finally chose to visit held in their past some secret, or secrets, which had never been divulged.

The secrets which beckoned me had to do with shipwrecks, buried treasure, ghosts, pirates, miraculous escapes and a variety of other strange occurrences. In every case, I found far more than I had anticipated. Several of the stories proved so fascinating that I was forced to return again and again to the scene of their origin.

Only by airplane travel could I keep pace with the clues which led me from Quebec to Atlanta, from Saint John's, Newfoundland, to Beaufort, North Carolina. With backtracking and sides trips, I logged approximately 53,000 air miles, or more than twice the distance around the world. I have been told that I am the only person to visit *all* the islands dealt with in this book, but I think I will not undertake the proof of that statement.

All of the maps and many of the drawings which appear in *Secrets of the North Atlantic Islands* are mine. I have never claimed more than passing fitness as a draftsman and need not, therefore, apologize for illustrations which are intended merely to make the book more interesting and understandable for the reader.

I have listed below persons who proved especially cooperative in producing this book. Several of them were far more helpful than I had any right to hope. Always helping me, although at times I know I taxed both her patience and her endurance, was my wife, Anna-Myrle Snow. Dr. Robert E. Moody was ever willing to advise me. Frank Lanzillo made the jacket illustration, and Robert M. Evans assisted greatly in his translation of one of the Anticosti incidents. John S. Arsenault, Alice Powers Blackington, James L. Bruce, Mme. Eugenie Faure Brugnani, Mrs. Elizabeth Cobb, Edward Dunn, Shirley M. Evans, Margaret Hackett, Francis F. Haskell, Frederick F. Hill, Vincent Holmes, Adeline Jones, Commissioner Frank R. Kelly, Boston Park Department, Harold Langley, Harriette Levensaler, John Light, John L. Lochhead, Gordon MacKay, T. F. M. Newton, Robert I. Nesmith, Foster M. Palmer, Joan Porter, Marion B. Rowe, Clifford K. Shipton, Irwin Smith, Alice Rowe Snow, Donald Burnham Snow, Winthrop James Snow, Victoria Zehringer Snow, R. Shirley Stinson, Mrs. R. Shirley Stinson, Janet D. Stuehling, Jack Stuewe, R. H. Tait, James Van Storey, Dr. Ralph A. Waldron, John G. Weld, and Walter Muir Whitehill also assisted.

Institutions to which I am indebted for help include the Bostonian Society, Boston Public Library, Harvard College Library, Boston Athenaeum, Peabody Museum, Essex Institute, American Antiquarian Society, Maine Historical Society, and the Mariners' Museum, Newport News, Virginia.

Winthrop, Massachusetts,   EDWARD ROWE SNOW
August 7, 1950.

In memory of
LOUIS VERNON HAEGG
my wife's father

CONTENTS

ILLUSTRATIONS

MAPS

LINE DRAWINGS

ILLUSTRATIONS

PHOTOGRAPHS

(The photographic supplement follows page 84.)

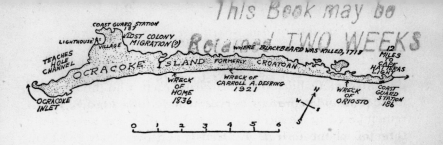

I. OCRACOKE

LONELY Ocracoke Island is a little-known sandy barrier with a long history of dramatic events. Fifteen miles long and a mile and a half across at its widest point, located between Portsmouth Island and Hatteras Island, it is part of the treacherous 190-mile reef which stretches down the North Carolina coast from Cape Henry to Cape Lookout. Blackbeard the pirate lived on the island; people from the Lost Colony are said to have settled there; the side-wheeler *Home* was lost just offshore; and a mysterious couple fleeing from England found temporary refuge on Ocracoke.

To reach Ocracoke and investigate its exciting past, we took off from the efficiently run little airport at Beaufort, North Carolina, with Leon R. Bridgers and Robert E. Lewis. As we flew over Portsmouth Island, where Roy Eubanks presides at the old coast guard station, we noticed aerial activity of a dangerous but vital nature off to our left. We soon learned that we were rapidly approaching an area where marine planes were dive-bombing an island target, creating an intense flash of orange-red flame followed by a drift of white smoke. Time and again the bombers dived at their target before we passed beyond their sight.

Before long, Ocracoke Island Light, one of the oldest in the country, appeared in the distance, and in no time at all we had circled low over Ocracoke Village and set down on the flat plain near the tower on the widest part of the island.

1

BLACKBEARD THE PIRATE

THE NOTORIOUS buccaneer, Edward Teach, who pillaged and murdered under the appropriate name of Blackbeard, is still remembered at Ocracoke. Teach had fourteen wives (only three of whom he legally married) and over forty children. It is a genealogical certainty that some of his descendants still live on the island.

There isn't much doubt, either, that Blackbeard was the most notorious, despicable and ruthless pirate who ever slit a throat or took possession of a woman prisoner. We have heard that there is honor among thieves, but Blackbeard made sure that his buccaneers would fear him rather than honor him.

During World War II, when I had been sent away from the North African campaign to a convalescent hospital in Bristol, England, I was interested to discover that this pleasant British seaport was the birthplace of Edward Teach. Blackbeard, the greatest cutthroat of them all, was born at Bristol in the year 1690.

By the time he had reached his teens, Blackbeard was already sailing the high seas under the command of a cold-hearted devil named Benjamin Thornigold. Without question, Thornigold gave Teach his first lesson in the use of terror as the most effective means of overwhelming a merchant ship on the high seas.

We first hear of Blackbeard as a pirate cruising with Thornigold in the West Indies. A short time later Thornigold and Teach sailed from New Providence for the American mainland, capturing several vessels in quick order. The prizes included a Bermuda wine pinky, a Havana sloop loaded with flour and a craft from Madeira with a rich cargo of silks and bullion.

Their next important capture was a large French Guineaman on which the spoils were valuable, the men soft and the women plentiful. By this time Teach, an apt pupil of a fearsome master, had risen high in the estimation of his captain. Encouraged by his obvious approval, Teach boldly approached Thornigold one day and asked if he could become commander of the latest captured ship. Thornigold roared in pleasure at his protégé's audacity, but nevertheless he shouted that Teach was getting too big for his breeches.

Teach had by now grown a horrible-looking black beard which, according to tradition, was unlike any other beard ever seen. It supposedly covered every inch of the pirate's face, growing up to his eyelids and hiding his ears. In fact, it is said that one couldn't tell where Teach's beard left off and his hair began. The pirate had let both grow extremely long to make himself more formidable and his victims more vulnerable.

Legend relates that when Thornigold finally gave his ambitious pupil command of a ship, the captain also bestowed upon him the name "Blackbeard," by which Teach was known until the end of his days.

When, a few years later, the British government issued offers of pardon to all pirates who would give up their profession, Captain Thornigold, who had a sizable amount of treasure laid away, sold his two vessels to Blackbeard and left the sea.

Blackbeard took the best ship, named her *Queen Anne's Revenge* and began a career of bloodthirsty conquest, pillage and murder never equaled in the annals of modern piracy. One of his memorable captures was near the isle of Saint Vincent, where he overcame the crew and passengers of the *Great Allan,* took all the supplies from her and burned and sank the ship. The men of the *Allan* who chose to live joined the pirates; the others were quickly massacred and their bodies thrown overboard.

Blackbeard next sailed for Bermuda. One dark night off the shores of the islands he noticed the lights of several vessels. In the morning he saw that they were three British

3

sloops, and boarding them in turn, he killed every man aboard who would not join his pirate fleet and then took over the vessels and their cargoes.

The next day Blackbeard fell in with two French ships headed for Martinique, one without cargo and the other heavily loaded with sugar and cocoa. Teach murdered everyone aboard both vessels. He then sailed for the North Carolina shore, where he soon got together with Governor Charles Eden of North Carolina, an official who never looked too closely into a lucrative business arrangement. Blackbeard told Eden that he had found the captured ships adrift at sea and Eden accepted his explanation. They shared the profits and Blackbeard sailed away for more booty.

Blackbeard kept a diary of his exploits, though little of it has been preserved. I quote an excerpt:

> *Such a day, rum all out:—Our company somewhat sober:*
> *—A damn'd confusion amongst us! Rogues a-plotting;—*
> *Great talk of separation—so I look sharp for a prize:—*
> *Such a day, took one with a great deal of liquor aboard,*
> *so kept the company hot, damned hot; then all things*
> *went well again.*

On April 9, 1717, Blackbeard's fleet reached the Bay of Honduras, where they overtook a ship and four sloops. When Blackbeard raised his famous pirate flag, the sailors fled ashore, for they knew their fate if they were caught. The ship was the *Protestant Caesar* of Boston, commanded by Captain Wyar. Blackbeard, chagrined that the men had escaped, burned the ship to the water's edge. He had a special hatred of Boston vessels, for the residents of that port had the unmitigated nerve to hang pirates when they captured them.

Finally, Blackbeard became such a menace to the ocean lanes that the British Navy decided they had to capture him. The man-of-war *Scarborough,* carrying thirty guns, was sent in search of him. One moonlight night the *Queen Anne's Revenge* and the *Scarborough* sighted each other. At dawn they came together. It was a long, hard-fought battle, with blood running into the scuppers of both ships, but Blackbeard, his men collapsing and dying all around him, would not surrender. The British captain ordered the *Scarborough* to retreat to the island of Barbados, and Blackbeard, licking his wounds, could now boast that he had defeated the Royal Navy. It was the first time in maritime history that such an event had occurred.

Blackbeard now sailed in triumph for Spanish America, where his fame preceded him everywhere.

During his return trip, he fell in with a certain Major Stede Bonnet, a Southern gentleman who had adopted piracy as a relief from boredom. Bonnet knew nothing of navigation, and Blackbeard suggested that he join the crew of the *Queen Anne's Revenge*. Bonnet agreed to give up his own ship and go aboard Blackbeard's as a lieutenant.

A short time later Blackbeard decided to take advantage of the royal proclamation of clemency and went ashore at Ocracoke for several months. Then, tiring of his idleness on the island, he went back to his old profession.

His first capture after emerging from his retirement was in the Bay of Honduras, where he overtook the sloop *Adventure,* placing Israel Hands (whom many of you have read about in Stevenson's "Treasure Island") aboard the *Adventure* as captain. Week after week passed with captures almost every day. Finally, Blackbeard took his fleet and headed north, accompanied by Major Bonnet, who by this time had learned enough navigation to become master of his own vessel again.

Arriving off the bar at Charleston, South Carolina, Blackbeard captured five vessels in two days, practically closing the port of Charleston, for no sea captain would sail while Blackbeard was waiting off the bar to pounce on his ship. With more than two hundred prisoners crowded aboard his flagship, Teach then sent his lieutenant, Captain Richards, to Charleston with a demand for a chest of medicine for the pirate fleet. Teach could afford to be arrogant, for aboard his ship as one of the hostages was a prominent citizen of Charleston, Samuel Bragg, one of the governor's councilmen. Captain Richards and his two assistants strutted through the streets of Charleston as they awaited delivery of the medical supplies. Only when they had returned to the pirate fleet with a giant chest of medicine worth over three hundred pounds did Blackbeard release all the prisoners.

There were many who referred to Blackbeard as the very devil himself. One night soon after his successful exploits at Charleston the pirate decided to give an exhibition of his Mephistophelean qualities. He took three of the more venturesome members of his crew aside, and, fixing his ferocious black eyes on them, told of his scheme. "Come," he roared, raising himself to his full height, "let us make a hell of our own and try how long we can bear it."

All four men descended into the hold. After Blackbeard had closed the hatches, he filled several large pots with brimstone and set them on fire. The four pirates remained in the hold, breathing the suffocating smoke into their lungs until all but Blackbeard shouted for air. Then he released the hatches and allowed the others to pull themselves up on deck, not a little pleased that he had held out longer than any of his men.

Next Blackbeard sailed to North Carolina, where he gave another demonstration of his own particular brand of wickedness. His ship loaded with gold and silver bullion and specie, Blackbeard decided to "clean house" and reduce the number of his men entitled to a share in the division of the spoils.

There were four ships in his fleet at that time, Major Stede Bonnet having sailed away on another mission. Blackbeard ordered the smallest of the fleet to stand by, had all the spoils removed to it, and then on the pretense of having the other three vessels careened for cleaning, he ran them toward the shore. Immediately after the ships were stranded, Teach chose forty of his men and with them went aboard the tender which he had kept aside, leaving more than three-hundred men ashore near the careened vessels. Then he sailed off with his picked crew. He never saw the others again.

But even forty men, Blackbeard decided, was too large a number. Reaching an island several leagues away where there was "neither bird nor beast nor herb," he sent ashore seventeen of his men ostensibly to find a suitable place for burying some of his treasure. Once they were on land, Blackbeard hoisted anchor and sailed away, leaving the seventeen marooned on the desert isle. Going ashore on another island, he divided the spoils with the remainder of the crew, reduced by his cunning from almost four hundred to twenty-three. Luckily for the marooned men, Major Stede Bonnet heard about the act and rescued the pirates, allowing them to join his fleet, which was then gaining fame of its own.[1]

Meanwhile, Teach had sailed for Bathtown, for an interview with his confederate, Governor Charles Eden of North Carolina. Teach told Eden that he had decided to retire from piracy again and wished for a pardon, which Eden as governor had the power to grant. Eden compliantly called together a Court of Vice-Admiralty. Its decision was a foregone conclusion and Edward Teach was adjudged an honest privateer again.

In North Carolina today you often hear the legend that Blackbeard fell in love with Governor Eden's daughter when he met her at the conclusion of one of his trips. Present-day historians point out the ruins of a brick tunnel which formerly ran from the water front to Governor Eden's home. This tunnel was believed to have been used by

---

[1] Bonnet was later captured by Colonel Rhet and hanged at Charleston, December 10, 1718.

Blackbeard in bringing his piratical spoils into the governor's cellar. It is said that the girl surprised the pirate one night as he was superintending the storing of goods in the basement of her father's home and that Blackbeard desired her at first sight.

With the consent of Governor Eden, the story continues, Blackbeard paid court to his daughter. The girl loved another, a sea captain who at that time was on the way home from England, but Blackbeard would not accept her refusal. He planned to kidnap the girl and sail away with her. Governor Eden warned his daughter of Blackbeard's plans, and in the middle of the night, accompanied by a Mrs. Margaret Palmer, Miss Eden is supposed to have taken refuge in the Old Marsh House at Bathtown.

Foiled in his plans, Blackbeard put to sea at once and lay in wait for the girl's lover. He captured and killed the young captain, cut off his right hand and packed it in a small silver casket. This grisly package he had delivered to Miss Eden as though it were a costly present. Upon opening the casket the girl cried out in horror and fainted dead away. Within a month she died and Blackbeard's revenge was complete.

Actually, the story, although worthy of Blackbeard, cannot possibly be true, for neither Miss Eden nor Mrs. Palmer was born until after Blackbeard's death, and the Old Marsh House was not built until 1744, over a quarter of a century after Blackbeard fought his last battle.

When Blackbeard was pardoned by Governor Eden's court, he acquired another woman as his wife and with her sailed north to the Isles of Shoals off the New Hampshire coast. There he lived happily with his bride for several weeks while supposedly burying a substantial treasure of silver bars and coins on the two islands of Smuttynose and Londoner. Just as he finished, his men reported a strong British fleet in the offing with one man-of-war on its way to

Londoner Island, and Blackbeard was forced to flee. Mrs. Blackbeard was left on Smuttynose Island to await the return of her husband.

Blackbeard never returned, however, and tradition tells us that the woman lived for many years at the Isles of Shoals until her death in 1735. It is said that her ghost still haunts the lonely isle.

Although he sailed away from the Isles of Shoals with English ships in pursuit, Blackbeard managed to reach his favorite resting place, Ocracoke Island, without being captured. There he went ashore to meet his many wives and children again.

He was not idle for long, however. He soon took a short cruise, during which he decided to again show the other pirates just how fiendish he could be. One evening as he was relaxing with his own men, sitting at table with his two trusty henchmen, Captain Israel Hands and Captain Richards, Richards saw a strange light flash in his leader's eyes. Then Blackbeard reached into his pocket and pulled out several fuses, which he began lighting and attaching to his hideous beard. This was his peculiar custom when he went into battle but he had never before adopted it under peaceful circumstances. The hint was enough for Richards, who fled to the deck above, but Hands had fallen asleep and had no idea what was taking place.

Blackbeard now began to chuckle to himself and cocked two of the many pistols which he always carried. Then he gave a great bellow, awakening Hands.

"What's the trouble?" asked the sleepy pirate, blinking and rubbing his eyes. Blackbeard smiled diabolically across the table.

"There's no trouble," he replied. "We're just going to have a little fun. It's a new game I've made up." Blackbeard drew in his breath, and at the same time held the guns under the table.

"Now," he shouted, blowing out the table candles to leave

the cabin in darkness, "here's something to remember me by!" In the blackness of the cabin, he crossed his arms and fired blindly under the table. Then he rushed up on deck, throwing the guns into the sea.

Israel Hands, badly wounded, was taken into his own quarters, and later carried ashore at Bathtown. When he recovered, the authorities placed him under arrest, for, unknown to the pirate, the forces of law and righteousness had finally united against Teach.

The British Government determined to destroy Blackbeard, for they had never forgotten his insult to the Royal Navy in forcing the *Scarborough* to retreat. The British took several steps at this time, the first of which was to see that Blackbeard was properly condemned as a pirate. Because the Governor of North Carolina could not be trusted to take action against his friend and confederate, it was arranged that Governor Alexander Spotswood of Virginia should issue his own proclamation. On November 24, 1718, Governor Spotswood offered a reward of one hundred pounds for Blackbeard, and corresponding sums for each member of his crew or the crew of any other pirate vessel.

Now the British Navy put Captain Robert Maynard in charge of an expedition to capture Blackbeard. Captain Maynard chose two crews from the men-of-war *Pearl* and *Lime,* then at anchor in the James River, hired two small sloops capable of sailing over the shoals around Ocracoke and lost no time in getting his expedition ready for sea. Sailing from Kicquetan on the James River, the two vessels reached the mouth of Ocracoke Inlet, where the spars and masts of Blackbeard's vessel were sighted.

On Ocracoke, Blackbeard saw the two sloops approaching, and stripped his own vessel for action, but by the time Maynard had reached a point off Ocracoke Village, darkness had fallen and the British leader wisely decided to anchor for the night. The channel was dangerous and the shoals were many.

With the coming of dawn, Maynard sent a small boat ahead to guide him towards Blackbeard's refuge, but in spite of all precautions, the sloops grounded many times. To lighten the vessels, Maynard first ordered all the ballast thrown overboard, and then he commanded that the water barrels be emptied. Finally, he approached within cannon shot of the enemy. Blackbeard opened the engagement by firing a cannon ball, but it failed of its mark and hit the water between the two sloops of the Royal Navy. Maynard hoisted his King's Colors at once, whereupon Blackbeard cut his anchor cable, planning to make a run for it if he could.

Blackbeard had a tremendous advantage with twenty cannon aboard, but he did not realize that the sloops had abandoned their heavy armament for the sake of greater mobility. The lighter vessel, Maynard's sloop, was able to slide over the shoal, but her companion ship maneuvered against a sand bar and stuck fast. Deciding to get action even though he must do it alone, Maynard ordered his sweeps put out. He rapidly closed the distance between his sloop and the pirate ship.

Soon the two opponents were near enough for hailing, and Edward Teach aimed his foghorn voice at the plucky representative of the British Navy. "Damn you for villains, who are you?" Blackbeard shouted, "and whence came you?"

"You may see from our colors we are no pirates," replied Maynard.

"Come aboard with your small boat!" suggested Blackbeard cannily. But the British captain was not to be caught.

"I cannot spare my boat, but I will come aboard of you as soon as I can with my sloop." This answer so upset the pirate that he rushed below for a quick drink of rum before continuing the conversation.

"Damnation seize my soul if I give you quarter or take any from you," the angered buccaneer roared.

Maynard's reply rang out across the water. "I don't expect quarter from you, nor shall I give any."

In spite of his bold words, Maynard knew that he was up against the strongest pirate in all the western seas, a brutal man with a staggering record of victorious battles and bloody captures.

In maneuvering for a good position, Blackbeard's craft ran aground, giving the British hope for a successful approach. But the tide came in and freed the pirate vessel. Shortly afterwards the wind died down completely. Again resorting to his sweeps, for Maynard was afraid that his prey would escape, the British officer drew up close to the notorious buccaneer.

Suddenly Teach, deciding that he would have to fight his way out, ordered his battery of guns made ready and gave the command to fire. It was a mighty broadside, and when the smoke died down twenty-nine of Maynard's men were either killed or wounded. Maynard ordered all survivors below and pretended that he, the helmsman and two sailors were the only ones aboard who were still alive. Blackbeard, his spirits rising at his apparent success, drew closer.

"Look at 'em!" he shouted. "Why, there's only three or four of them still alive! All the rest are knocked on the head. Let's jump aboard and cut the others to pieces! Let no one live to see sunset!"

And jump he did, with fourteen of his men. Maynard then signaled for his own sailors below to rush up on deck. The element of surprise made it an even fight, for Maynard had twelve men and Blackbeard fourteen.

Both captains spotted each other at the same moment and both fired instantly. Blackbeard missed fire with his first pistol and then again with his second. But Maynard had lodged a bullet in the pirate's leg. The buccaneer still had his cutlass, however, a mighty weapon which two ordinary men would have had difficulty in swinging. The opponents parried for a moment, and then Blackbeard brought his heavier blade down on the British officer's sword, snapping it off at the hilt.

"Now I've got you!" shouted the triumphant pirate. But he had spoken too soon, for just as he drew back for his final thrust, an alert British marine stabbed him in the throat.

Shrieking like a wounded beast, Blackbeard turned against his new attacker, but he was soon hemmed in at all sides. On and on he fought with cutlass and pistol, until he was bleeding from twenty saber thrusts and five gun wounds. Bending over to fire once more, Blackbeard was seized with a terrible convulsion and tottered for a moment in helplessness. His cutlass and pistol clattered to the deck. Then the mighty pirate dropped dead before the man who had sworn to capture him, Robert Maynard of the Royal Navy.

By this time Maynard's other sloop had arrived on the scene and her crew boarded the pirate ship on the opposite side. The marines rushed below just in time to prevent the explosion of Blackbeard's ship, for they caught a giant Negro about to throw a blazing torch into an open powder barrel. The Negro and the remaining pirates surrendered.

Before sailing away from Ocracoke, Captain Maynard himself boarded the pirate ship and went into Blackbeard's cabin, where he found many letters and papers, among them incriminating correspondence between Governor Eden, the Governor's collector, the secretary to the Governor and Blackbeard. There was other correspondence with certain traders from New York, but the Eden letters were particularly damning. No wonder the Negro crewman had tried to blow up the ship!

With this incriminating evidence on hand, Captain Maynard ordered Teach's head severed from his body and suspended from the bowsprit of the victorious sloop,[1] and the British vessel sailed into Bathtown, displaying this grisly emblem of victory.

Respecting no authority, when Maynard reached Bath-

---

[1] Blackbeard's skull was later obtained by one of the influential men of Bathtown, who had part of it lined in silver in a strange manner, after which the bolder members of the man's family would drink toasts from it.

town he took a squad of men to the Governor's storehouse. Here he ripped open the doors and discovered eighty hogsheads of sugar, sixty of them belonging to the Governor and twenty to his secretary, Mr. Knight. The eighty barrels for Eden and Knight had been declared by Blackbeard as their part of the booty in a recent capture. Although Governor Eden managed to weather the storm, his secretary, made of weaker material, fell sick with the "fright," and died within a few days of the shameful discovery.

Fourteen of the captured pirates were hanged a short time later; a few of the remainder were pardoned. Among those pardoned was Israel Hands, Stevenson's character in "Treasure Island," who was allowed to sail back to England, where he occupied himself as a professional beggar for many years.

What happened to the fabulous Blackbeard treasure?

There are two important incidents which would indicate the possibility that Blackbeard did bury treasure at the Isles of Shoals. The first occurred some time before 1820 when Captain Samuel Haley of Smuttynose Island uncovered five bars of silver on the shore. After realizing $3000 from the sale, he devoted some of the money from his unexpected find towards building a breakwater across to Malaga Island.

The second incident took place during World War II. At the height of the conflict several government representatives went ashore on Londoner Island where they made some interesting discoveries. Mrs. Prudence Randall, daughter of the Reverend Frank B. Crandall, owner of Londoner Island, told me the following story about their visit:

> *Government men who went ashore on our island without permission found definite indications that there was a substantial amount of silver still buried on the landing side of the beach facing the Star Island Hotel. The*

exact location is about halfway across the half-moon stretch of the beach.

We have been told that Blackbeard buried his loot here. He buried silver bars on our island and his crew buried some silver bars and a considerable quantity of pieces of eight over on Smuttynose. Captain Haley found the silver bars on Smuttynose Island but never located the pieces of eight. The remainder of that treasure is just below the water line on the beach east of the breakwater at Smuttynose.

We were told that our silver bars, probably worth thousands of dollars, are so far down in the sand that it would be a very costly experiment to locate them and bring them to the surface. Actually, I have been within a few feet of their location.

Both my father and I agree that there is no doubt that the treasure is still buried down in the sand between the high and low water marks. Yes, we'll share fifty-fifty with any ambitious person who cares to search for it, after they have our permission in writing to land on the island.

The sand shifts so rapidly out there after every storm that whereas you might know where to look one week, why the next week everything would be changed. But the silver doesn't move much, as it is too heavy, and it's there waiting for someone with money and a feeling for adventure to go after it. The government men gave it up, saying that it would take several thousands of dollars for dredges and pumps.

Prudence Randall

Did Blackbeard himself leave any clues as to where his treasure was buried? It is said that on the eve of his last battle, one of Teach's henchmen questioned him about it. The pirate's reply was typical: "Nobody but the Devil and

15

myself know where my treasure is, and the longer liver of the two shall have it all."

Teach died as he had lived. One of the most ferocious pirates of all times, he ended his career as he probably would have chosen, fighting a worthy opponent in the throes of a struggle to the death.

THE FEMALE STRANGER

ANOTHER STORY connected with Ocracoke Island, one of the strangest on record, cannot be substantiated except in part. It begins in the year 1790, when Lord Arthur Sutledge returned to his home in Lancaster, England, after graduating from Oxford University. Self-satisfied, rather reserved in bearing, Sutledge set about what, in his position of wealth and refinement, he felt would be a fairly easy conquest of the lady he wished to marry, Miss Anna Seaton. She accepted his attentions and their engagement was soon announced. But during an angry quarrel, and for a reason never revealed by either party, the engagement was broken off, and the very next year Miss Seaton married Edward Brimmer of Preston.

Two years later the couple were blessed with a baby girl, whom they named Ellen Jane. The birth of the child appeared to have restored friendly relations between Lord Sutledge and the Brimmers. When Anna Brimmer began failing in health in 1804, and the next year her doctor recommended a long ocean voyage as a means of regaining strength, Lord Sutledge volunteered to have his own family nurse take over the care of little Ellen until the Brimmers returned. Sutledge saw the happy couple off at Portsmouth aboard the proud East Indiaman, *Earl of Abergavenny*, on February 1, 1805. A week later he learned that the ship had gone down with the loss of 247 people, including the Brimmers.

After a few months Lord Sutledge legally adopted little

Ellen. As the years passed and Ellen matured, she grew more and more to resemble her mother, the woman to whom Sutledge had once been engaged. On Ellen's twentieth birthday he could stand it no longer. Breaking down emotionally as he sobbed out his story, he told the girl that she was the daughter of the woman he had once hoped to marry. The following afternoon Sutledge came to Ellen quietly and asked for her hand in marriage. Already upset by his revelation of the day before, Ellen was stunned by his request and terribly embarrassed. Not wishing to hurt him more than she could help, she pleaded for a few days in which to consider his proposal. He agreed readily, believing in his enthusiasm that he would soon become a bridegroom.

Actually, Ellen was in love with a young surgeon in the British army named John Trust. The next evening at their usual rendezvous on the terrace back of the Sutledge home, she told John of the proposal. Since there seemed no immediate answer to the problem, the lovers decided to let matters rest. Perhaps, they thought, a solution would present itself.

One night the inevitable happened—Lord Sutledge discovered the pair in each other's arms. Sutledge, his dreams crashing down, became enraged. He attacked the surgeon but was thrown off; undaunted, he grabbed a cane and rushed again at Trust. The young doctor defended himself by pushing Sutledge head over heels down the terrace steps.

Tragically for all concerned, Sutledge hit his head against an iron scraper on the lower step and lost consciousness. Realizing his serious condition, Trust called the local doctor, who announced that there was no hope. Lord Sutledge, he said, would die within a few hours.

As predicted, Sutledge died before midnight, and the two lovers, conferring hastily, decided that their only chance was to flee to Liverpool that night. They arrived early the next morning and were married within a few hours. Then, hiring a small fishing craft, they succeeded in reaching Trust's brother, Captain Harold Trust of the British sloop-of-war *Defense*, anchored off the Downs.

Once safe in Captain Trust's cabin, the couple told him all the details of their frightful experience. The next afternoon the daily newspapers were sent aboard ship, carrying the information that John Trust and Ellen were being hunted as murderers. The lovers' flight to Liverpool and subsequent marriage had been discovered. Luckily, the *Defense* was soon to leave on a West Indian cruise. Before the couple were detected, the sloop sailed from England. Five weeks later her anchors rattled down in Bridgetown Harbor, Barbados.

Farewells were said ashore at Bridgetown one night, and the *Defense* sailed away. The fugitive pair soon obtained passage aboard an American sailing vessel which set them ashore at Ocracoke Village on Ocracoke Island. Using assumed names, they could probably have lived there for the remainder of their lives free from danger. Unfortunately, however, Ellen had developed ship fever. There was no doctor at Ocracoke and John Trust realized that he would have to take her to a city on the mainland where she could be properly treated. Finally, Captain James Low of the schooner *Echo* from Antigua agreed to sail them to Alexandria, Virginia. By this time Ellen was desperately sick.

On October 9, 1816, the *Echo* reached Alexandria. A carriage took John and his sick wife to Gadsby's Tavern, which still stands in that illustrious city. A doctor, hastily summoned, told John that there was little hope for Ellen's recovery.

A few days before her death, Ellen called to John late one night and asked him to promise her to act according to her instructions.

"Please listen carefully," she began. "I know it isn't long that I have to live, and I don't want you to be caught and sent back to England. Let's keep our secret. Promise me that you won't put my name on the gravestone."

John finally consented, and Ellen was greatly relieved. She died on October 14, 1816, and was buried in Saint John's Episcopal Cemetery in Alexandria. The inscription on the stone has made it famous the world over. The title FEMALE STRANGER, was the anonymous phrase John Trust used to designate his wife. He had respected her dying wish and omitted her name from the stone. But as a final gesture of recognition, he placed her age on the tomb, twenty-three years and eight months, with a poem expressing his love for her and a quotation from the Bible.

Eventually, Trust journeyed to New York and obtained employment. He worked hard and faithfully for fourteen long years. Then, in 1831, the theft of a sum of money in his office placed everyone under suspicion, and Trust was questioned about his background. When he gave Alexandria, Virginia, as his birthplace, the authorities discovered that he was not telling the truth. But to tell the truth would have involved him in the death of Lord Sutledge, and so Trust remained silent and was sent to prison for eight years because of a crime he did not commit.

Released from prison in 1839, John Trust returned to Alexandria to visit the tomb of his wife. Then he attempted to obtain employment, but as he was aged beyond his years, no one wanted to hire him. And so Trust drifted into the woods north of Alexandria, where he built himself a shack on the Potomac River, spending his time doing odd jobs, fishing and hunting. By 1845 he was well known in the vicinity as "Cabin John."

The cabin which he had built was beautifully situated near a pleasant meadow, bounded on one side by vine-clad hills and on the other by several inspiring valleys. As he wished to visit Ellen's grave as often as possible, John built himself a small skiff. In it he would row down the river and into Hanley Creek, which ran past the Alexandria cemetery. When he finally reached the grave of his loved one, he placed flowers on the tomb and rested by its side for several hours

19

before rowing the long distance back to his cabin. John Trust kept up this strange ritual for many years, and was perfectly contented with his existence during this period. While not seeking companionship, he never shunned it and thus became known as one of the interesting characters along the Potomac River.

In 1851 he began to realize that the infirmities of age were upon him; no longer could he row down the river and back to pay his respects at the tomb of the FEMALE STRANGER. After careful deliberation, he decided to chance a letter to his brother Harold in England, asking him to come to America for a farewell conference. Unfortunately the letter wasn't delivered for almost a year, as it followed the naval officer to China and back to England. Then, as soon as Harold could arrange his affairs, he obtained a leave of absence and sailed to America.

When Harold Trust finally neared the shack along the Potomac, neighbors told him that no one had seen his brother for more than a year. Trust proceeded to the cabin but he realized that something was wrong the moment he saw the building. Its door was hanging loose from one hinge and the entrance was barred by heavy cobwebs. Pushing aside the webs, Harold strode into the shack. There was no sign of his brother. He hunted desperately for some written word or message which John might have written, and finally his patience was rewarded when his eye caught a letter nailed to an upper shelf. The letter was marked "Harold." He opened it and read:

> Dear Brother,
> I have waited longingly for you to come but now I realize it is too late. Bury me with her in the Episcopal Cemetery at Alexandria. Her grave is marked a FEMALE STRANGER. Take me there by water at night.
>
> John

Harold strode out of the hut, folding the letter as he went.

That afternoon he and the neighbors scoured the underbrush around the cabin. Finally, as the sun was setting, they located the bones of luckless John Trust hidden in a tangle of weeds beside a small brook which he was said to have loved. The skeleton was identified by a family ring encircling one of the fingers. Harold quickly made the necessary arrangements to carry out his brother's final instructions. He ordered the cabin utterly destroyed at once and took John's remains back to Alexandria.

Two nights later a group of silent men rowed up Hanley Creek, carrying an unusual burden in their craft. They were soon at work in the cemetery. Removing the cover of the tomb marked FEMALE STRANGER, they placed John Trust's last mortal remains beside the skeleton of his long-dead wife. When the tomb was sealed, Harold Trust paid off the silent workers, who quietly moved away into the night, haunted by the strange affair in which they had participated.

The following morning Harold Trust left Alexandria for New York, and within a few days he had sailed for England with the strange secret locked in his breast.

Many of the landmarks in the story of the ill-starred couple can be visited today. Ocracoke Village has hardly changed since 1816, and Cabin John, where John Trust lived on the Potomac River, is plainly marked on any atlas or map just a few miles up the river from Washington. Gadsby's Tavern, where Ellen Trust died in 1816, still stands in Alexandria, Virginia, with a metal plate set into the door frame of the room in which she passed away. But most interesting of all is the famous inscription on the cemetery stone which reads:

To the memory of a
FEMALE STRANGER
whose mortal sufferings terminated
on the 14th day of October 1816
Aged 23 years and 8 months

21

This stone is placed here by her disconsolate
Husband in whose arms she sighed out her
latest breath and who under *God*
did his utmost even to soothe the cold
dead ear of death

How loved how valued once avails thee not
To whom related or by whom begot
A heap of dust alone remains of thee
Tis all thou art and all the proud shall be

To him gave all the *Prophets* witness that
through his name whosoever believeth in
him shall receive remission of sins

Acts. 10ᵗʰ Chap. 43ʳᵈ verse.

THE LOSS OF THE "HOME"

THE SHIPWRECK of the famous paddle-wheel steamer *Home* on October 9, 1837, was one of the outstanding disasters along the Atlantic Coast during the first half of the nineteenth century. It created a sensation all over the country and aroused intense feelings of compassion for the victims and their unfortunate families. As late as 1900 the wreck of the *Home* was still talked about with awe and intensity up and down the Atlantic seacoast.

When a ship engaged in the usual pursuits of commerce goes down with her crew, it is regarded as an unfortunate event, and the public feels pity for the little circle of mourners. But with the sinking of a passenger vessel carrying great numbers of men, women and children from all walks of life, the average person experiences real sorrow as the details are made known. It is then that the awful dangers of the sea are brought home to all of us.

Like the loss of the steamer *Portland* off Cape Cod in 1898, the wreck of the *Home* in 1837 is that unusual type of marine catastrophe which holds public attention for years after the tragedy would normally be forgotten.

The paddle-wheeler *Home* was launched from the yard of Brown & Bell at New York in April, 1836. Fitted for sea at the foot of Delancey Street, she was ready for travel a year later. No expense had been spared to make her interior appointments equal to those of the finest hotels of the period, but the structural weaknesses of her hull were readily apparent to men of the sea. In fact, expert examination of the *Home* would prove that she was never intended to sail the high seas! Her beam of twenty-two feet was totally inadequate for her length, two hundred and twenty feet. In speed, this floating palace was among the fastest of the day, and her owner, Mr. James B. Allaire of New York, was very proud of this feature of his ship.

All went well on the *Home's* voyage from New York to Charleston, South Carolina. On her second trip the *Home* broke the speed record between the two ports, negotiating those rather stormy coastal waters in the amazing time of sixty-four hours.

When news of this swift journey became known, many who would ordinarily have traveled by other means were attracted to the *Home*. The voyage between New York and Charleston was advertised to prospective customers as a trip of less than three days; the same journey had taken their parents one or two weeks to complete!

There was talk that after a few more trips the *Home* would be groomed for a spectacular journey across the ocean. The merits of the vessel were so widely discussed that whispers of doubt as to her safety were dismissed with a tolerant but contemptuous smile by her owner, Mr. Allaire.

On the afternoon of Saturday, October 7, 1837, the *Home* was scheduled to sail. Excitement over the voyage reached a feverish pitch. Many who had not planned to make the trip were carried away by the enthusiasm of the crowd and boarded the vessel in New York. Possibly fifteen persons sailed on the *Home* who failed to give their names to anyone ashore. Because of this circumstance, the total number of persons on board the *Home* was never definitely known. We are sure, however, that there were forty-five in the crew and ninety known passengers, of whom about forty were women and children. James B. Allaire, the owner's nephew, was among the passengers, for his uncle had certain theories about the performance of his vessel which he wished to have tested on the high seas.

At exactly five o'clock the crew removed the gangway, and farewells rang through the air as the paddle-wheels began pushing the *Home* seaward. Passing through the Narrows, the steamer was proceeding at better than twelve knots. When she reached the new Captain Gedney Channel, the pilot was confused by what was then known as the Romer Buoy, and the steamer grounded heavily on a shoal. She hung there for more than three hours until the incoming tide freed her. Then, after a private conference between Mr. Allaire and Captain Carleton White, the steamer proceeded down the bay.

Drawing abeam of Sandy Hook Light, the *Home* veered to starboard and began her long trip toward distant Charleston. On and on the paddle-wheels carried her, until by Sunday morning there was much talk among the passengers and crew of a record passage between Sandy Hook and Charleston.

That evening the wind changed and came strong from the northeast. The waves built up to eight and ten feet in height, and after a few violent wrenchings, the steamer began to take in water. The storm grew in force and intensity, and by midnight the *Home* was wallowing in the dangerous seas of a mighty gale, a predicament for which she had never been built.

The rolling, pitching and straining of the ship soon weakened the engine-bed, and the paddle-wheels were slowed down. Whenever a sea caught the *Home* under her port guardrails, the ship listed sharply to starboard, throwing the port paddles out of water, where they vibrated alarmingly as they turned uselessly in the air. Sometimes it was ten or twelve minutes before the captain could bring the *Home* around and get the ship back on an even keel.

James B. Allaire was much embarrassed by this sudden turn of events. He had made the journey to satisfy his uncle that the *Home* could reach England, and here she was in difficulty on a trip from New York to Charleston! He retired to his stateroom and did not appear for hours.

Meanwhile, the crew set emergency sails on the masts. This steadied the ship for several hours, but after sunset Sunday the storm grew more and more intense. The seams in the hull widened, the water streamed in and it required the struggles of the entire crew to keep the pumps from losing their battle with the sea. In spite of their frantic efforts, around midnight the water in the hold began to climb, slowly but inexorably. Inch by inch it rose, until Captain White was so frightened that he sent out an appeal for help to all able-bodied men. Handbasins, buckets, pails, chamber pots and pans were called into service as bailers. Many of the panic-stricken women volunteered for duty. But in spite of everything, the water rose higher and higher.

With the coming of dawn, the bleak, forbidding shores of Cape Hatteras were seen ahead, and soon Cape Hatteras Light was visible twenty-three miles away. Captain White ordered the course changed so that the *Home* would clear the terrible reefs which surround Hatteras Island, and before long the lighthouse faded from view. By two o'clock in the afternoon it was agreed that the danger of hitting the shoals was over, and a new course was chosen to bring the *Home* nearer to land. Captain White decided to beach her on the nearest shore if there was no other alternative.

Hour after hour the *Home* had been weakening and working loose. By this time the bow actually rose and fell three or four feet from the rest of the vessel's framework with every successive wave! A short time later the entire hull began to work up and down, bending and twisting as though it were a deckload of laths which had been swept overboard. This sickening motion roused terror among the passengers, and many gave up all hope of survival and consigned themselves to their Maker. Others made desperate preparations to save themselves and began cutting blankets into long, thin strips with which to secure themselves to spars or timbers when the ship went to pieces. (The two life preservers on the boat had been appropriated by two of the men passengers, and the *Home* carried only three lifeboats for passengers needing twice that number.)

At six o'clock Monday night water reached the engines; they gave a final quiver of vibration and died. In the strangeness of that unexpected silence, every passenger felt that the end could not be far away. Beyond sight of land, the ship was running before the wind with her emergency sails, but without the engines her speed was more than cut in half.

Shortly before nine o'clock that night the storm clouds broke asunder, revealing a light high in the heavens. It was the moon, shining eerily through the rifts in the clouds. By its pale light the distant shores of Ocracoke Island were visible, and soon afterwards the atmosphere cleared enough to reveal the friendly flashes of its lighthouse.

Captain White decided to beach the *Home* at Ocracoke Island, and gave orders to the helmsman to that effect. Nearer and nearer the straining side-wheeler came toward the beach. Soon the moonlight revealed close at hand the glistening backs of the great waves as they hurled themselves up on the shore, and Captain White ordered all hands to prepare for the violent shock when the two-hundred-and-twenty-foot vessel would hit the sand. By ten o'clock the *Home* was in the outer breakers, and soon a mighty wave worked itself under the stern, lifted the *Home* high amidships and sent her forefoot crunching to pieces as she struck bottom more than four hundred feet from the island itself.

There was instant chaos and confusion. Above the noise of the breaking timbers could be heard the desperate shouts of men, the high shrieks of women and the children's piteous cries of terror. The *Home* settled into the sand and began to break up. Mr. Allaire had come out on deck some time before to talk with Captain White, and after a hasty conference, they ordered the women and children forward so that they would be nearest the shore. The screaming and wailing continued with husbands and wives clinging together and children clutching their mothers as the various groups were escorted forward. Still blowing a gale, the wind pushed the giant billows through the weakening structure of the *Home* and on toward the shore, where they broke with a thunderous crash.

By now most of the women and children had reached the forecastle. Several waves swung the *Home* around until her bow was headed at an angle toward the beach. Then a tremendous comber formed, and there were shrieks of alarm as this mountainous sea began to rush toward the doomed ship. Catching the women and children on the forecastle in its powerful grasp, the wave pulled them all into the ocean together. All but two of the women were drowned at once. Of the children only one, a boy of twelve, was thrown up on the beach alive.

The two women who had survived could be seen clinging desperately to fragments of wreckage as they floated toward the island. Mrs. LaCoste of Charleston, an elderly woman of tremendous size, had lashed herself to a deck settee before the wave washed her off the forecastle with the others.

Shipwreck news always travels rapidly, and as Mrs. LaCoste struggled feebly toward land, the islanders were there waiting for her. Each wave carried her closer to them, until finally a giant wave caught the terrified woman and carried her along at an alarming speed. As it broke against the sand, it swept Mrs. LaCoste high on the shore. Then when it started to recede, the undertow began to pull her out to sea again. At that moment the islanders rushed into the surf and rescued her.

Mrs. LaCoste was so heavy that she had extreme difficulty in walking, yet this almost helpless Charleston lady was one of the two women swept off the ship who survived to tell her thrilling story!

Out on the wreck of the *Home* plans were made to launch a craft into the sea. The jolly-boat was put over and three men jumped aboard. Before they could push off, a wave caught the boat and capsized it, drowning the men. Another wave then snapped the lines and sent the empty jolly-boat to wreck itself on the shore. The long-boat was dropped into the sea and twenty-five passengers scrambled in. Another great wave caught them, capsized the long-boat and drowned every one of the twenty-five persons.

A short time later large fragments of the paddle-wheeler began to break away from the hull of the vessel, and many of the braver men attached themselves to the floating timbers. A few of them reached shore in safety. The *Home's* smokestacks began to totter shortly afterwards, and the port stack fell just as a woman passed beneath, carrying her baby toward the upper deck. Both mother and child were killed instantly.

A Mrs. Schroeder of Charleston had lashed herself to a deckrail brace, when a wave swept her overboard. Still tied to the brace, she dangled there, submerged with each passing wave. Mr. Vanderzee of New York noticed her helpless position. Reaching down over the side, he seized her by the clothes and held her up for some time, but was unable to pull her over the rail. Finally, the strain proved more than he could stand, and he was forced to release her. As she dropped into the water again the brace gave way. When a wave caught her and threw her up on the shore, she frantically dug her feet into the sand and clung to the brace. In spite of her efforts, the undertow pulled her halfway down the beach. Still tied to the brace, she rolled up again with it before the next great billow thundered on the shore and engulfed her. Time after time she reached a position on the beach almost above the high tide mark only to be swept out by the next sea. By now, her strength was rapidly leaving her. Just as Mrs. Schroeder lost consciousness, a summer visitor at Ocracoke, a man named Littlejohn, saw her struggles. He rushed into the water and saved her, cutting her free from the brace.

Mrs. LaCoste and Mrs. Schroeder were practically naked, and the natives carried them up the beach and covered them with sand as protection against the cold. They were later taken to the home of William Howard on the island.

Out on the *Home,* the Reverend George Cowles of Danvers, Massachusetts, was struggling to help his wife to safety. The well-known minister always experienced a "strong and invincible dread of the sea" but had been persuaded to take the voyage because of the fast passage of the *Home.* While he was helping his wife reach the ruins of the quarterdeck, Reverend Cowles met Steward David Milne. The steward was the son of a minister, and Reverend Cowles comforted him with a verse from the Bible. Placing his hand on Milne's shoulder, he said:

"He that trusts in Jesus is safe, even amid the perils of the sea." Those words were the last the minister was to utter, for just as he finished speaking another great wave swept across the forecastle, and when it was gone both Reverend Cowles and his wife had vanished.

The *Home's* forecastle snapped off a short time later. On it were Captain White and seven men. They floated ashore in safety, and all eight were rescued. Of the estimated one hundred and fifty persons who went aboard the *Home* in New York, twenty passengers and twenty of the crew survived. On reaching land, most of the men were forced to walk and run up and down the beach to keep warm, for they were stark naked.

By noon they found themselves "among a set of savages" from Ocracoke Village. But there were several families who did everything in their power to help the survivors, and these benefactors included the Howards and the Wahabs, leading families on the island today. Soon the pitifully depleted ship's company was housed and fed. Before the end of the week, the forty survivors had been taken by inland water craft toward their respective destinations.

In all, twenty dead bodies from the *Home,* including that of Mrs. Cowles, washed ashore and were buried by William Howard in his cemetery.

It is easy to criticize a sea captain after a disaster, and several passengers from the *Home,* led by a Mr. C. C. Cady, claimed that Captain White was intoxicated most of the journey. However, Steward Milne quickly came to the captain's rescue, and defended him warmly.

"Captain White drank only two glasses of absinth cordial all the time during the trip," said Milne. "It was a passenger, Captain Alfred Hill, who was drunk and others confused the two. Captain White didn't eat, sleep or lie down in his office until he was entirely worn out by fatigue and watching day and night at the wheel."

At the time of the disaster India rubber life preservers were just coming into use. There were only two aboard the *Home,* but both successfully carried two passengers ashore. One of these survivors remarked that had the side-wheeler been supplied with a hundred and fifty life belts instead of two, there would have been few deaths that October day in the great surf off Ocracoke Island.

THE "ARIOSTO"

In 1899 Ocracoke Island was the scene of the worst ship-wreck of the year, in which twenty-one lives were needlessly sacrificed. The steamer *Ariosto*, laden with a valuable cargo of wheat, cotton, lumber and cotton-seed-meal, had sailed from Galveston, Texas, in December, 1899, bound for Nor-folk, Virginia. Here she was to refill her coal bunkers for a trip to Hamburg, Germany, with thirty in the ship's company.

As the *Ariosto* approached Cape Hatteras on the night of December 23, her commanding officer, Captain R. R. Baines, was only mildly disturbed to notice a rough sea driven by a southwest wind, for the sky was clear overhead. By mid-night, however, thick weather set in; there was a heavy rain and the waves grew higher and higher.

At 3:45 the next morning the chart room telegraph bell rang. Captain Baines jumped up to answer it, but before he could act, the *Ariosto* hit bottom with a thumping crash. The captain rushed out onto the bridge to discover that the steamer was entirely surrounded by white water. He imme-diately sent up several rockets of distress. A short time later he could see that they were answered on shore.

Unfortunately, Captain Baines did not realize that his ship was only seven hundred yards off Ocracoke Island, two miles southwest of the life-saving station. He believed him-self aground on the dreaded Diamond Shoals, and, afraid that the *Ariosto* would slide off the bar and sink into deep water, he ordered two boats put over.

Within half an hour, both the pinnace and the lifeboat were launched with twenty-six of the crew aboard. Captain Baines ordered the occupants to "get away clear" and stay in the lee of the vessel until daylight. He remained aboard the *Ariosto* with three of the men.

The pinnace weathered the gale for half an hour before the swift-moving tide carried her out of the lee of the ship.

She soon capsized. A few minutes later the lifeboat was also swept away and capsized. One by one, the sailors sank to their death in the icy water. Only five survived.

Seaman Elsing, a powerful swimmer, battled through the breakers without help and reached shore; Fireman Petersen and Seaman Saline were able to swim back to the *Ariosto* and were soon hauled aboard. Fireman Henroth clung to wreckage until he reached land, collapsing as the Ocracoke life-savers pulled him from the water. As we shall see, the fifth survivor, Boatswain Anderson, had the narrowest of all escapes.

As dawn broke in the eastern sky, Keeper Howard of the Ocracoke Station ordered the international flags MK set, indicating to the survivors on the *Ariosto* that they were to stand by their ship until rescued. Keeper Howard had first learned of the wreck from Surfman Guthrie who had been hiking the beach on duty at 4:00 A.M. when he noticed the masthead lights of the ship just off the shore. The life-savers had done everything in their power to prevent the sailors from leaving their ship in the lifeboats. Because their efforts failed, twenty-one lives were lost. But there were still six men out on the wreck.

As a result of a hurricane the previous August a deep gully ran through the island and it was only with the assistance of seven civilians from Ocracoke Village that Keeper Howard's men were able to ford the gully and pull the life-saving gear to a point opposite the doomed ship.

The first shot from the Lyle gun was fired at 5:45 A.M., but the steamer was still six hundred yards from shore, and the line dropped into the sea. As the life-savers pulled the spent line ashore, it caught onto a heavy object and the men pulled with great difficulty. Finally, the object was hauled up on the beach. It was a man—unconscious but still alive! He was the boatswain, Anderson, who had been in the capsized lifeboat. While struggling to swim ashore, he had felt the line fall across his body. He had managed to fasten it around his arm just before he lost consciousness.

By eleven o'clock the *Ariosto* was only four hundred yards off the beach, and a Number Four line was shot across her bow. The life-savers sent out the breeches-buoy and hawser, but the *Ariosto* was by now rolling horribly in the surf, making it almost impossible to operate the tackle.

The men on board the wreck watched their chances, however. Soon the first sailor jumped into the breeches-buoy and started on his perilous trip to safety. Then, one by one, the crewmen took their long journey to the beach. Finally, only Captain Baines remained aboard. It was quarter past two that afternoon when he jumped into the canvas carrier and started ashore. Ten minutes later he landed safe and sound on the beach.

Captain Baines wrote a letter to Keeper Howard some time after the shipwreck, and it was signed by all nine survivors. In it, he said:

> ... *That such a lamentable loss of life occurred is not in any way to be attributed to the want of diligence, promptitude or lookout of Captain Howard and staff, and we are unanimous in our conscious declaration that their action in the matter was all that could be done, and is deserving of the highest commendation.*

THE "GEORGE W. WELLS"

THE GIANT SCHOONER, *George W. Wells,* from Boston to Fernandina, Florida, ran into a severe tropical hurricane on September 3, 1913, and early that same afternoon, with sails blown away and distress signals flying, she was driven ashore in a sinking condition six miles southwest of the Hatteras Inlet Life-Saving Station. The *Wells* had already been sighted by the crews of two stations fourteen miles apart on Ocracoke Island, and when she finally grounded four hundred yards off the beach, the life-savers were ready to help her. Within twenty minutes the first Lyle gun was fired. Because of the high winds, however, the line failed to reach the foundering ship. Two other attempts were also unsuccessful.

Captain York of the *Wells* now let into the raging sea a small spar with a line attached. Twenty minutes later the spar was retrieved on the beach, and the line was secured to a regular breeches-buoy apparatus with the whip line. The schooner's crew soon hauled out the apparatus and made it fast.

The straining and twisting of the schooner snapped the whip line, but the original line was still intact. The life-savers attached another line to the original, and this was sent out to the ship and made fast. Then the tackle on shore parted. The life-savers worked feverishly for half an hour before the tackle was repaired and all was in readiness for passengers on the wreck to come ashore.

Three children, two women and a man passenger were landed safely on the beach, and then the crew was brought ashore. Captain York was the last to leave his schooner. The entire ship's company was escorted to the Hatteras Inlet Station on Ocracoke Island, where they were taken care of for several days.

The great 2970-ton schooner *George W. Wells* was the first six-master ever constructed. She was built by Holly M. Bean at Camden, Maine. Strangely enough, she had collided with the second six-master ever built, the *Eleanor Percy*, off Cape Cod in the fall of 1904. Both vessels survived the crash. At Ocracoke, however, the *Wells* was totally wrecked, and her timbers are still to be seen from time to time at the lonely island.[1]

---

[1] Another wreck at Ocracoke in the same storm was the British steamer *Glensen* of Whitby, England. Bound from Newport News to Brunswick, Georgia, she was wrecked two miles south-southeast of Ocracoke Station. All on board, twenty-four in number, were saved.

Since Aycock Brown wrote his *Saturday Evening Post* story about Cape Hatteras and Ocracoke Island in 1940, life there has changed considerably. Mrs. Charlotte O'Neal, the island's midwife, has passed away, and two others have taken her place, Mrs. C. F. Williams and Kathleen Bragg. Tom Howard has retired as postmaster and his daughter-in-law is now in charge. Amasa Fulcher's general store was bought out by Garrish and O'Neal, and Fulcher is dead. George Gaskins, the man who "escaped both shipwreck and marriage," has died.

Aycock Brown, the island's historian, told me that he went there in 1928 to spend two weeks and stayed seven years. A former editor of the Beaufort, North Carolina, *News,* he published six issues of the *Ocracoke Island Beacon.* At present he runs a column in the Greensboro paper called "Covering the Water Front" and is prominent in the Lost Colony National Park activities at Manteo.

One of our objectives at Ocracoke was to visit the wreckage of the *Carroll A. Deering,* which had been washed ashore at various places on the island. I had promised to bring back a souvenir from her to my friend, Carroll A. Deering, for whom the ill-fated five-master was named.

The story of the *Deering* has remained one of the unsolved mysteries of the sea ever since she was discovered abandoned, caught in the dreaded Diamond Shoals, on January 31, 1921.[1] Not a single member of her crew was ever seen again, dead or alive.

The largest fragment of the *Deering* to be found on Ocracoke includes her capstan; it is located exactly halfway down the island's shore, seven and a half miles from either end.[2]

---

[1] I tell the *Deering's* story in full in my *Mysteries and Adventures Along the Atlantic Coast.*

[2] Aycock Brown visited the wreck shortly after the hurricane of 1944, finding the capstan section completely washed clear of sand, and made a fine photograph of it at that time. Now the wreck is sanded over again and the capstan barely shows above the surface of the beach.

From it, I secured several fragments of timber and three long iron spikes to take to Carroll Deering.

In exploring the island, we saw some of the wild ponies which still roam the sand dunes at Ocracoke, but we were disappointed to learn that Pony Penning Day, the exciting auction which used to be held on the Fourth of July, is a thing of the past. Formerly, there were from three to four hundred untamed ponies at Ocracoke, but now there are not over sixty and only an occasional pony is sold. The ponies live on beach grass, which is plentiful, and find water by pawing down with their hoofs anywhere on the island to a depth of eighteen inches.

In Ocracoke Village we met Mrs. Stanley Wahab. Her husband, who, we learned later, was responsible for bringing electricity and other improvements to Ocracoke, is a descendant of an Arabian, Tom Wahab, who was cast ashore on the island in 1780, the only survivor of a disaster at sea. Tom Wahab's son married a daughter of Tom Howard, descended from a member of Blackbeard's crew who settled on Ocracoke, founding what has become the leading family of the island.

The various cemeteries at the island well repay the time spent studying their stones. The Wahab-Howard cemetery has about thirty-seven graves, the most interesting of which is that of Warren O. Wahab. Read the dates carefully:

SACRED
TO THE MEMORY OF
W A R R E N   O .   W A H A B
SON OF
JOB AND ELIZA WAHAB
BORN SEPTEMBER 10th 1885
DIED SEPTEMBER 14th 1842

The same cemetery reveals that Agnes Howard, widow of William, the grandson of William Howard the first, died in 1857 and bears the unusual inscription:

She was!
But words are wanting to say what.
Think what a wife should be:
She was that!

After visiting the graveyard we walked down toward the
lighthouse, and beyond the white sides of Ocracoke Light
we could see the buoys out in the channel. We had noticed
many memorials to the earlier inhabitants of Ocracoke, but
where, I began to wonder, was a reminder of the notorious
pirate, Edward Teach, who had made the island his home
for many years? I found my answer on U. S. Government
Chart Number 1232. There, clearly designated, and
bounded by those same buoys at which we were looking,
was Teach's Hole Channel. Now that his old residence has
been torn down, the channel is the only memorial of Ocracoke's most famous, and infamous, citizen!

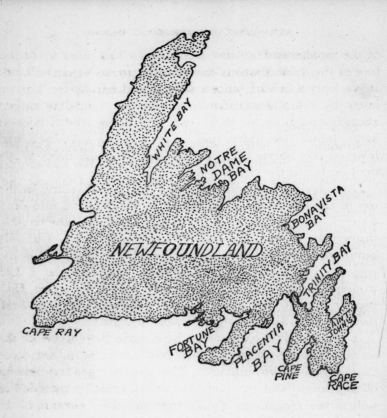

II. NEWFOUNDLAND—
THE GREAT ISLAND

I WANTED next to visit Newfoundland, for I felt sure that this great outpost of the North American continent would reveal many secrets to me. The airplane was again my choice as a means of travel. Ten hours after leaving Boston we approached the rocky coast of Newfoundland in a gale which rocked and pitched our plane. Then, at the height of the wind, word came over the wireless that a fearful wreck was even then taking place on the shore of Newfoundland.

It was my thrilling experience to fly down over the wreck

of the motorship *Harcourt Kent,* which had piled up at the foot of the Saint Shotts cliffs in southeastern Newfoundland. It was only a quick glimpse we had of the freighter, but we knew by radio that there were eighteen Canadian sailors aboard, struggling for their lives. When we landed later at Saint John's, we heard that several daring fishermen had lowered themselves over the cliffs and rescued every single man on board the wreck.

Later I visited the cliffs of Saint Shotts. Climbing to the top of the hill where overhanging ledges drop off into deep water, I thought back over the history of many of the terrible shipwrecks which have occurred in the vicinity. Literally hundreds of vessels have been wrecked at the foot of the jagged cliffs around me. The ships whose stories I had studied with most interest were the British transport *Harpooner* in 1816, the steamer *Anglo-Saxon* in 1863, the *Scottish King* in 1898 and the *Assyrian* in 1902.

It is impossible to mention here more than a few of the terrible marine disasters which have occurred at and near Cape Race, Newfoundland. The almost legendary wrecks of the *Comus* and the *Lady Sherbrook* must be included as well as the *Helgoland,* the *Herder* and the *Laurentian.* In 1873 the cable ship *Robert Low* went to the bottom, followed in 1890 by the *Hanoverian* and the *Grasbrook.* The *Texas* piled up on the ledges in 1896, and two years later the *Abbeymore* crashed to her doom. In 1902 the bark *Aquitaine* was lost, and the *Lusitania* foundered the same year. The full list is a long one, too long to set down here.

Radio, radar and other modern devices to aid navigation have greatly reduced the number of shipwrecks in the vicinity of Cape Race, but for many years the residents of the area could depend for part of their living on a disastrous shipwreck every so often. While they did everything possible to save lives, they were also ready to salvage the cargo of an unfortunate vessel which lay shattered on the rocks below their cliffs.

Cape Race has often been called the world's most important headland because of its proximity to ships traveling the Great Circle Course. Thousands of craft every year are reported by the observer at the Cape, and other thousands pass by in bad weather undetected. Without question, many of the most terrible tragedies in the entire maritime history of the New World have occurred where the rugged Newfoundland cliffs meet the sea. All types of vessel have sunk into the waters at the foot of the mighty precipices around Cape Race. Brigs, barks, schooners, ships, steamers, tankers, freighters and even battleships lie broken at the foot of the jagged cliffs.

The region is continually threatened by fog. It appears without warning, winter and summer, in rain, snow or sunshine. The ocean currents are eternally confused here, as the warm Gulf Stream vies for mastery with the icy Arctic Flow. The conflicting currents produce a strong northerly sea-river which smashes against the headland at Cape Race, one branch running up the eastern coast toward Saint John's, and the other pouring into Saint Mary's Bay.

The western-bound vessel comes under the influence of these currents hours before drawing abeam of Cape Race. If it is foggy or stormy, her captain may find himself in danger on what is called the Cape Race Front. The eastern-bound navigator is drawn by the current heading toward Saint Mary's and may find himself in a treacherous position on Cape Race Back, as the natives call it.

The residents of Trepassey told me that there wasn't a reef, rocky headland or rock-bound island that didn't take its name from one or more shipwrecks which had occurred nearby. In one thirty-mile strip of jagged coast every crevice has lodged some fragment of wreckage. At the foot of the tall, stately cliffs the ocean bottom is covered with broken hulls, and each little cove has become a graveyard for scores of victims taken from the sea.

The native fishermen here are brave and philosophical,

but practical about the wrecks which occur near their homes. They are heroic in saving lives of the victims of those terrible disasters, but after the last person has been taken off a wreck, their attitude changes. Then they become the salvagers of the coast and must be dealt with in businesslike fashion.

In 1879 three freighters were wrecked less than two miles from each other in a single day during a siege of heavy fog. A small fishing dory put out to rescue the crew of one of the freighters, and after getting the first two loads ashore, went back for the captain and his officers. "Thank God you noticed us on the ledge out there," exclaimed the captain of the wrecked freighter. "I don't know how to express my thanks." "You're welcome," one of the fishermen replied laconically. "We've been up these three nights since the fog got thick, waiting for you to strike, and you didn't disappoint us." The fisherman and his mates then proceeded to salvage the freighter's goods.

In the old days the Newfoundlander needed "a few wrecks" to get him through a hard winter. An illustration of this is a conversation held between the late Monsignor Power, Bishop of Saint John's, and the Reverend Father Hennebury, whose parish included Cape Race.

"How do you think your people will get along this coming winter?" the Bishop asked.

"Very well, your Excellency," the priest answered, "with the help of God and a few good wrecks."

The people of Newfoundland have more than reciprocated for what they salvaged. At the turn of the present century, one man was known to have buried 229 bodies of shipwreck dead. The government had never advanced him a penny for all his work. Many others in the same community had received the Royal Humane Society's medals for outstanding bravery in rescue work.

On many occasions the people of Newfoundland have warned the owners that their stranded vessels would not last more than a day or two, at most, only to have the owners commission salvage ships at great expense from Halifax which arrived after the broken vessel had completely disintegrated. On other occasions the sinking wrecks have pulled the salvage ships down to their doom.

Knowing all this, the natives like to go aboard with their own methods of salvage before it is too late. It usually pays the owners to co-operate. An example of what may happen to a stubborn owner occurred in 1902, when the steamship *Assyrian,* sailing for Montreal, grounded just below the Cape lighthouse. The owners, seeing her rest easily on the strand, decided to wait for a wrecking tug. The tug arrived at the end of a week and began to free the *Assyrian,* but that very afternoon a gale swept in and snapped her back. As her stern drifted ashore, the wrecking tug was caught and destroyed also. The *Assyrian's* freight, worth $420,000, was a total loss. If the Newfoundlanders had been allowed to begin salvage work at the time of the shipwreck at least a quarter of the cargo would have been saved.

On another occasion the Cape Race fishermen noticed a bark drifting in on the rocks. They launched their dories and rowed out. When they climbed aboard they discovered that she was a Bergen bark bound for Quebec in ballast to load lumber. The only commodity she carried was rocks for ballast. One of the fishermen expressed himself in no uncertain terms: "I don't know what the Almighty is thinking of this year. First he sends us a bad fishery, and now he sends along a damned Norwegian bark loaded, of all things, with rocks."

Another amusing salvaging story concerns the wreck of the *Scottish King,* in 1898. This ship slid in over a reef near Seal Cove at the height of a furious gale. She ripped her bottom badly but then proceeded to slide in on a natural cradle in shallow water, where she came to rest, buoyed perfectly by the rock formation. When the storm died down, there was a frantic scramble to lighten her before she snapped apart. The cargo included several hundred cases of Apollinaris water. The ship also carried two thousand cases of the best champagne, but the fisher folk of Newfoundland were not too familiar with either the taste or the value of that beverage.

The natives enjoyed the effervescing alkaline qualities of the mineral water until their stomachs rebelled. When they finally came upon the champage, they were too suspicious to sample it, and a sharp Halifax trader bought the whole expensive consignment from them at ten cents a bottle.

In 1902 the French bark *Aquitaine,* sailing for Saint Pierre and Miquelon, slid up on a Newfoundland reef in a remote part of the coastline. When her crew reached shore, they told the natives to take as much of the cargo as they wished. By the time the authorities heard of the wreck, two days had elapsed. The natives had used those two days to advantage. The revenue men soon took over the vessel, but not before fully fifty per cent of the cargo had vanished for regions unrevealed. Without question there are still many quarts of choice beverage from the *Aquitaine* preserved in some out-of-the-way fishing village, awaiting an occasion for celebration.

Prominent in the list of disasters along the rocky Newfoundland coast is the tragedy in which the British transport *Harpooner* was hurled to her doom in 1816. Aboard were 385 men, women and children returning from Quebec to London after the War of 1812. Most of the passengers were attached to the Fourth Veteran Battalion of the British Army. There was also a canine passenger on board. Before leaving Quebec, the *Harpooner's* master, Captain Joseph Bryant, had purchased a fine Newfoundland dog which he named "King." By the time they were a week at sea the captain and the dog were close friends.

On Saturday morning, November 9, 1816, the *Harpooner* was proceeding on her course past Newfoundland when a violent gale of snow and rain hit the area. Soon the mighty seas were pushing the transport off her route toward the great cliffs of Saint Shotts. At eight o'clock that night the second mate's watch was called, and an hour later came the cry dreaded by all sailors: "Breakers ahead! Breakers ahead!"

A moment later the *Harpooner* hit heavily and then slid off the reef, only to crash against another. The vessel began to fill and settled over on her larboard beam, half submerged, but supported by the rocky ledges which surrounded her.

In the midst of these disastrous events the dog King rushed up to his master and seized his coat sleeve, pulling him in the direction of the cabin. And the dog was just in time, for the cabin was ablaze from several lighted candles which had overturned in the crash. Captain Bryant, with the help of a dozen sailors, soon put out the flames. He knew then that King was not only a good friend but a reliable assistant.

A short time later a mighty wave picked up the *Harpooner*, lifted her completely off the ledges, and sent her wallowing in the heavy seas closer to shore. All was now hopeless confusion. Many men, women and children rushed up on deck; scores of others drowned in their cabins.

Again the ship hit on a gigantic undersea ledge and lodged there fast on the rocks. This time the masts were toppled by the force of the blow. Several passengers tried to float ashore on them only to be dashed to death at the foot of the cliffs.

By four o'clock the next morning, when the storm seemed to let up, Captain Bryant had to devise some way of getting his passengers ashore. He knew that the *Harpooner* could not stay afloat much longer. As the first step in his plan, he asked his mate, Mr. Hadley, to take four men in the jolly-boat and try to reach a rock on shore.

Ten minutes later the men pushed off in the jolly-boat, the mate frantically trying to steer with the tiller as his crew rowed with all their strength. Several giant waves swept in and nearly capsized them, but finally they managed to reach the shelter of a huge rock a hundred yards away from the *Harpooner*. Just as they were about to land, the jolly-boat was smashed to pieces under them. The five men scrambled to safety, however, and soon they had climbed up onto the highest point of the rock. There they discovered that the rock was still a good distance from the shore itself. Nevertheless, it was so high that they would be safe there indefinitely.

Mr. Hadley now shouted across to Captain Bryant: "Let your log line float in so we can secure it." The captain signaled to show that he understood. Soon the log line began to drift in toward the rock. It came closer and closer, and then suddenly the current swept it away from the rock. Time and again, the log line was rereeled and let over, but always the current proved too strong.

Parts of the ship were now breaking off and drifting toward the rocky shores. Captain Bryant realized that at any moment the *Harpooner* might break up altogether and that all on board would be lost. Then he had an idea born of desperation.

The captain called his dog King. Talking in an encouraging tone to the huge animal, he tied the log line to the dog's collar. Then he pointed to Mr. Hadley on the rock.

"Go get him!" shouted the captain, and a moment later King sprang from the rail into the sea.

From his perch on the rock, the first mate began whistling and shouting to the dog. Fifty yards from the ship, however, King encountered a heaving mass of wreckage which swept him under the surface of the sea. When he emerged, it was seen that a small timber had caught in the log line. King seemed to be having difficulty in breathing, and Captain Bryant ordered the dog pulled back to the ship. The order came just in time, for King was choking because of another fragment of wood twisted between the line and his collar.

45

"I'll know better now," said the captain, and removed King's collar.

"Do you still want to try it?" he asked King. The dog wagged his tail and barked eagerly. "All right, then, but this time we'll do a better job of it."

The captain looped the log line around King's shoulders and secured it with a bowline. Then he patted the dog once or twice before signaling him to jump. King sprang into the swirling seas again and made for the rock where the mate was waiting with his men. This time King swam much more easily, and the men played out the line rapidly as he neared the rock. Soon he was caught in a giant swell and with a mighty crash he was pushed high up on the rock within a few feet of the waiting men. Before they could reach him, however, the undertow snatched the dog back into the swirling seas at the foot of the cliffs.

When the next wave broke the men were ready. The mate had locked arms with the others, forming a human chain. As King was again lifted high on the rock, he swept in past Mr. Hadley, who made a frantic try for him and missed. But as the undertow began to pull the dog out again, the log line came in near enough for the mate to grasp it. "Hold on," he shouted, and the men fought with all their might to prevent the deadly undertow from carrying King back into the ocean once more.

For a split second it seemed that both men and dog would be dragged out into the boiling sea, but the sailors clung desperately to the rocky crevices on the ledge, and the crisis passed. A moment later King was well above the water as the wave receded far down the rock. The men were able to pull him up to safety. When the next swell thundered against the mighty boulder, King and the five men were beyond its dangerous reach.

The mate shouted to the captain that King had arrived safely with the log line. The captain now tied a heavier line to the end of the log line and signaled ashore for the sailors to pull away. Finally, the heavy line reached the rock. The sailors then retrieved from the sea enough timbers to build a makeshift tripod. When the tripod was secured to the rock, several of the *Harpooner's* crew decided to attempt swinging hand over hand along the hundred yards of line between the ship and the rock.

The *Harpooner* had struck at nine o'clock Saturday night, November 9, and it was almost Sunday noon when the first sailor swung out and started for shore. He landed on the rock amid cheers from the other survivors. A short time later a block was rove on and a sling arranged. One by one the survivors were hauled up onto the huge boulder. Only one passenger who attempted the trip failed to gain the rock. This unfortunate man was struck by a gigantic sea as he swung out onto the line, lost his hold and fell to his death in the ocean!

Each trip in the sling took ten minutes, and late Sunday afternoon there were still over one hundred and forty people left on the ship. Since the storm seemed to be going down, several of the men decided to risk throwing themselves into the sea and swimming for shore. Most of them perished immediately.

Around four o'clock Sunday afternoon it was decided that the women should try to ride the sling. The first woman to make the attempt was a soldier's wife, who was expecting a child at any moment. Her husband was placed in the sling first in order to hold her in his arms, and then the trip shoreward began.

All eyes were upon the couple as they moved slowly toward the rock. The survivors watched tensely as a wave swept over the pair. When it had passed, they could see that wreckage had caught in the block. The next wave freed the line, however, and the soldier and his wife neared the great rock where the men waited to help them. Now the most difficult part of the task was at hand—hauling the double load up the face of the boulder.

The men on the rock went down the line hand over hand to reach the couple, now almost submerged by the surf. Finally, they succeeded in pulling the husband and wife to safety. Less than two hours later, sheltered from the wind and spray by the other survivors, the soldier's wife gave birth to a baby boy.

By now the situation on the *Harpooner* was desperate. The vessel could not last much longer; the sun had set and there were still over a hundred survivors waiting to be taken ashore. But at seven o'clock Sunday night, the heavy rope, frayed by constant working and swinging across the sharp rocks, snapped in two. There was no way of replacing the line, and many gave themselves up to despair. The tide slowly rose again, and great waves swept completely over the wreck. The *Harpooner* was going to pieces.

The first break came around midnight at the stern. Then, at four o'clock Monday morning, the *Harpooner* split in two up to the forecastle. In the mad scramble for safety, dozens were swept overboard to their death, and soon the ship was almost bare of human life. Captain Bryant stayed aboard his ship until almost the last, when a gigantic wave caught him and pulled him under. He was never seen again.

The very last person to leave the broken vessel was an old subaltern, Lieutenant Mylrea of the Fourth Veteran Battalion. Over seventy years of age, he remained on the vessel until everyone else had either been rescued or lost. Then he thought of his own life and leaped into the sea. Miraculously, he floated in to the rock and was pulled to safety. Of the last one hundred aboard the *Harpooner,* over fifty were drowned.

The 177 survivors remained on the rock until dawn. The men were able to start a fire, and carried the soldier's wife and baby near its warmth.

At daybreak, November 11, 1816, on Monday morning, it was low tide. The storm had gone down enough for five men to wade ashore. A mile away they found the home of a fisherman. They were taken to Trepassey, and by Wednesday evening, November 13, all but five of the survivors had reached that town to be billeted in the homes of the good people there. Near the wreck at Saint Shotts, in the fisherman's house, the soldier, his wife and newborn baby were

recovering from their terrible experience. All survivors reached Quebec the following spring.

In the tragedy of the *Harpooner* 208 persons lost their lives. King, the dog, saved the lives of more than 155 of the 177 survivors. Someone, sometime, should erect a monument on the great cliffs of Saint Shotts in memory of King, the heroic Newfoundland dog.

On April 27, 1863, the steamer *Anglo-Saxon* was approaching Chance Cove, Newfoundland, in a thick fog. Her captain was more than ordinarily anxious to meet the news boat and deliver dispatches from Europe. The telegraph cable extended from Cape Race to the United States, and westbound steamers threw overboard sealed packets at the Cape with the latest press dispatches from Europe. It was now the height of the Civil War, and sea captains vied with each other to meet the news boat first so that their messages could be telegraphed by cable to New York.

Before she reached the waiting news boat, the *Anglo-Saxon* crashed at full speed into a rocky headland ravine. Her voyage was over.

The scenes which followed have rarely been equaled in the terrible history of disasters at sea. The great liner, with 444 persons aboard, was slowly battered to pieces as the rocks held her in the mammoth gully in which she had crashed. Sheer, towering cliffs surrounded her and there seemed to be no means of escape.

The captain had blown his signals of distress for five long minutes before the steam failed, and the fishermen from the nearby villages were already on their way to the wreck. When they saw that the *Anglo-Saxon* was foundering at the bottom of a precipitous cliff, they almost gave up in despair. But one fisherman did not give up and ordered the others to hurry home for long lines of rope. When they returned he made a boatswain's chair. Then he had himself and seven other men lowered down from the top of the cliff to a rocky abutment one hundred and fifty feet above the broken steamer. Here he set up a tripod with block and tackle.

Into the block he rove several hundred feet of line and then gave careful instructions to the other men. They were to lower him down the face of the cliff, until he was just above the foaming waves. He would then order someone to jump from the steamer and he would reach down into the water, pull the survivor across his knees and both would be hoisted up to the top of the cliff. It was a wild, fantastic scheme, but the fisherman was unable to watch the people on the wreck drop to their death without trying to do something to help them.

When the fisherman reached the water's surface, the stern of the *Anglo-Saxon* had been shattered, and there were two hundred frantic survivors crowded on the forecastle. Several men were willing to attempt the jump. One leaped into the sea, swam across the waveswept gully, and was seized in an iron grip by the hands of the fisherman.

The survivor was pulled into the boatswain's chair, and the other rescuers on top of the cliff began the long, hard pull to bring their double load to safety. Time after time the same plan was carried out, but finally darkness prevented any further rescues that evening. Early the next morning the fishermen were out on the cliffs again. One hundred people were brought to safety by the end of the second day.

The forecastle of the *Anglo-Saxon* was still wedged into the gully the following morning. By noontime the last living person had been removed from the wreck. In all, 127 survivors had been rescued from the *Anglo-Saxon*. Three hundred and seventeen were drowned.

As the men on shore worked to save the passengers, the women and children of the neighborhood guided them away from the cliffs and into their warm homes. Later, when the storm subsided, those bodies which could be found were buried in a common grave on the hilltop.

The last great disaster along the shores of Newfoundland was a double shipwreck which occurred during World War II. On February 18, 1942, the American destroyer *Truxton* and the cargo vessel *Pollux* ran aground during very bad weather. Although the full details were never made public, it is known that there were 119 drowned from the *Truxton* and eighty-five lost from the *Pollux*. Before the war the *Pollux* had been known as the *Comet,* a mail steamer which ran from New York to Cuba.

For many years after the wreck of the *Harpooner* in 1816, ships carried Newfoundland dogs on board to be used in case of disaster. The last known wreck involving one of these famous dogs occurred in December, 1919, when the steamer *Ethie,* with ninety-two passengers aboard, ran ashore at Bonney Bay, Newfoundland. The surf was so high and treacherous that it was impossible to launch the lifeboats.

A Newfoundland dog aboard the *Ethie* had a small line placed in his mouth and with it he swam through the boiling seas to reach shore. As in the case of the ill-fated *Harpooner,* a heavier line was then sent in. The fishermen from a nearby village set up a tripod on the beach and rigged a boatswain's chair. Everyone aboard the *Ethie* was eventually landed ashore, including a tiny infant, which was transported across the raging seas in a mail-bag.

A famous poet and a famous painter are both associated with Newfoundland dogs. George Gordon, the great poet known as Lord Byron, was the owner of a superb Newfoundland which he called "Boatswain." Born on the Great Island in 1800, Boatswain soon became one of the closest friends Byron ever had, and when the dog died in 1815 at Windsor, England, the poet wrote a beautiful epitaph in his memory. Byron said of his canine friend:

> *Beauty without vanity,*
> *Strength without insolence,*
> *Courage without ferocity,*
> *And all the virtues of man without his vices.*

The eminent Scotch painter, Sir Edwin Landseer, often portrayed the black and white Newfoundland, and one of his best paintings shows the dog with a little child he had saved from drowning. Copied all over the world, the painting did much to popularize the breed.

Unfortunately, World War I with its food shortages nearly brought an end to Newfoundland dogs in England. Many of them were destroyed because they required large amounts of food. Their loss is also felt in America, where the growing tendency for small homes and apartments lessens considerably the popularity of dogs of this variety. It is sad to see that such a kindly, capable animal is being allowed to die out.

The history of Newfoundland, I found, is fascinating and varied, beginning with the explorations of John Cabot in 1497, up to the present day.

Newfoundland is the great outpost of a mighty continent. With scarcely a fort or a gun, she stands firm and invincible, unassailed and impregnable. Until 1948 she rejected affiliation with Canada, but now the Great Island has become a part of that neighborly nation to our north. Newfoundland has a small population compared to many other Canadian areas, although its settlement reaches back through the years.

John Cabot first sighted Newfoundland in 1497, sailing there on his ship the *Matthew* from Bristol, England, in one of the fastest cross-Atlantic voyages recorded in that century. Leaving Bristol on May 2, 1497, he reached Newfoundland less than four weeks later on May 27. Making the most of his discovery, Cabot went back to England with news of his good fortune and received ten pounds as a reward from Henry VII, August 10, 1497. This sum compares favorably with the purchase of Nahant, Massachusetts, for a suit of clothes and the acquisition of Manhattan Island for $24.

From the beginning, the English made use of the fine fishing grounds which surround Newfoundland. King Henry, on February 3, 1498, presented Cabot with a pension of twenty pounds, and gave exclusive rights to "John Kabotto" to fish around Newfoundland at his own expense. In 1501 Cabot lost his exclusive rights, and others were allowed to fish in Newfoundland waters.

On June 11, 1583, Sir Humphrey Gilbert sailed from Plymouth, England, with five small vessels, bound on an expedition to discover the Northwest Passage to China. Only four of his ships reached what is now St. John's harbor on August 3. At Saint John's, Gilbert found a hardy community of Basque fishermen ruled by an admiral and he acquired possession through the ancient English custom of turning over a sod and waving a hazel wand. After exploring extensively along the Newfoundland coast and losing another of his ships, the *Delight,* he gave up his plans to find the Northwest Passage and started back for England. On his return trip he was overtaken by a terrible hurricane, and was last seen on September 9, 1583, aboard his sloop the *Squirrel.* With his final known words he shouted across to a larger vessel in his fleet, the *Golden Hind,* that he was "as near heaven by sea as by land." Neither Gilbert nor his little 10-ton sloop was ever seen again.

After the defeat of the Spanish Armada in 1588, England embarked on further exploring and colonizing activities. In 1610 Sir John Guy founded a company to exploit Newfoundland's resources. Guy did much to turn the fishermen of Newfoundland against him and they retaliated by destroying his supplies and burning his sawmill. In 1615 Captain John Mason, an Oxonian who wrote the first book on Newfoundland, soon had matters in hand again. Then Sir William Vaughn began a colony of Welshmen at Trepassey Bay, later selling out to Lord Baltimore.

In 1662 Charles II of England, for reasons which are still mysterious, granted the French permission to send a colony of their own countrymen to Grand Placentia, Newfoundland. After many vicissitudes of war and peace, the Treaty of Utrecht, signed in 1713, took away all French rights to the soil of Newfoundland. The French were still allowed to fish off its shores, but it can be said that from that moment on, the cause of France began to fail in America.

Although a French fleet captured Saint John's on June 27, 1762, the English recaptured it the same fall. In the Treaty of Paris which followed in 1763, France lost everything in

America except the tiny islands off Placentia known as Saint Pierre, Miquelon and Langlade.

Pirates have often ravaged the shores of Newfoundland. In the year 1612 Captain Peter Easton, with forty ships at his command, sailed for Newfoundland, to plunder the fishing villages and shipping along the coast. Stealing munitions and supplies, he persuaded over a hundred volunteers to join him and forced four hundred other Newfoundlanders into piracy against their will.

On June 4, 1614, Captain Henry Mainwaring also ravaged the fishing vessels off Newfoundland and pressed four hundred more natives into his pirate fleet, inducting one man out of every six. The next year Mainwaring sailed for Spain, but was later pardoned by the government and sent to the Barbary Coast. There he fought against the Barbary pirates, one of whom was Captain Peter Easton, the former ravager of the Newfoundland coast, who had joined the African group in 1613.

By far the most spectacular pirate who ever visited the shores of Newfoundland was Captain Bartholomew Roberts. Roberts, unlike most buccaneers, never touched liquor. Tea was his strongest drink. He made his men retire every night at nine o'clock, and if one of them seduced a woman, the penalty was death! Gambling, dice rolling, and card playing were forbidden on his vessel. But in spite of his restrictions (or perhaps because of them), Roberts captured more ships than any other marauder of the sea. Four hundred vessels of all types fell before his disciplined buccaneers.

When he reached northern latitudes, Roberts set his eyes on the coast of Newfoundland. He debated long as to the best way of overcoming the fishermen there. His method was unusual, if not unique.

He sailed into Trepassey Bay with trumpeters blaring forth and drummers beating steadily away. In less than two hours of terrific fighting Roberts destroyed or sank all but one of twenty vessels anchored in the bay. Going ashore, he plundered the settlements and burned the fishing flakes and warehouses. When he gathered the Newfoundland fishermen together, seeking volunteers to join his fleet, he declared that he had never asked a man to become a pirate against his will. In spite of Roberts' tactful technique, not one fisherman would join his crew, and the gentlemanly pirate sailed out of Trepassey Bay with his original force of buccaneers. The people of Newfoundland never forgot his brief visit.

Newfoundland, since World War I, has been considered a British Dominion, and as the years went by its financial condition grew so serious that the mother government set up a Royal Commission of Inquiry. On February 22, 1933, Lord Amulree was appointed to conduct a thorough investigation into Newfoundland's problems. His report recommended that Dominion rights be suspended until such a time that the island again became self-supporting.

The British House of Commons agreed to make good the budget deficits of Newfoundland, and the island Parliament was suspended for the emergency. The Governor and a Commission of Six, appointed by the United Kingdom, took office February 16, 1934, with full legislative and executive powers.

Finally, in 1948, the people of Newfoundland held an election to decide whether they should return to the self-government of the past or confederate with Canada. A majority voted to confederate with Canada, and so on March 31, 1949, Newfoundland and its possession, Labrador, became part of Canada. At the present time the Prime Minister of Newfoundland is Joseph R. Smallwood.

Many Americans have come to know Newfoundland for its airport at Gander. Indeed Gander, with a population of 3000, has been called one of the world's most important landing fields. Its airport has an area of one square mile, and in the thirty months ending December 31, 1948, at least 350,000 passengers, or more than the entire population of Newfoundland, landed at Gander.

I returned from that airport with a deep feeling of respect for the hardy race of people who have wrestled with destiny on the Great Island for more than 450 years. They deserve much commendation for their brave fight against the terrible limitations of weather, climate and sparse economy.

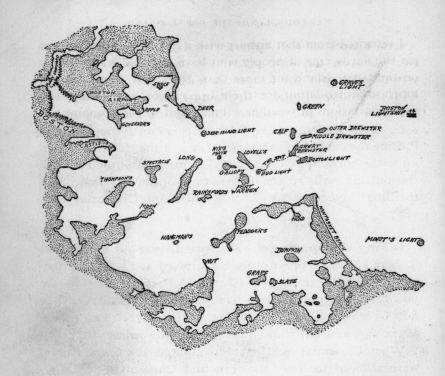

III. ISLANDS OF BOSTON BAY

PROBABLY no comparable area in the entire United States
has been the scene of so many interesting and exciting events
as the islands of Boston Bay. Since they are almost at our
doorstep in Winthrop, Massachusetts, we decided to visit
them by the old Indian method of water travel—canoeing.
We made plans to paddle to Boston Light and the six other
islands I had chosen to explore: Castle Island, Apple Island,
Nix's Mate, Lovell's Island, George's Island and Noddle's
Island, a total journey of twenty-seven miles in Boston Harbor. Of the thirty-five islands and lighthouses in the area,
we were to visit seven.

Up an hour before dawn, Mrs. Snow and I crammed

several knapsacks with cameras, notebooks and food. As the sun rose over the bay, we carried the canoe down to the water's edge, put the knapsacks aboard and paddled away with the incoming tide. Fifty minutes later we rounded old Hospital Point, and beached our canoe on the sands of historic Castle Island, where Fort Independence stands today. Pulling the canoe high above the reach of the tide, we walked up to the entrance of the venerable fortress, and then around the outside walls to the Dearborn Bastion, the scene of a thrilling adventure which took place on Christmas Day, 1817.

During the summer of 1817, twenty-year-old Lieutenant Robert F. Massie of Virginia had arrived at Fort Independence as a newly appointed officer. Most of the men at the post came to enjoy Massie's friendship, but one officer, Captain Green, took a violent dislike to him. Green was known at the fort as a bully and a dangerous swordsman.

When Christmas vacations were allotted, few of the officers were allowed to leave the fort, and Christmas Eve found them up in the old barracks hall, playing cards. Just before midnight, at the height of the card game, Captain Green sprang to his feet, reached across the table and slapped Lieutenant Massie squarely in the face. "You're a cheat," he roared, "and I demand immediate satisfaction!"

Massie quietly accepted the bully's challenge, naming swords as the weapons for the contest. Seconds arranged for the duel to take place the next morning at dawn.

Christmas morning was clear but bitter. The two contestants and their seconds left the inner walls of the fort at daybreak for Dearborn Bastion. Here the seconds made a vain attempt at reconciliation. The duel began. Captain Green, an expert swordsman, soon had Massie at a disadvantage and ran him through. Fatally wounded, the young Virginian was carried back to the fort, where he died that afternoon. His many friends mourned the passing of a gallant officer.

A few weeks later a fine marble monument was erected to Massie's memory. Placed over his grave at the scene of the encounter, the monument reminded all who saw it that an overbearing bully had killed the young Virginian.

THE MASSIE DUEL AT CASTLE ISLAND

Feeling against Captain Green ran high for many weeks, and then suddenly he completely vanished. Years went by without a sign of him, and Green was written off the army records as a deserter.

In 1827 an obscure young man enlisted in Battery H, Boston, and was sent out to Fort Independence on Castle Island. Although he signed the register as Edgar A. Perry, he was really Edgar Allan Poe, destined to become America's greatest writer of stories of horror and fascination. One day young Poe saw the marble monument to Massie's memory, and after reading the inscription, asked the older soldiers for details of the duel.

According to the story which Poe finally gathered together, Captain Green was so detested by his fellow officers at the fort that they decided to take a terrible revenge on him for Massie's death. They had learned that the captain had killed six other men in similarly staged duels and that not one of the victims had been at fault! Gradually their hatred toward the despicable bully grew, until Massie's friends, enraged by Green's continual boasting, determined to take a life for a life.

Visiting Captain Green one moonless night, they pretended to be friendly and plied him with wine until he was helplessly intoxicated. Then, carrying the captain down to one of the ancient dungeons, the officers forced his body through a tiny opening which led into the subterranean casemate. Following him into the dungeon, they placed him on the granite floor.

By this time Green had awakened from his drunken stupor and demanded to know what was taking place. Without answering, his captors began to shackle him to the floor, using the heavy iron handcuffs and footcuffs fastened into the stone. Then they all left the dungeon and proceeded to seal the captain up alive inside the windowless casemate, using bricks and mortar which they had hidden close at hand.

Captain Green shrieked in terror and begged for mercy, but his cries fell on deaf ears. The last brick was finally inserted, mortar applied and the room sealed up, the officers believed, forever. Captain Green undoubtedly died a horrible death within a few days.

Realizing the seriousness of their act, Massie's avengers requested quick transfers to other parts of the country, but several of the enlisted men had already learned the true circumstances.

As Edgar Allan Poe heard this story, he took many notes and several of the other soldiers reported Poe's unusual interest in the affair to the commanding officer of the fort. Poe

61

was soon asked to report to the post commander, and the following conversation is said to have taken place:

"I understand," began the officer, "that you've been asking questions about Massie's monument and the duel which he fought?"

"I have, sir," replied Poe meekly.

"And I understand that you've learned all about the subsequent events connected with the duel?"

"I have, sir."

"Well, you are never to tell that story outside the walls of this fort."

Poe agreed that he would never *tell* the story, but years afterwards he did *write* a tale based on this incident, transferring the scene across the ocean to Europe and changing both the characters and the story itself. He named the tale "The Cask of Amontillado."

In 1905, eighty-eight years after the duel, when workmen were repairing a part of the old fort, they came across a section of the ancient cellar marked on the plans as a small dungeon. They were surprised to find only a blank wall where the dungeon was supposed to be. One of the engineers, more curious than the rest, spent some time examining the wall. Finally, by the light of his torch, he found a small area which had been bricked up. He went to the head engineer and obtained permission to break through the wall. Several lanterns were brought down and a workman was set to chipping out the old mortar. An hour later, when he had removed several tiers of brick, the others held a lantern so that it would shine through the opening.

What the lantern revealed made them all join in demolishing the walled-up entrance into the dungeon. Twenty minutes later it was possible for the smallest man in the group to squeeze through the aperture.

"It's a skeleton!" they heard him cry a moment later, and he rushed for the opening, leaving the lantern behind him.

Several of the others then pulled down the entire brick

barrier and went into the dungeon where they saw a skeleton shackled to the floor with a few fragments of an 1812 army uniform clinging to the bones.

The remains could not be identified but they were given a military funeral and placed in the Castle Island cemetery in a grave marked UNKNOWN.

The Massie monument came to achieve a fame which attracted thousands of visitors to old Fort Independence each Sunday, especially after a bridge was built out to the island in 1891. But in 1892 the monument was moved, along with Massie's remains, across to Governor's Island, and set in a new cemetery there. Massie's skeleton was dug up again, however, in 1908, and taken, with the monument, down the bay to Deer Island to be placed in the officer's section of Resthaven Cemetery. Then, in 1939, Massie's bones were removed from the Deer Island grave, and taken, with his tombstone, across the state to Fort Devens, in Ayer, Massachusetts.

Thus, after his death, Massie became the Roving Skeleton of Boston Bay, a man who was buried four times in four different places within a period of 122 years.

Crossing the harbor again in our canoe, we arrived at the Boston airport. After a hike along the beach beside the runways, we reached what remains of old Apple Island, where a strange Englishman lived for nineteen years.

The early history of William Marsh is not known, but we are certain that he landed mysteriously at Germantown, Massachusetts, in 1813, at the height of the war with England. To quote from a century-old volume, he had "with him two females, one of whom passed as his wife and the other as her assistant." Taking possession of a small house on the shore, he lived in Germantown for many months in complete isolation. Many of his neighbors wondered why he had chosen to cut himself off from normal association with others. Whenever he went to town for supplies, he never spoke to anyone unless it was absolutely necessary; even then he kept the conversation at a bare minimum. He always paid for what he ordered in Spanish doubloons and English crowns.

Several months later, after a severe winter, Marsh's neighbors began to speak openly against him and to "throw out frightful innuendos." Whether their objections were on moral, social or spiritual grounds is not quite clear, but the Englishman and his two ladies were denounced as unearthly beings, strongly imbued "with the scent of brimstone." In May, 1814, the people of Germantown demanded that the Marshes leave the neighborhood.

Marsh, realizing that he could not remain, purchased a small 10-ton sloop, loaded it with all his worldly goods and sailed out of Quincy Bay with the others of his family aboard. At this time he obtained the services of a Negro boy, Black Jack.

Having been rudely treated by the people of Germantown, Marsh decided to cruise around the harbor, going ashore on many of the delightful islands as the months went by. When he needed provisions he would land at Point Shirley, and on several occasions appeared there with his faithful Negro servant to purchase a week's supply of food.

The island which appealed to him more than any of the others was Apple Island, situated halfway between Governor's and Snake Islands. It was here that he decided to settle when the first chilling blasts of winter arrived. On Apple Island was a snug colonial mansion which had been built before the Revolution by the Hutchinsons of Boston. Marsh decided to buy the property and move into the home. Move in he did, but it was not until 1830 that he could find the owner and acquire legal possession.

Meanwhile, the Marsh family thrived. Each year another child was born on Apple Island until the young Marshes numbered an even dozen. But still, according to those who went ashore there, Marsh always retained a silent, unfriendly attitude. Visiting Boston once a year, he made a vivid impression as he strode down State Street wearing a long red cloak. Always, both in Boston and on his island domain, his bearing and manner were mysterious.

As the years passed, strange tales of William Marsh and Apple Island began to circulate around the harbor. The Marsh residence was said to hold a trapdoor which would drop unwanted visitors to their death in a pit far below the level of the cellar itself. Some claimed that Marsh was a retired privateer; other, bolder persons called him a pirate.

William Marsh died in 1833, and his house was completely destroyed by fire two years later. His widow and children moved off the Island, establishing residence in Boston.

Years later, Oliver Wendell Holmes visited Apple Island and went up to the ruins of the burned dwelling. The stories he had heard about Marsh so impressed Holmes that he felt he had to see the house where the mysterious Englishman had lived. Later he wrote a poem about William Marsh and Apple Island, calling it "An Island Ruin." It reads in part:

> They told strange things of that mysterious man;
> Believe who will, deny them such as can;
> He lived at ease beneath his elm-trees' shade
> Did naught for gain, yet all his debts were paid;
> They said his house was framed with curious cares,
> Lest some old friend might enter unawares;
> That on the platform of his chamber's door
> Hinged a loose square that opened through the floor;
> Touch the black silken tassel next the bell,
> Down with a crash, the flapping trapdoor fell;
> Three stories deep the falling wretch would strike,
> To writhe at leisure on a boarder's pike.
> He came, a silent pilgrim to the West,
> Some old-world mystery throbbing in his breast;
> Close to the thronging mart he lived alone;
> He lived; he died. The rest is all unknown.

Almost every year from 1850 until 1946, people used to

65

go ashore at Apple Island to search in vain for the hypothetical buried gold of William Marsh. The last of his famous elm trees was cut down in 1938, and later almost all the soil of the island was removed as runway fill for the Boston airport. William Marsh's grave and skeleton went along with it. Now when the giant overseas planes from England land at the Boston airport they often pass over the remains of an Englishman, William Marsh, who died with his old-world secret still "throbbing in his breast."

Before starting for the outer limits of Boston Harbor we decided to paddle around East Boston, formerly Noddle's Island, and then over by Thompson's Island. Dodging between ferry boats and tugs, we finally reached the site of the old Donald McKay shipyards on Noddle's Island, across the harbor from the Boston Navy Yard, where the venerable warships, the *Constitution* and the *Constellation*, are moored in varying stages of decrepitude.

We stepped out of the canoe for a moment at the spot where Donald McKay built his vessels, the clipper ships, the most beautiful sailing craft ever constructed. It was here that McKay's skill and daring were allowed to reach their heights. From this very point his genius sent the *Flying Cloud,* the *Lightning,* the *Sovereign of the Seas* and his master ship, the *Great Republic,* into the waters of Boston Harbor to sail all over the world, breaking record after record.

When we had paid our respects to the clipper ships of a century ago, we returned to the canoe and paddled slowly out by Thompson's Island,[1] where we had discovered four Indian skeletons in 1941.

---

[1] The Farm and Trades School has been at Thompson's Island since 1833, a school for worthy but unfortunate boys. Headmaster William M. Meacham has run the school since 1926. An ideal environment which is so closely associated with the natural, beautiful life at the island has influenced generation after generation of New England youth. If the proud parent who raises one son to manhood is said to have done the community and his country a

Half an hour later we landed at the strangely shaped marker known as Nix's Mate, located at the entrance to Boston's inner harbor. There are many stories about the marker, most of which are not true. The famous legend of Nix's mate is the most interesting:

Late one summer's day in 1689, as darkness descended on the waters of Boston Bay, a Captain Nix was guiding his ship toward the wharves of Boston. Darkness caught him at the entrance to the harbor, however, and Captain Nix anchored for the night off a small twelve-acre island between Long and Lovell's Islands. During the night screams were heard coming from the anchored vessel, and in the morning the captain was found murdered. The others in the crew accused the mate of the crime, but he protested that he was innocent. He was judged guilty of the murder, however, and taken to the nearby island to be hanged. With his last words he declared that the island would gradually wash away and thus prove his innocence.

The mate was hanged. Gradually as the years passed the island did wash away, thus apparently proving the innocence of Nix's mate.

But actually, there is no record in Boston history of any Captain Nix having been murdered and his mate hanging for the crime. In those days, moreover, the British Admiralty laws were very strict, and the accused in any marine crime had to be tried within the limits of Boston proper, never on a harbor island. As final disproof, the island was known as Nix's Mate in 1630, or fifty-nine years before the alleged crime.

The island actually got its name from a trivial misunderstanding in 1630 between one William Coddington and a Dutch pilot aboard the *Jewel*, one of John Winthrop's fleet.

worthy service, think what we owe this Thompson's Island organization, which has supplied fatherly interest and guidance to several thousand times that number. The Farm and Trades School is a splendid example of what can be done for the worthy boy of today.

Coddington pointed at the island and asked for its name, and the pilot thought he wanted to know the Dutch word for the surf crashing against the island's shore. "Nixie Schmalt," answered the pilot, "I do not know how to spell it, but it mean the Wail of the Water Spirits." Coddington set it down on his map as "Nix his Mate Island," and the years have changed it to Nix's Mate.

The island's connection with hanging, of course, came from several pirates who were first executed in Boston and then strung up in chains at Nix's Mate as a warning to other pirates. Perhaps the most outstanding buccaneer to hang in chains at Nix's Mate was William Fly, who was executed in Boston with two of his men on July 12, 1726. Afterwards, according to the local newspaper, he was taken down the harbor to "Nick's Mate, about 2 Leagues from the Town, where the abovesaid Fly was hung up in Irons."

By 1805 Nix's Mate had washed away to such an extent that the Boston Marine Society erected a seawall around what had once been a twelve-acre island to save it from complete destruction. At present there is a large black and white cement pyramid erected on top of the seawall.

In ten minutes we crossed the Narrows which separates Nix's Mate from Lovell's Island. Here we visited the old lighthouse keeper's home, where in 1782 the French man-of-war *Magnifique* was wrecked. A treasure went down with that ship, and as the years passed it was covered with sand which by 1900 created a bar reaching across to Lovell's Island. Shortly afterwards two range lights were erected on the island. In 1920 the lighthouse keeper, Charles H. Jennings, was digging in his back yard when he came across several blackened discs. He scrubbed them vigorously to remove the dirt and rust and found that they were gold pieces, obviously from the *Magnifique*. When he went to Boston, he sold several of them for $29 each.

Unluckily for Jennings, he left the island on his vacation

shortly after his discovery. He always believed that the substitute lighthouse keeper dug up the remainder of the *Magnifique's* treasure, estimated at about $7000. At least, when
Jennings returned from his vacation, there was a yawning
hole in his back yard at the spot where he had found the
gold pieces. He never discovered any more of the treasure.
The lighthouse was torn down in 1940 when the army occupied the entire island.

After visiting the lighthouse sites we walked up to the
top of Lovell's Island, where we paused at a giant boulder
known as Lovers' Rock. Here on December 4, 1786, fifteen
people, among them two young lovers, who had been shipwrecked on the island crawled in under the huge rock for
protection against the terrible blizzard that had destroyed the
Maine packet on which they traveled. Their shelter proved
totally inadequate. By morning the entire group had frozen
to death. They were found that same afternoon by a fisherman who crossed over from another island after the storm
died down. The shipwrecked lovers were embraced even in
death, and they have given the giant boulder the name by
which it is known today—Lovers' Rock.

We walked back to our canoe, but because it was low
tide we paddled only as far as the Great Brewster Spit, a bar
two and a half miles long which ends at Great Brewster Island. Then we hiked across another bar half a mile long to
Little Brewster Island on which stands Boston Light, illuminated for the first time on September 14, 1716, and the
oldest lighthouse in America.

We met the keeper, who invited us to climb to the top
of the tower. There, ninety-eight feet above the sea, we
looked out at two other lighthouses, Graves Light, off to the
north, and famous Minot's Light, about nine miles to the
south. Minot's Light is the second tower of the same name,
the first having fallen into the ocean on April 17, 1851, carrying two keepers to their death. By 1860 another lighthouse
had been erected in the same spot. This commanding tower,

a hundred and fourteen feet high, is now known as Lovers'
Light, because its flash, 1-4-3, spells out I L-o-v-e Y-o-u to the
lovers along the shore.

Gigantic waves crash in vain against the granite sides of
Minot's Light, known as the most dangerous lighthouse in
America. Because of its hazardous location, the lighthouse
was made automatic in September, 1947, and today only occasional visits of inspection are made to this world-famous
beacon off the Cohasset, Massachusetts, shore.

After climbing down Boston Light, we hiked back to the
end of Great Brewster Spit where old Bug Light formerly
stood, and paddled half a mile to the westward to Fort Warren on George's Island.

Fort Warren is most famous for its use during the Civil
War. Here were imprisoned Confederate Commissioners
James Murray Mason and John Slidell, as well as the Con-
federacy's Vice-President Alexander Hamilton Stephens.
The famous marching song *John Brown's Body* was written
at Fort Warren during the war, and played there for the first
time by the Brigade Band in 1861.

THE LADY IN BLACK

NEARLY ALL the islands of Boston Harbor have a ghost or
two connected with their history, but the most dramatic and
famous of them all is the Lady in Black, who for eighty years
is said to have haunted Fort Warren and George's Island.

Back in the early days of the Civil War a young soldier, a
bridegroom of a few months, was captured in battle and sent
up to the northern bastion of Fort Warren at George's Island, where he was imprisoned in the Corridor of Dungeons
along with several hundred other Southerners. He soon
wrote to his wife, telling her sorrowfully of his unfortunate
capture and of his deep love and loneliness for her. The letter was passed through the battle lines and was eventually
received by the girl. On learning of her husband's fate, she

determined to leave her pleasant home, travel up the coast, reach Fort Warren and free her husband.

The girl got in touch with a blockade runner who agreed to take her up the coast. She then obtained a suit of men's clothes and an old pepper-box gun and had her hair cut short. Two and a half months later the blockade runner set the "young man" ashore at Cape Cod. There she stayed in the home of a Southerner, and a week later she had established herself in Hull, Massachusetts, at the house of another Southerner. Now less than a mile away from George's Island, for the next few days she studied the fort through a telescope until she had entirely familiarized herself with the section of the bastion which held the famous Corridor of Dungeons.

On the first stormy night, when the rain was coming down with such driving force that it obscured all vision, her Southern host rowed the girl across to the island and left her on the beach. Crouching on the shore, she watched the two nearest sentries, soaked to the skin, methodically patrolling their posts. They strode slowly and automatically toward each other, and then, turning on their heels, walked slowly away—back to back, of course. She estimated that there was almost a minute and a half after they turned when she could run the gauntlet.

Watching alertly, the girl grasped the bundle which held her gun and a short-handled pick. At the exact moment when the two men began to walk in opposite directions, she stole toward the spot where they had met. A minute later she had reached a hiding place in a tangle of shrubbery a short distance away. She lay there in the rain until they came back, met and walked off again, back to back. Then she rose quickly and scrambled over the cover-face outside the bastion where her husband was imprisoned. Except for the sentries some distance away, the entire fort seemed asleep.

Standing there alone, she recalled a tune which she and her husband had used to signal to each other. She began to whistle it softly at first and gradually louder. There was no answer. Could it be that her husband had been transferred to another Yankee prison since she had received his letter? A score of possibilities flashed through her mind.

She decided to risk everything by giving a final shrill, piercing whistle. When she had finished, she threw herself down on the banking. There was complete silence for several minutes, but finally an answering whistle came from within the fort. Looking up cautiously at the walls of the bastion, she noticed that there were narrow slits in the stone some distance above her. From one of these slits, a rope of cloth emerged and dropped lower and lower until she could grasp the end.

"Hang on," cried a voice, and a moment later she had been pulled up, bundle and all, to the seven-inch slit in the granite wall. Several hands lifted her up so that she could squeeze through the tiny aperture. Soon she was in the arms of her husband.

A short time later hurried conferences were held among the six hundred Confederate prisoners inside the Corridor of Dungeons. With the arrival of the girl and the short-handled pick they saw the chance they had been waiting for. Instead of digging a tunnel out of the fort and escaping aboard the schooner which Southern sympathizers would provide, they decided upon a bolder idea. They would tunnel from one of the dungeons located at an outer corner of the bastion and dig toward the inner part of the fort. They planned to come up from under the parade ground where they could break into the arsenal, arm themselves, capture the small garrison of eighty Union soldiers and take over the fort. Then they would climb up on the parapets, turn the 248 guns of Fort Warren against Boston and besiege the city. This plan, they believed in their enthusiasm, would change the entire course of the Civil War, and victory for the South would be assured.

Beginning work on the tunnel before the guards arrived

for the morning check-up, the prisoners piled earth in front of the tunnel's mouth in the dungeon. Whenever the guards appeared a group of prisoners sat down on the fresh earth, completely concealing the tunnel from view.

As the weeks went by, the tunnel was lengthened and its direction was plotted and replotted. The earth they dug was laboriously carried back into the Corridor of Dungeons by the prisoners, who used their shirts and jackets as containers. Each windy night they threw the dirt out of the narrow slits in the walls of the bastion. Finally, those who were engineering the project believed that the tunnel had reached a point between the granite wall of the fort and the center of the parade ground.

The next night the prisoners were to make the final upward thrust toward the surface of the parade ground. At one o'clock in the morning a young lieutenant swung the pick vigorously against the top of the tunnel. The pick went through the earth and smashed against the granite wall which is inside the parade ground. The plotters had miscalculated.

One of the sentries guarding the area heard the sharp sound of the pick below and suspected what had happened. He shouted a warning to the next sentry, who passed the word down the line to the guardhouse. The sergeant in charge visited the scene and heard the sentry's story. Immediately the entire fort was on the alert.

At that time the commanding officer of Fort Warren was Colonel Justin E. Dimmock of Marblehead, veteran artillery expert, who was formerly in charge of Fortress Monroe. Ten minutes after the sentry heard the suspicious noise on the parade ground, Colonel Dimmock made a surprise visit to the Corridor of Dungeons. There he caught several of the prisoners scattering dirt outside the walls.

One by one the Southerners were taken out into the dry moat, until the Corridor of Dungeons appeared completely empty. But eleven prisoners were missing when roll call was taken. A careful examination of the corner dungeon revealed the opening of the tunnel.

Colonel Dimmock shouted down to those in the shaft, "You have failed, so you might as well come out and surrender."

The unhappy Southerners crawled out of the tunnel. After a few words with her husband, the girl had decided to make a final attempt for freedom. Their plan was this: The young soldier would crawl out and quietly surrender. Afterwards, they hoped, the guards would count the prisoners and finding them all accounted for, relax their vigilance. The wife would then appear behind the Union soldiers, cock her gun, and order them to surrender. It was a radical plan, born of desperation.

The young husband emerged from the tunnel. The guards counted the prisoners, found that they were all present, and began moving the last of the Southern prisoners to a new place of confinement. Colonel Dimmock announced that in the morning the tunnel would be filled up and sealed off with cement. Then, just as the prisoners were leaving the dungeon, the girl sprang out of the tunnel and ordered the guards to surrender.

"I've a pistol and I know how to use it," she shouted.

Colonel Dimmock thought quickly. He advanced slowly towards the girl, his hands raised in surrender. Slowly his men followed him, forming a circle around her. Then, with a rapid motion, the colonel hit against the barrel of the gun, knocking it to one side as the girl fired. The gun was old and rusty, and it exploded. A fragment of metal passed through the brain of the young husband.

Two days later the soldier's lifeless body was buried in the lonely cemetery of the fort. The following week his desolated widow was sentenced to be executed as a spy.

On the morning of the girl's execution her guards asked if she had a final request. "Why, yes," she replied. "I'm tired of wearing this suit of men's clothes. I'd like to put on a gown once more before I die."

A search of the entire fort revealed only some black robes which had been worn during a theatrical performance given by the First Corps of Cadets the summer before. It was in this costume that the lady was hanged an hour later. That afternoon her body was cut down and placed in the Fort Warren cemetery by the side of her husband.

As time passed, the guards at the fort were shipped away, and recruits arrived to take their places. But the key men, eight in number, stayed on. One of them, a private named Richard Cassidy, had witnessed the execution of the Southern girl and it was his duty night after night to patrol the cover-face where she had been hanged. The other men joked with him, warning him to watch out for the "Lady in Black." He laughed with them, but actually he was not too pleased with his duty.

One night, seven weeks after the execution, Private Cassidy came running toward the guardhouse, screaming at the top of his voice. Finally, he was calm enough to tell his story. He had been patrolling his post and was thinking about the execution when suddenly two hands came out of the night and fastened around his throat. He squirmed and twisted until he faced the being who was trying to choke him and saw to his amazement that it was none other than the Lady in Black. Then he summoned all his strength, broke free from her grasp and ran for help.

The guardhouse rocked with laughter as Cassidy finished his story, but it was no laughing matter to Cassidy either then or the following morning when they sentenced him to thirty days in that same guardhouse for deserting his post.

Ever since that night, it is said, the Lady in Black appears from time to time. In the winter of 1891 four officers walking out through the massive sally-port looked ahead into the fresh snow and saw several footprints made by a woman's slipper. As no woman was then living at the fort, they held the ghost of the Lady in Black responsible.

During World War II, one unfortunate sentry went stark, raving mad when ordered to patrol the area where the execution had occurred. He was placed in the island hospital to recover, but his condition went from bad to worse, and he was finally taken to an institution, where he is to this very day.

A few years after World War II ended, non-commissioned officers were allowed to have their wives and families living at the fort. One woman, known for her practical jokes, heard about the Lady in Black and decided to play a prank on her next-door neighbor. She removed her false teeth, smudged her face with charcoal and let her long, black hair down over her shoulders. Completely dressed in black, she threw a huge black shawl over her head and started for her neighbor's back door.

Not realizing what a terrible sight she presented, the prankster knocked on the door and, as it was opened, she bared her toothless gums and screamed. Her neighbor gave a single horrified glance and slumped to the floor in a dead faint. It was fully half an hour before the poor woman recovered her senses. During that time this modern Lady in Black vowed that if her friend recovered she would swear off practical jokes forever.

The most recent story involving the Lady in Black occurred in 1947 and was told to me by Captain Charles I. Norris of Towson, Maryland. Captain Norris was alone on the island one night, reading in the first-floor library of his house on the post, when something tapped him on the right shoulder. He turned, but there was no one in the room. As he began reading again, he felt another definite tap on his left shoulder. Again there was no one to be seen. He had just started to read again when the upstairs phone rang. Leisurely putting down his magazine, he climbed the stairs and picked up the telephone. A man's voice said, "Operator speaking. Number, please."

Captain Norris asked the operator who it was that had been calling him. "Why," answered the operator, "your wife answered and took the message, sir!"

"My wife!" cried the startled captain. "My wife is not on the island."

Captain Norris was completely bewildered and went downstairs to sink exhausted into a chair. There were no more manifestations, but he decided that only the Lady in Black could account for the tapping and the mysterious telephone call.

Since 1946 thousands and thousands of interested visitors have gone ashore at Fort Warren and walked through the Corridor of Dungeons. Although the graves of the Lady in Black and her husband have long since been moved from the island, one of the commanding officers had a spurious tomb built into the floor of one of the casemates at the Corridor of Dungeons. Originally planned as a surprise to the lady guests at an officers' dance, the casket, which is merely a great wooden box set flush in the dirt of the casemate, proved such an overwhelming success that it has been allowed to stay there ever since.

Whenever newcomers enter the Corridor of Dungeons, the ritual first performed at the officers' dance is repeated. A small soldier, or perhaps a girl, is dressed in black and taken up to the casemate ahead of the others. The "Lady" of that particular occasion is placed in the coffin and the lid is closed over her. The unsuspecting guests enter the casemate and gather around the story-teller, who, with proper embellishments, tells the tragic history of the Lady in Black. At the end of the story, and usually with a flourish, the narrator swings open wide the cover of the casket, whereupon, with a blood-curdling scream, the Lady in Black leaps to her feet. Visitors who have been fortunate enough to see this performance are never likely to forget it.

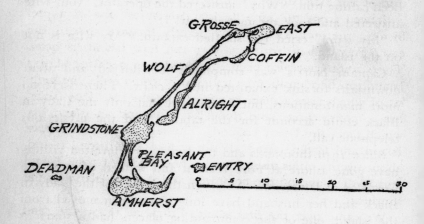

BIRD ROCKS

BRION

G·ROSSE EAST

COFFIN

WOLF

ALRIGHT

GRINDSTONE

PLEASANT BAY

DEADMAN

ENTRY

AMHERST

0 5 10 15 20 25 30

IV. THE MAGDALENS

MY MOTHER'S father, Captain Joshua N. Rowe, went off to sea at the age of twelve under unusual circumstances, and, while on a voyage through Cabot Strait and the Gulf of Saint Lawrence, his ship was wrecked at lonely Amherst Island in the Magdalen group. Ever since I heard the story of my grandfather's shipwreck I have wanted to visit the island where he was marooned.

And now I was on my way, winging through the sky on the final lap of a six-hundred-mile hop from Boston. The twin-engined Cessna was purring beautifully, and I hoped to land by noon, for we had started at eight that morning. Prince Edward Island was now below us, and soon the Magdalens were off on the horizon.

The Magdalen Islands are located fifty-six miles due north from Eastern Point, Prince Edward Island. In the old days, it was quite a feat to reach them, but today, with the Maritime Central Airways running at least two planes a week to Grindstone Island and often to Amherst Island, the isolation of the Magdalens is a thing of the past.

Viewed from the air, the islands remind one of a prehistoric monster which leans slightly forward toward the east. Entry Island forms its feet and East Island its head. The islands have also been compared to a necklace. Entry Island can be identified by its lavishly tinted cliffs, the highest of which rises a sheer 559 feet from the sea. East Island has a "conspicuous sand dune," a pond and an island bay which faces the Great Lagoon. The lagoon runs from East Island and Coffin Island all the way to Grindstone Island, about twenty miles distant, and is bounded by Grosse Island and Wolf Island on the northwest and Alright Island on the southeast.

We came over the first island, Entry, at 11:55 A.M., and then flew out in a wide circle that brought us over all twelve islands. Then we landed at the airport on Grindstone Island.

The Magdalen Islands were discovered by Jacques Cartier on his voyage to the Gulf of Saint Lawrence in 1534. They were originally known as Brion, Rameés and Araynes. "Rameés," the early name given the entire group, indicates that the islands are connected by bars. "Les Araynes" means that the islands of Grosse and those to the south are connected by sand.

Island naming is of interest to many. The Magdalen who ultimately lent her name to the island group was Magdalen Honfleur, wife of François Honfleur, who settled there in 1663. Brion Island was named by Jacques Cartier in 1534 in honor of Philip Chabot, Sieur de Brion. Amherst Island is named for General William Amherst. Grindstone Island is so called because of the coarse white sand which forms its principal headland, Cape Meule. Alright Island comes from a sailor's term, the meaning of which is lost in obscurity.

As at Saint Paul's Island, many of the ledges and reefs around the Magdalens were named because of the shipwrecks they caused. There were Columbine Shoals, Andromache Roche, Meule Roche, Old Harry Head, Glawson Patch, Rochers du Dauphin, Quero Ground, Anse à la Cabane, Doyle Reef, Newhall Ground, Le Fond George, Anthony's Nose and Pierre de Gros Cap.

In 1663 the islands were conceded by New France to François Doublet Honfleur, for whose wife the group was named. His family used the islands as a fishing base until 1719, when the French Government leased them to LeCompte de Saint Pierre.

In 1763 only ten families lived at the Magdalens, all engaged in walrus and seal hunting. Soon afterwards an American shipper named Gridley established a trading and fishing post on Amherst Island. For many years he did a thriving business, sending walrus tusks, skins and oil to New England. During the Revolution, Gridley's property was partly destroyed by the enemy, but he re-established his post after the war ended. By this time, however, the walrus had almost completely disappeared and the seals were becoming wary of landing at the islands. Gradually the post lost its importance and was abandoned, but even now the ruins of this trading center can be seen.

Gradually the Magdalen inhabitants, both French and English, forgot the walrus and the seals and adapted themselves to the cod and herring fishing industry. They did very well at it. Of course, if the ice brought a herd of seals against the shores, they went out and killed them. Nevertheless, depending mainly on fishing and farming, they were able to live happy and prosperous lives.

In 1798 the Magdalens acquired a new owner, Boston-born Isaac Coffin, commander of a frigate which had transported Governor-General Dorchester of Canada to Quebec. In the course of their trip, a furious gale had arisen, and Governor Dorchester feared that the frigate would never reach port. When the storm subsided as they passed the Magdalens, the relieved Lord Dorchester asked Captain Coffin if he would not enjoy the gift of the islands. The captain accepted with pleasure. At his death in 1839 the islands went into the possession of his nephew, John Townsend Coffin, of the Isle of Wight. In 1860 there were 2651 people living at the Magdalens under the lenient rule of the Coffin family.

The most fantastic *true* story I have ever heard was told me one night while I was visiting Grindstone Island. It is called the Miracle of Le Bourdais.

In the year 1872 there was a terrible blizzard which hit Grindstone Island shortly after church services on Sunday, December 15. The storm continued with such fury that few island inhabitants left their homes for several days. On Thursday, however, during a lull in the blizzard, three brave lads decided to go down to the beach. Reaching the water's edge, they found the wreckage of a ship scattered up and down the shore at the foot of the cliffs and beyond the high tide mark.

For several hours the three boys gathered salvage from the wreck. When it grew dark, they lighted flares and began to make their way homeward. As they passed a large mass of wreckage, there emerged from behind it a gigantic creature, eight feet high and snow white, which advanced on them slowly, uttering guttural, inarticulate noises. Dropping their flares and their spoils, the boys fled to their homes.

The next morning the storm returned in full force, but that afternoon conditions were relatively normal. News of the wreck had spread quickly, and about twenty men went down to the shore where the disaster had taken place. Few of them had paid any attention to the strange story of the three boys, dismissing the huge white creature as a giant white owl, or, at worst, a polar bear which had come in on an ice floe.

The men worked all that day at the wreck, which they found had been loaded with wheat and was named the *Calcutta*. They were able to save several tons of wheat but very little else. However, the spars and rigging, anchors and chain were located and stored for future use. When the sun went down the men concluded that the day had been a profitable one and, lighting flares, began their homeward journey across the frozen marshes and fields.

As they passed a haybarn, again without warning, an enormous white shape eight feet in height reared up at them from out of the snowdrifts and slowly advanced. The creature was so frightful that every last man dropped whatever he was carrying and ran as fast as he could for home, screaming with terror.

Reaching the village, the men lost no time in calling at the home of Father Charles Boudreault to tell him of their fantastic experience. The good Father tried to comfort them as best he could, but their fear was so deep-seated and their vision so vivid that the men couldn't forget it. "All right," Father Boudreault told them. "Tomorrow I shall accompany you to the scene of your encounter. Now all of you go home to your good wives and say no more about it."

Early the next morning Father Boudreault appeared in front of the church, and soon a dozen men joined him, each armed with a gun. The others decided to stay at home and protect their wives—or so they claimed.

After an hour's walk the party reached the haybarn, but a light snow the night before had obliterated all evidence of the strange encounter. The men returned to the village and decided to search again after lunch. That afternoon the tide was out, and the group walked along the beach to the scene of the wreck. Afterwards they continued across to the haybarn without finding a sign of the huge white creature.

However, as Father Boudreault walked across the meadow in back of the barn, he saw something that excited him. "Come over here!" he called to the others. Soon they were

THE HORROR OF GRINDSTONE ISLAND

all gathered around him. "Look!" The men glanced down into the snow to discover several impressions of the strangest footprints they had ever seen. The prints were about twenty-two inches long and almost twelve inches wide. What unusual creature could have such a foot?

Father Boudreault followed the tracks for a short distance and soon realized that it was a two-legged something which he was tracking in the snow! But what two-legged animal could this be? And the men had claimed it was eight feet high!

On and on they walked, as the afternoon sun dropped lower and lower in the sky. Father Boudreault continued to walk in front of the others, but they were all on the alert, their guns ready to shoot whatever the thing might be— ghost, giant or polar bear. "What can it be?" each man said to his neighbor. A polar bear, after all, doesn't walk on its hind legs, nor were there men eight feet tall roaming around the Magdalen Islands.

Then, far in the distance, they saw a huge form, evidently on its side, down on the beach. They approached the gigantic creature slowly with their guns ready for action. By this time the sun had set. As soon as the men lighted their flares, Father Boudreault advanced alone toward the form in the snow. Then he was at the side of the creature. He reached out and touched it. When he told the men that his hand had encountered frozen snow, they were more perplexed than ever, for they doubted that there could be an icy ghost.

Father Boudreault now walked around to the other side of the creature. It was indeed huge, more than nine feet in girth and almost eight feet long. Still the priest did not know what it could possibly be. Several of the men crowded behind him, and in the light of their flares he could distinguish what appeared to be the head of the creature. And what a head it was—almost four feet wide and three feet long!

84

The last of the *Carroll A. Deering*

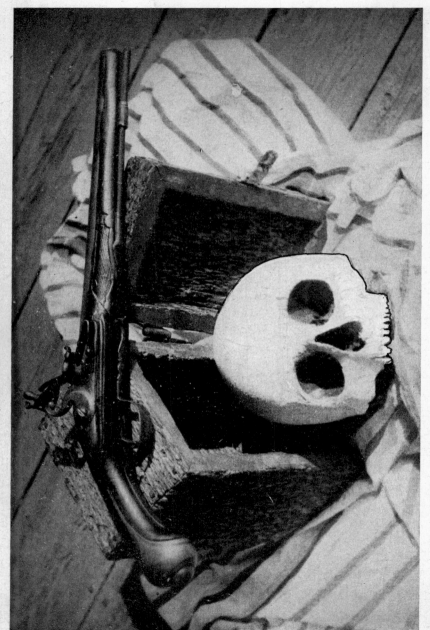

The skull of the famous pirate Blackbeard, photographed with one of his pistols

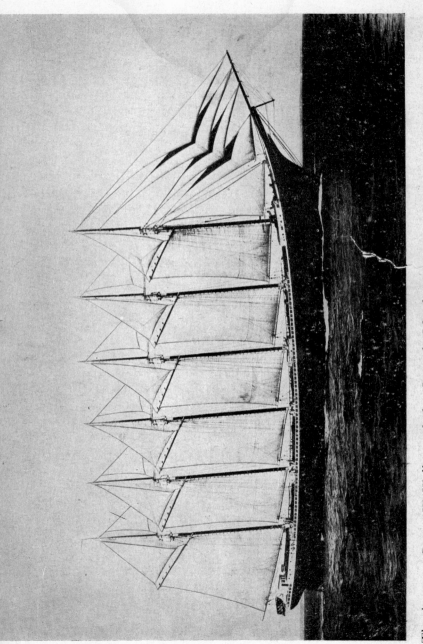

The six-master *George W. Wells*, wrecked at Ocracoke Island

Boston Light, erected in 1716, the oldest lighthouse in America

Interior of Castle Island, Boston Harbor. The dungeon is located immediately below the last arch.

The famous Lady in Black whose ghost still haunts Fort Warren. This picture was taken just before she was

America's most dangerous beacon, Minot's Light

The shipwreck of the *Grand Design,* Mount Desert Island. After a painting by Howe D. Higgins.

Where privateer William Kidd actually buried treasure at Gardiner
Island, New York

Captain Kidd's famous cave at Deer Isle, Maine

t Pierre, with its landing strip in the foreground

pwreck at Saint Pierre

united
death only
Parte

·MOTTO·INSIDE·THE·RING·

·DESIGN·ON·THE·SEAL·OF·RING·

THE·POT·IN·WHICH·THE·MONEY·AND·RING·WERE
FOUND·AT·RICHMOND·ISLAND, MAY·11TH, 1855.

Coins, ring and pot found at Richmond's Island, Maine

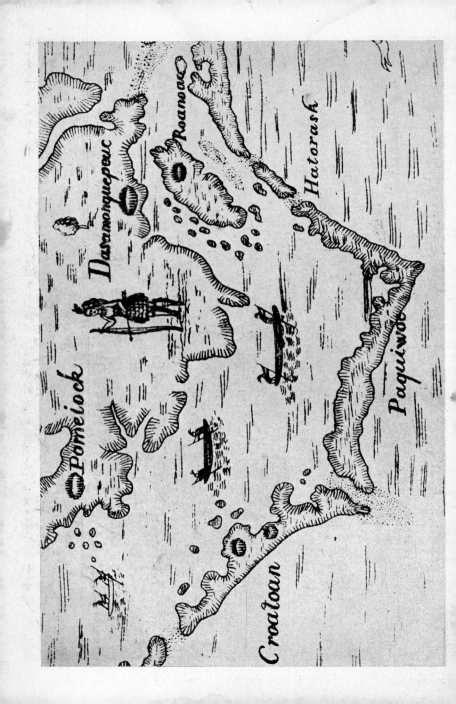

hes claimed to have been left by the Lost Colony, declared fraudulent

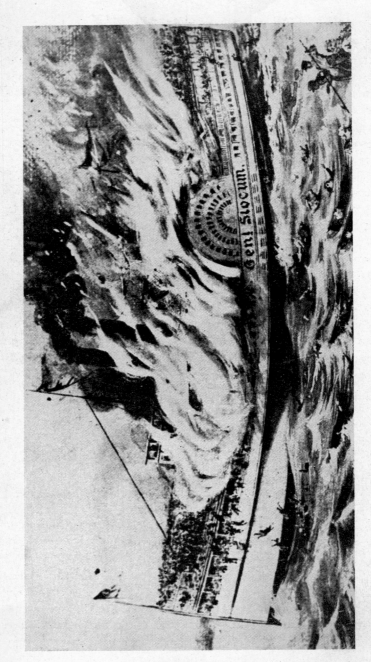

The *Slocum* disaster in New York harbor

"Hold the torches closer," Father Boudreault told the men, and soon there was good illumination by which to examine the creature's head. The priest crouched down on his knees to look more closely, and now he could distinguish two cavities where eyes were located. But the entire body, except for its eyes and mouth, was so covered with ice and snow that it was still impossible to tell what sort of creature it really was.

Then the eyes began to open and close, and a horrible inarticulate moan came, it seemed, from the very depths of the creature's soul. Again and again the weird moan issued forth.

In a moment the huge creature's massive arms, two feet thick and four feet long, began to move, feebly at first, and then with more strength.

The priest leaned over to see more clearly, and as he did so, his overcoat flew open, revealing his Roman collar and breastpiece, with a silver cross dangling below. The creature now appeared to be considerably excited, and its unhappy moans grew more agitated. Then, as Father Boudreault leaned closer and closer the creature made a final effort, and the priest heard the single word: "Father!"

"Mon Dieu!" shouted the priest. "Incredible as it seems, this creature is a living man. We've got to get him to the nearest house. He's been frozen by the blizzard, and the snow was caked over him until it is actually from one to two feet in thickness. Let's carry him away. Come on, men."

Several of the Canadians went down to the shore, where they found a piece of planking nine feet long and of sufficient width. It took every man present to help carry the huge form back to the village, for the ice and snow made its total weight over a thousand pounds.

That night the men and women of Grindstone Island worked far into the early morning hours, first chopping away the outside ice, and then thawing away that portion nearest the flesh with heavy cold towels. Gradually a human form emerged from within the fantastic shape which had been brought into the house: a man six feet eight in height and weighing, without ice and snow, no less than three hundred and ten pounds! It was his enormous physique which had kept him alive.

Later the man was questioned by Father Boudreault. He was found to be Auguste Le Bourdais, the first mate of the wheat ship *Calcutta* and the only man saved. He could only recall that after the wreck of his ship he had clung a full day and night to a fragment of wreckage in the sea, and that during the days after he reached the shore he had eaten nothing but snow! The sight of Father Boudreault's cross had evidently given him back his senses, but that Auguste Le Bourdais did not perish during his long exposure in below-zero weather is rather short of miraculous.

Le Bourdais' sufferings were terrible as his limbs began to thaw. Soon he was wishing that he had died in the wreck. A week after his rescue, the islanders realized that they would have to cut off his badly frozen legs. It took ten men to hold him to the table while the amputations were made. But he lived!

When the ice flows melted at the end of May, 1873, Le Bourdais was taken to Quebec for another operation. His legs were further shortened so that he could be fitted to peg legs. He later returned to the Magdalen Islands and eventually founded the government telegraph office there. Even with peg legs, he could stand up against anyone in a fight.

In 1877 S. G. W. Benjamin visited the Magdalens by the Pictou steamer *Albert*. He described the terrible havoc which befell the Gloucester fishing fleet as it lay in Pleasant Bay, off Grindstone Island, in August, 1873. When the wind shifted from a westward gale to an easterly blow, thirty-three fishing vessels were cast ashore on Amherst Island within an hour.

Twenty-four years before the Gloucester fleet met disaster

on Amherst Island, my grandfather, Captain Joshua Nick-
erson Rowe, was wrecked at the same location.

As I have said, my grandfather went to sea at the age of
twelve. One late summer, on his first voyage, he was aboard
the fishing schooner *Checker,* off the Magdalen Islands. On
the night of September 8, Captain Kimball, his master, anchored the *Checker* in the lee of Amherst Island for protection against the strong westerly breeze. During the night
the wind came around to northeast, and before morning a
gale was blowing. Then the storm began to push the *Checker*
toward the shores of Amherst Island. Twelve-year-old
Joshua kept a diary of what happened:

> *We tried to get underway but on account of a strong
> current and heavy sea our only hope was to trust to
> Providence and our good anchors. Not ever being at
> sea before, I thought it would be best for me never to
> go again if I could get on shore again.*
>
> *At 9 a.m. Sept. 9, 1849, we piled up on Amherst Is-
> land. We stayed ten days in a tent made of our own
> sails. There were some inhabitants on this side of the
> island but they were not disposed to help us any. In
> fact, they stole our provisions that we took from the
> wreck. We recovered part of it.*

Later a kindly Magdalen Islander took the shipwrecked
sailors into his house and gave them warm cereal served in
dishes which the islander had salvaged from an earlier
wreck. Unknown to the kindly but ignorant benefactor,
the dishes were actually chamber pots.

Young Joshua Rowe reached his home in Maine the following summer, but changed his mind about not going to
sea. He followed the ocean for the rest of his life.[1]

---

[1] He became first mate aboard the record-breaking clipper ship *Crystal
Palace* and was later owner and captain of the former slaving yacht *Wanderer.*
During the Civil War he was a Naval officer and at the time of the Klondike
Gold Rush he was captain of a steamer carrying passengers to Alaska, where
he died of pneumonia.

One winter, two men named Chenel and Welsh were out in a dory off the Magdalens when a gale blew them out to sea. Then a change in the wind took them back to the mouth of Grand Entry Harbor. There they became trapped in the floe, and Allan Clarke and John Payson went out on the thin ice to save them. Clarke advanced farther than Payson, crawling along the jagged pack ice with two dory oars and a rope. Finally, he reached the boat, rove a line through the painter and hauled the two men almost to shore. Then Payson and the others hitched a horse to the dory and pulled it high on the beach. Clarke had been struggling on the broken ice continuously for almost eight hours, and his clothes were frozen stiff. He collapsed after he had saved the others. For this daring rescue the Canadian Humane Society awarded Clarke a beautiful bronze medal.

The story of Farmer, the ocean-going horse of Entry Island is well known at the Magdalens. In March, 1925, Farmer was traded by his owner, Richard McLean, who took the horse over the ice to Amherst Island, three miles away. Then he drove the animal across Amherst Island, up along Grindstone, Wolf and Grosse Islands, where he delivered him to the new East Island owner. But Farmer became homesick, and in June galloped back across the route he had come, swam the three miles to Entry Island and reported to his old owner. He had come more than fifty-five miles under strange conditions but he had accomplished his purpose. Richard McLean allowed Farmer to stay on Entry Island for the rest of his days.

The wreck of the *Miracle* in 1847 was a fireside topic at the Magdalens for many years. The *Miracle* was a full-rigged Irish immigrant ship, sailing from Liverpool to Quebec, thirty of whose 408 passengers died of fever while crossing the ocean. On May 4, 1847, while approaching the Gulf of Saint Lawrence, the ship ran into a heavy southeast snowstorm and crashed against the shores of East Point on East Island. Captain Elliott had the masts cut down in order to save the ship. Then two boats were launched, but both capsized and sixty-four immigrants drowned. Finally, the storm began to abate, and the other survivors were able to reach shore in safety. To this day the keel of the old *Miracle* appears out of the sand from time to time.

The airplane has brought a decided change to the Magdalens, for it means the difference between isolation and civilization during the long winter months. Many years ago, to bridge the lonely gap between summers, Jean Joseph Le Bourdais, son of the "ice monster," began the publication of an island newspaper, *Le Bulletin*. He continued it even after the coming of the year-round airplane to the Magdalens. One of his most unusual stories dealt with a polar bear which roamed the islands from an ice pack twenty-five years ago. The bear seemed to have decided on a principle of neutrality toward humans, and he became almost a tame pet. With the coming of spring, he disappeared on an ice field which floated out to sea.

From earliest times, mail had been sent ashore in the winter by setting a barrel adrift so that the favoring currents and winds would carry it to the mainland to the south of the islands. The barrel, marked "Magdalen Island Mail," more often than not arrived at either Prince Edward Island or Cape Breton in a week or ten days. With the advent of the telegraph cable, the old ways of communication were forgotten, but in 1908, when the cable snapped, leaving the island in isolation with supplies getting low, the old cask method was brought back into use. A small barrel was properly marked and set adrift with a tin sail secured to it. It arrived in Cape Breton in eight days and the islanders' message of distress was taken to the government officials. The icebreaker *Stanley* was promptly sent to the rescue.

Today there are about ten thousand persons living on the Magdalens. The French predominate, but about six hundred of the residents are of English origin. The French are Roman Catholic and the English are members of the Church of England. The two nationalities are largely separated, with Grosse Island and Entry Island populated mostly by the English, Grindstone mostly by the French and all the other islands overwhelmingly by the French.

Each island has its own characteristics. Entry Island is very mountainous though the farm land is excellent. The cliffs on the island actually overhang the sea in many locations. Formed into a thousand unusual shapes, and brilliantly tinted with a mixture of red sandstone, ocher and gray gypsum, the towering crags completely outclass the better known rocks of the famous Channel Islands. A hundred feet from the main part of Entry, Devil's Island is a strange, isolated mass which rises three hundred feet into the air.

Grindstone is the business center; the main airport, the post office, the radio station and the bank are all located there.

Alright Island is another land of varied colors, with purples, grays, yellows, reds and browns intermingled in its cliffs. Long white sand dunes in the foreground and wooded hills above the cliffs give the entire island a pleasant, varicolored effect.

From Pleasant Bay off Grindstone one gets a typical view of Amherst Island. The village there has been called "a curious little town composed of perhaps fifty houses straggling up the flanks of Demoiselle, a conical hill, which on the sea side falls nearly two hundred and eighty feet."

A geologist's paradise is at Cap Rouge on Grindstone Island, where a visitor can fill his pockets with bloodstones, agates, chalcedony and jaspers.

Although scores of geologists have visited the islands and have written many chapters of their findings, it was not until recently that geology proved profitable there. During the winter of 1947 the Quebec Manganese Mines, Ltd.,[1] began operations at Grindstone Island, searching for manganese. A power shovel cleared an area in one location so that the engineers could send down a diamond drill. At forty-nine feet the drill brought up high grade ore containing fifty-three per cent metallic manganese. It is estimated that well over a hundred thousand tons of the metal is in the vicinity. Since every ton of steel requires fourteen pounds of manganese, and most sources in North America are low grade, it would appear that the Magdalens are at last coming into a prominent part of the world's economic picture.

In addition to the mining industry, there are now four fish freezers, eight producers' cooperatives and seven consumers' unions. *Time* Magazine, on November 17, 1947, said in summarizing these activities, "the industrial revolution is bringing the Magdalens—once known mostly for their sea birds, especially gannets—out of the mists at last."

But the only true village in the Magdalens is at Grand Entry, which is actually the western tail of Coffin Island. The village has the Magdalen rarity of a real street (covered with sand though it is) with houses on both sides for more than four hundred feet.

Deadman's Island always catches the eye of the passing sailor. It seems to lie floating in the water like a dead man in a shroud. Many a luckless vessel has crashed against its sheer cliffs, with a few fragments of wood or clothing all that remained of a happy group of voyagers who had sailed down under the sea forever.

When poet Thomas Moore saw Deadman's Island for the first time on a dark September evening in 1804, he composed a fitting ode to it, linking it with a phantom vessel which may have been the *Flying Dutchman*:

---

[1] This group sold its assets to Royran Goldfields and in April, 1950, was asking for annulment of its charter.

91

DEADMAN'S ISLAND

There lieth a wreck on the dismal shore
Of cold and pitiless Labrador,
Where, under the moon, upon mounts of frost,
Full many a mariner's bones are tossed.

Yon shadowy bark hath been to that wreck,
And the dim blue fire that lights her deck
Doth play on as pale and livid a crew
As ever yet drank the churchyard dew.

To Deadman's Isle in the eye of the blast,
To Deadman's Isle she speeds her fast;
By skeleton shapes her sails are furl'd,
And the hand that steers is not of this world!

The two loneliest of the lovely Magdalens are Brion Isle and the Bird Rocks, respectively, nine and sixteen miles away from East Island, the closest of the main Magdalen group. Brion Island was once said to be so desolate that even rats could not live there. It is the graveyard of many a fine ship, and cases of starvation and cannibalism are reported to have occurred there. Today, however, the lighthouse keeper and his wife dwell on the island in the company of a happy and prosperous farmer.

The single island of the Magdalens which impresses me more than any of the others, however, is Gannet Rock, or Great Bird Rock. Connected by an underwater shoal to Little Bird Rock, the reddish sandstone island presents a startling appearance when seen for the first time. It resembles a beautifully colored and gigantic airplane carrier anchored forever in the gulf.

Bird Rock has been visited by several famous people, including Jacques Cartier in 1534, John James Audubon early in the nineteenth century and Franklin D. Roosevelt in 1939. But the man who will be most remembered there is

Arthur Griffin, nationally known photographer from Winchester, Massachusetts. His color pictures of the gigantic rock gave pleasure to millions of people in 1949 when they were published in *The Saturday Evening Post*.

The winters at Bird Rock Lighthouse are especially terrible, for the isolation here is well-nigh complete. It is a seven-acre kingdom on a rock barely two thousand feet long and nine hundred feet wide, and except for a tiny plot of grass, it has no vegetation at all. For a good part of the year, the Gulf of Saint Lawrence is blocked by ice, and no ship ventures forth.

When spring arrives, however, there is excitement enough for all. Then the seven-acre rock becomes a great rookery, crowded with gannets, bridled guillemots, foolish guillemots, razor-billed auks, kittywakes and puffins. In springtime the keeper and his family must be careful in walking around their domain to avoid stepping on nests and eggs.

When the great ornithologist Audubon visited Bird Rock he was fascinated by the many specimens he saw there. Another distinguished visitor was Dr. H. Bryant of Boston, who has described his visit to Little Bird Rock:

> *The landing is very difficult at all times, as it is necessary to jump from a boat, thrown about by the surf, onto the inclined surface of the ledge, rendered slippery by the fuci which cover it, and bounded toward the rock by a nearly vertical face. The landing once effected, the first part of the ascent is comparatively easy, being over large fragments and broad ledges; but the upper part is both difficult and dangerous, as in some places the face of the rock is vertical for eight or ten feet, and the projecting ledges very narrow, and the rock itself so soft that it cannot be trusted to, and in addition rendered slippery by the constant trickling from above, and the excrements of the birds that cover it in every direction.*

The unfortunate and unnecessary Bird Rock Disaster is still a topic of conversation during the long wintry nights at the Magdalens.

Shortly after the turn of the present century, there was a prolonged spell of thick, dense fog in the Magdalen area. In those days there were no automatic fog horns to warn away ships at sea, and a cannon was fired at regular intervals during the heavy weather, day after day and night after night. Finally, the three keepers, John Turbid, Paul Chenel and John Pigeon, grew so tired of carrying only three charges of gunpowder at a time to the cannon, as regulations required, that they took the whole barrel over to the cliff. This had been forbidden in order to minimize damage in case of an explosion.

One day, soon after the keepers began this forbidden practice, the cannon backfired, and the priming cap flew into the open powder barrel. In the explosion which followed Chenel and Pigeon were blown to pieces. One of the keeper's children was also killed, but Turbid, who had been blown into the sea, survived to swim ashore and make his way back to the lighthouse.

Another disaster at the Rock occurred during the seal-catching season. In the month of December the seals penetrate the Gulf of Saint Lawrence in great herds. By the middle or end of March the female seals climb up on the floating ice to have their young, which they nurse with great care and tenderness for the next three weeks. During this nursing period they stay on the ice and do not venture near the water. It is at this time that the sealers land on the packs and kill the animals by clubbing or shooting.

The winds of March usually push one or two of the giant ice packs, loaded with seals, against the Magdalen Islands. The ice stays grounded near the coast until the wind changes, and the news of its arrival soon spreads all over the Magdalens. Bells are rung and guns are fired, and entire families stop whatever they are doing to join in the seal hunt.

In one year, 1864, six thousand seals, each worth $3.00, were slaughtered by the islanders.

The men and boys stay out on the ice fields, but the women return home at meal-times and prepare food which they often carry for miles across the ice to their menfolk. When enough seals have been killed, the men remove the skin and fat and tie the pelts together. Sometimes their loads are very heavy, and their progress toward home is slow. As they start for home the wind may change, carrying them out to sea on the ice floe before they realize their danger.

One year around the turn of the century Keeper Whalen, his son and Assistant Keeper Joseph Pigeon went out on the ice and killed many seals. They had taken along a galvanized iron flatboat for safety. But that night the wind blew so hard that they were unable to navigate the boat through the tossing ice cakes. Before morning both Whalen and his son had frozen to death. Pigeon was still alive and decided to make an effort to reach Bird Rock. He climbed out of the flatboat and made his way out over the bobbing, crashing ice pack. It was a terrible journey as he battled his way through the masses of ice. Time and again he abandoned all hope, but toward morning the wind shifted, and the pack began to float toward the Magdalens again. Pigeon was soon in sight of Bird Rock.

Battling his way across the lolly, or soft ice, Pigeon reached Bird Rock late that afternoon, where he told the tragic news of death to Mrs. Whalen. The two of them continued to run the lighthouse until help came more than a month later.

Another ice catastrophe occurred several years later. Around 1910 Keeper Telesphore Turbid, his son and Keeper Damien Deveaux went out on the floe after seals, leaving Mrs. Deveaux alone on the island. The wind came up and they floated off toward the south. The lighthouse keepers soon froze to death, but young Turbid somehow reached Cape Breton Island alive. Here he was rescued in an unconscious condition and cared for by the natives. As he was taken to the hospital, he revived long enough to tell his tragic story.

Then young Turbid said, "Annie Deveaux is all alone at the Rock. Will you save her?" Within an hour, Turbid died.

The following morning the government icebreaker was pushing through the ice, and three days later Annie Deveaux, a solitary prisoner at Bird Rock for four weeks, was rescued.

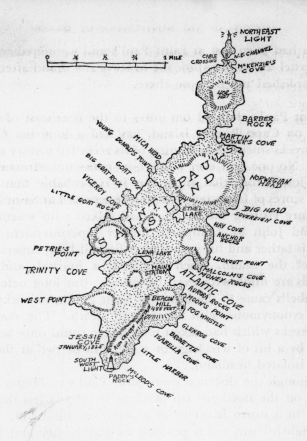

The map shows Saint Paul's Island with the following labels:

NORTH EAST LIGHT
N.E. CHANNEL
CABLE CROSSING
McKENZIE'S COVE
HOT HEAD
BARBER ROCK
MICA HEAD
MARTIN POWER'S COVE
YOUNG DONALD'S POINT
GOAT COVE
BIG GOAT ROCK
VICEROY COVE
LITTLE GOAT ROCK
SAINT PAUL'S ISLAND
NORWEGIAN HEAD
ETHEL LAKE
BIG HEAD
SOVEREIGN COVE
HAY COVE
ANCHOR ROCKS
PETRIE'S POINT
LENA LAKE
LOOKOUT POINT
TRINITY COVE
MAIN STATION
MALCOLM'S COVE
MONEY ROCKS
ATLANTIC COVE
AURORA ROCKS
WEST POINT
MOON'S POINT
BEACON HILL 455 FEET
FOG WHISTLE
GLENROE COVE
BRUNETTE COVE
JESSIE COVE JANUARY, 1825
ISABELLA COVE
SOUTH WEST LIGHT
LITTLE HARBOR
McLEOD'S COVE
PADDY'S ROCK

Scale: 0   ¼   ½   ¾   1 MILE

V. SAINT PAUL'S ISLAND

AFTER an hour's sail from North Cape, we neared the precipitous cliffs of Saint Paul's Island in Cabot Strait. On the east side of the island we found Atlantic Cove, and soon headed shoreward in the dory.

The landing at Saint Paul's is always a difficult one, and we had a particularly bad time getting ashore in the crashing surf. But we finally landed safely, and half an hour later stood at the top of a long incline, looking back at the turbulent waters we had just left. I thought of the many vessels

97

which had been lost at Saint Paul's and wondered whether that cruel sea would allow me to leave the island after I had accomplished my purpose there.

Saint Paul's, located ten miles to the northeast of North Cape on Cape Breton Island, has had a long list of fatal shipwrecks since the beginning of its recorded history around 1825. No one will ever know how many unfortunate ships were lost before that time, but it is probable that scores upon scores of forgotten vessels were wrecked at Saint Paul's.

Before visiting the island, I had talked with seventy-five-year-old John M. Campbell, former superintendent there. He, his father and his grandfather had all been superintendents of the island. Each one kept a journal, and their records are filled with exciting stories. But long before the Campbells came to the island of Saint Paul's, its rocky cliffs were synonymous with terror and death. The countless shipwrecks which had taken place there could only be identified by a bit of wreckage or a skeleton or two at the base of an isolated headland.

Although the distance from Saint Paul's to Money Point Light on the northern tip of Cape Breton is less than ten miles, in a storm it might as well be ten thousand. When the frightful surf starts pushing its way higher and higher up the rocky ledges of Saint Paul's, no one can land on the island and no one can leave it. During a gale, Saint Paul's could be no more effectively cut off from the rest of the world if it were on another planet. At the height of winter, when the dreaded ice packs crash against the island, its coastline is even more fearsome.

Although the island is scarcely two and three-quarter miles in length and only a mile in width, the contours of its cliffs, chasm and outer beaches are so intricate that its shore line measures eleven miles. Because of the constant surf, there are few days when the base of the cliffs can be explored. Almost every bay or rocky ledge, and more than a score of headlands and coves, have been the scenes of shipwreck and tragedy.

The four really important locations at Saint Paul's are North (or Northeast) Light, South (or Southwest) Light, Atlantic Cove on the east and Trinity Cove on the west. Atlantic Cove was the island headquarters for many years. There are two inland lakes, Lake Ethel to the north and Lake Lena to the south. Yellowish-brown streams flow from these lakes into both Trinity Cove and Atlantic Cove.

Seagulls are often found at Saint Paul's, and the great auk, now practically extinct, once lived on its rocky crags. As large as a goose, with short wings and a white breast, the bird could be identified by a milk-white spot under its right eye. Before the species disappeared altogether, museum collectors offered as much as $1500 for a single auk.

At two locations the island's rocky masses rise to a height of more than four hundred feet. The highest point of all looks down into Atlantic Cove and forms a geographical triangle with the cove and Lake Lena. Four hundred and eighty-five feet above the sea, this peak is the southern point of the triangle, with the lake the northwest point and Atlantic Cove forming the third apex to the northeast. Once called Beacon Hill, this peak is now known as Crocan Mountain. The other high area is on the rocky northern peninsula of the island and looks down across the chasm toward North Point Light which is on a tiny separate island all its own. You can only reach North Point Light by climbing into a hanging chair built along the lines of a breeches-buoy and pulling yourself across the chasm on the cable over the water far below. It is a great adventure.

The island's two lighthouses are officially listed as lying in the Cabot Strait at the entrance to the Gulf of Saint Lawrence. They have been illuminated since 1837. North Point Light burned down in 1916 but was soon rebuilt, and its beacon now shines steadily from a white octagonal structure forty feet high, 126 feet above the sea. South Point Light is a red cylindrical iron tower twenty-seven feet high, standing 156 feet above the ocean. Its light flashes four times every twelve seconds. Also on Saint Paul's is a fog diaphone at North Point Light; a radio direction-finder at Atlantic Cove which at times is operated as a radio-beacon; and a marine telegraph, weather, and ice report station at South Point Light.

I had come to Saint Paul's to delve into its fascinating, if relatively short, history of shipwrecks, tragic disappearances and fierce island loyalties. Several weird ghost stories made my task an even more interesting one. In collecting the facts, the journals kept by the three Campbells proved invaluable.

The name of Campbell will never be forgotten by the brave men who live at Saint Paul's Island. The first of the family to live there was John Campbell, who came in 1837 to oversee the building of the lights and remained as the island's first superintendent.

Three of John Campbell's children were born deaf and dumb, and two of these unfortunates died in childhood of tuberculosis. Campbell had at least two other children, Malcolm and Samuel. Samuel succeeded his father at the station in 1874, bringing his two-year-old son out to the "rock" in 1876. The boy's name was John M. Campbell, and it was he whom I interviewed in 1950.

John M. Campbell remained on lonely Saint Paul's until 1890, and returned again in 1904, remaining as its superintendent until 1918.[1] The Campbell family, therefore, has played a most important part in affairs at Saint Paul's for eighty-one years.[2] Later we shall quote from the tens of thousands of words which the Campbells recorded in the journals they kept out on the cruelly isolated rock.

John M. Campbell prepared a list for me of vessels

---

[1] John M. Campbell was also in charge of Sable Island from 1919 to 1921.

[2] There is no superintendent at Saint Paul's today.

wrecked at Saint Paul's. They were the *Jessie, Mitchell, Wave, Deodata, Margaret, Marie Casabona, Canadian, Venesian, Viceroy, Anna, Alfred Taylor, Emperor, Glenlevit, Ollivete, Warwick, Barbara, Norwegian, Duncan, Jane, England's Queen, Pallas, Royal Sovereign, Glenroe, Brunette, Thistle, Isabella, Minerva, Enchantress, Vanguard, Briton Elliot, Turrett Bay, Helena, Arcola* and the *Elliot*. For every known disaster there are two unknown wrecks in the stormy waters beyond the island cliffs.

Mariners learned to fear the rocks of Saint Paul's long before the beginning of recorded history at Cape Breton. There is good reason to believe that at least one Spanish galleon, driven far off its course, crashed to its doom against the granite sides of this natural bastion.

For years fishermen brought up gold doubloons from the sea bottom at the base of one of the cliffs. Their technique was to dip long poles into pitch and with them, reach down to the floor of the ocean. Doubloons adhered to the pitch and scores of them were brought to the surface. The fishermen's crude methods were not effective in recovering the heavy bars of gold and silver which were undoubtedly part of the cargo, and most of the treasure from the galleon is believed to be still in the water at the base of that cliff.

John M. Campbell told me that one of the keepers discovered a crocan, or jug, containing five hundred sovereigns in a rocky crevice some distance above the waves. Evidently a shipwrecked sailor had hid his treasure in a safe place and died before it could be removed. The area where the jug was found is still known as Crocan Cove, at the foot of Crocan Mountain.

One event in the island's history I most wanted to investigate was the wreck of the barque *Jessie,* a disaster which occurred before Saint Paul's was inhabited and offered protection to ships at sea. I therefore visited Jessie's Cove, named for the ill-fated barque, in an effort to recapitulate the terrible tragedy which took place there in the year 1825.

The barque *Jessie* sailed from Prince Edward Island on December 24, 1824. There were twenty-eight persons on board, including Mr. Donald MacKay, who owned the *Jessie*, and a Mr. Forbes of Pictou. As the barque left the Gulf of Saint Lawrence and entered the Cabot Straits, she was caught by a terrible snowstorm. On January 1, 1825, the *Jessie* crashed to her doom against the granite cliffs of Saint Paul's.

There were heart-breaking scenes as the passengers and crew on board the foundering ship pulled themselves ashore. Soon the little group of survivors erected a lean-to from canvas sails and spars. Later they built a huge bonfire, in an effort to signal the fishermen at Cape North. But the days went by without help. Finally, their food was gone, and, one by one, the survivors perished on the lonely island.

Mr. Donald MacKay of Prince Edward Island kept a diary[1] describing the shipwreck and the terrible days on Saint Paul's after the disaster. His last entry was on March 17, 1825.

Several weeks later, as was their custom, fishermen went ashore at Saint Paul's to search the island for wrecks. They found what remained of the *Jessie* and discovered the little camp with the bodies of the survivors who had built it. The fishermen soon spotted Donald MacKay's beautiful overcoat, which had been made for him by his wife, as well as one hundred guineas he carried in his clothing. All the bodies were stripped of valuables, and the fishermen vanished with their spoils from the grim island.

As the weeks passed, Donald MacKay's wife began to worry about her husband and remembered him as she had last seen him, dressed in the fine warm overcoat she had made. When the weeks turned to months, she gradually

---

[1] His diary was later sent to Boston and "placed in the museum" but I have been unable to locate it anywhere in Massachusetts. Incidentally, its author is not to be confused with Donald McKay the famous shipbuilder.

realized that her husband would never return to her on Prince Edward Island.

One day as she went into the village store for supplies a strange thing occurred. On the other side of the store she seemed to see her husband standing at the counter. Rushing over, she discovered her mistake. The man was a stranger, wearing a coat which resembled the one she had labored so long to make. And then she realized, from the buttons on the sleeve, that it was her husband's own garment.

"Where did you get that coat?" the excited woman shouted. "Tell me this instant!"

The stranger tried to bolt out of the store, but he was caught by a dozen willing hands and brought back to Mrs. MacKay. She then pulled open the overcoat to reveal her husband's initials, *D.M.*, which she had embroidered on the lining.

"Explain why my husband's initials are inside your coat pocket, can you? Where is my husband?"

The stranger realized that the game was up. He confessed everything, including the fact that he had taken the one hundred guineas, and returned the coat and the money to Mrs. MacKay.

The distraught widow immediately made plans to go to Saint Paul's. She went ashore with a group of men, found the camp site and the pitiful remains of her husband. His body and that of the captain were brought back to Charlottetown. Most of the others from the *Jessie* were buried on the island.

The funeral services at Charlottetown made a deep impression on the residents of Prince Edward. Donald MacKay and his companions had not died in vain, for, as a result of their terrible fate, mariners demanded that a shelter and a lighthouse be built on Saint Paul's.

The first published account of a visit to Saint Paul's Island was written by Mr. John Adams, the architect who was chosen to plan the lighthouse there. Sailing from Quebec in June, 1830, on the Government brig *Kingfisher,* he landed at Saint Paul's on July 14.

Mr. Adams found the island directly in the route of ships sailing to and from the Gulf of Saint Lawrence. Its cliffs, he wrote, were nearly perpendicular and surrounded by deep water. The architect noted how easy it would be for a vessel to crash against the rocks in fog and vanish forever.

When Mr. Adams and his party landed, they found the graves of seventeen persons from Miramichi, who had been wrecked at Saint Paul's several years before. The bodies had been discovered the following summer by sailors who landed on the island and looted the dead. Adams saw the remains of a shelter located in a sort of hollow. Here the shipwrecked men had huddled under a canvas covering before they died of starvation.

The architect wrote of another vessel, a British transport, which had been wrecked on the island around 1813. This vessel was probably the *Royal Sovereign.* Of further wrecks he tells us:

> *We minutely examined every cranny around the Island in the ship's launch, and occasionally clambered on the rocks at the bases of the cliffs, but found no shelter. In all these bays and indentations, which are very numerous on the western side, we found remains of former wrecks piled up there high and dry—deals, staves, pieces of bulwark, planks of boats, &c., &c. plainly indicative of past misfortunes.*

One day Captain Bayside of the *Kingfisher* was cruising along the island cliffs when he found the fragments of a bowsprit, a broken canteen and a piece of planking, on which the figures 8.o were distinguishable.

When John Adams explored the island he discovered a strange water-filled area near the center of the island in which a man might sink to his death if he made one unfortunate misstep. This treacherous section was covered with a luxuriant growth of bog grass which was mixed with an abundance of a marshy plant known as the *Sarracenia Purpurea,* called *Lunette au Cochon* by the Canadians. What appeared to be solid ground was actually a matwork of decayed roots and fibers resting on water. One of Adams' companions sank a leveling rod twenty-two feet down through the soft mass without touching bottom!

When he had thoroughly explored the island, Architect Adams returned to the mainland. He had decided that a single lighthouse placed on Beacon Hill, the highest part of the island, and shining from a height of five hundred feet would be the best illumination. In this opinion he was opposed by others who believed that two lights, one at each end of the island, would be of greater advantage to navigators.

On February 5, 1831, John Adams read his report on Saint Paul's before the influential Literary and Historical Society of Quebec, and in the summer of 1832 the New Brunswick Government sent a vessel to Saint Paul's for the purpose of building a shelter at Trinity Cove.

Strangely enough, on the other side of the island at the same time three men, headed by a Mr. MacKenzie from Cape Breton, were constructing a similar shelter. It is said that neither party knew of the other's existence, but this is hard to believe in view of the fact that the island is barely a mile wide. There must have been some venturesome souls in both camps.

At the height of the following winter, the *Great Britain* from Hull, England, went ashore on the ledges near Trinity Cove, and all but four of those aboard were drowned. When the survivors reached shore safely, one of them climbed around the precipitous sides of Saint Paul's, looking for help. He then crossed the island and discovered the Cape Breton Humane Station.

Mr. MacKenzie ordered his two assistants to care for the

sailor while he went to search for the remaining survivors. Following footsteps in the snow, he soon found two other sailors, frozen to death. Then he followed the footsteps of the fourth man to the clearing where the New Brunswick Humane Station at Trinity Cove was located. MacKenzie entered the shelter and found that the fourth man was being cared for. He was in hopeless condition, however, and died in great pain a short time later.

Evidently the two camps were jealous of each other's importance. Shortly after the wreck of the *Great Britain* the men at the Cape Breton station ran short of food when their relief ship failed to appear, and they asked those at the New Brunswick shelter to divide supplies with them. Instead, White, in charge of the station, suggested that he would care for the surviving sailor from the *Great Britain* to allow more food for the three men of Cape Breton. But the sailor refused to leave the camp of his saviors, and there matters rested. With the coming of January, a real crisis was at hand.

On January 6, 1833, with their food gone and no sign of the promised relief ship, MacKenzie, his two men and the sailor left in an open boat for Cape North, ten miles away. They were caught in a snowstorm and nearly capsized by the high waves and strong wind. By ten the next morning, however, they were sailing into Ingonish, half frozen and covered with snow, but safe.

On Saint Paul's, the men of the New Brunswick station had their own adventures. In the fall of 1833 White was blown out to sea when an oar of his boat snapped as he was returning from a ship. He was later rescued by a vessel which took him to England, and Donald Moon was chosen to take his place at the island.

A large, rambling house at Trinity Cove was finished and was often used as a place of refuge by shipwrecked sailors. But the Cape Breton Islanders eventually won out over the

New Brunswick men when the government chose Atlantic Cove as the site for the main rescue station.

In 1837 John Campbell of Argyleshire, Scotland, was appointed by the British Government as superintendent of Saint Paul's Island. His first task was to direct the building of the main station and two lighthouses. I have before me as I write the journal John Campbell kept while he was on the island. During the summer of 1843 his oldest son Malcolm, or Malcom, as the superintendent spells it, was taken seriously ill, and Mr. Campbell sent for a doctor from the mainland. We quote from his journal:

1843

July 11. Fresh breezes from the South with rain most all day. Nothing doing outdoors. Doctor Foreman of Sydney arrived here on Sabbath to attend my oldest boy Malcom who was dangerously sick of a disease which I did not understand, tho I pretend to be something of a quack. The boy however recovered ere the doctor arrived. He drew a tooth which was troublesome to the boy and gave him one dose of physic for which he had the effrontery to charge me 30 (thirty) pounds. He maintained his grounds and talked about the respectability of the medical profession and such stuff. I had however to pay to this extortioner the sum of twenty pounds not that I was at all afraid that he could recover any such sum by legal means, but I did not really want to have anything more to do with so barefaced and shabby a fellow. It is such fellows as Foreman that lower the medical profession in the estimation of the public. Such cannot make a living but by such grasps, when a windfall of this kind comes in the way it is generally spent or expended in the gratification of their appetites. The fellow is sitting in the room while I am writing this and I can assure the reader that I have enough to do to keep old Adam down—

Other excerpts followed. The journal describes the beginning of scores of incidents but seldom the end, often leaving the reader unsatisfied. He mentions a wreck but doesn't give its name:

> *July 15, 1843. The schooner* Mary Ann *Captain Muggan with Frazer the diver on board left for Sydney with iron and some chains taken from the wreck.*
>
> *July 21. Charles Muggan with Mr. Thos. R. Frazer the diver on board arrived today from Sydney to work again at the wreck. Strange the wreck stands it so long. The quantity of iron in her bottom keeps her together and keeps her from rising with the sea.*
>
> *August 14. Visited the S. West Light and landed three chaldrons coal here and one chaldron at Atlantic Cove. Proceeded in the evening to the N. E. Station and landed coal there until dark.*
>
> *August 17. Fresh breezes from the south with fog and rain. Visited the southwest light. All well.*
>
> *Dr. Tho. McCulloch the principal of the Dalhousie College, Halifax, has written to me to procure for him specimens of the St. Paul rocks and I have been this day with my men employed in collecting them.*
>
> *October 25. Light winds from the Northwest cloudy and dark. Landed from the* Greyhound *the following articles for the humane establishment Namely one case containing 12 pairs of trousers 24 pair shoes and 12 jackets. One case containing 240 yards lampwick for lighthouses also provision and coal.*
>
> *November 21. Light wind from the North a fine day but shifted to South East about dark visited the North East Light all well took Launch and had a view of both Lights off Atlantic Cove after dark they pleased me with the motion of the South West Light was exactly what I wished to be One minute and a half dark and ½ minute flash.*

November 24. Fresh breezes from the N. E. a fine day for the season of the year Killed a cow today for winter beef Men in the afternoon geting fire wood

December 19. Fresh breezes from the N. W. with frost visited the N. E. Light all in goode order No sails in sight. I imagine that the fall fleet are all past so that in all probability we shall have no wrecks this fall indeed without dense fog or a thick snow storm there cannot be a wreck on St. Pauls; at least while the lights are kept in good order which will always be the case, if the Lord will, while I continue Superintendent.

January 18, 1844. The billows of the Atlantic dashing and foaming are certainly worth looking at they dash against the cliffs with such violence that the spray rises high against the side of the mountains perhaps to the height of three hundred feet. How wonderful of God are Thy works.

January 29. A great gale of wind from the North East with snow and drift ice driven passed the Island with great violence great sea round the Island. What a long and dreary winter we have in this country especially on this wave worn north. Upwards of seven months without any communication with any part of the world. Revolutions and great changes may take place even in Nova Scotia without my hearing anything about it until it be over.

March 20. Saw a schooner in the ice about four miles from the island in a Northwest direction. Sent some men out to her on the ice she proved to be the Mermaid of Sydney on a sealing voyage.

March 22. The Brigantine Niger of Sydney Captain McCloud anchored off the southwest coast of St. Paul's this afternoon on a sealing voyage They are out 28 days and have only killed three seals. I hope however they may succeed

March 25. Captain Ross and one of his men called

upon me this morning His old crazy schooner was very leaky and seemed to be much alarmed about her I boarded her with Captain Ross and certainly no man in his senses would risk his life even in the middle of summer in such a trap They were also nearly out of everything being about 5 weeks in the ice so that I found that I must give them provisions or keep them all on the island 20 men for the period of 7 weeks I therefore remembered the old proverb of two evils choose the least and gave them a barrel of flour tea some fish blocks of fall.

April 19. Light winds from the south very warm weather saw two vessels in the ice today. The lights doing well Killed 56 seals today. I have now 364 seals on shore a great help to support my poor family

May 8. It is really a backward spring. I am not as yet able to send a boat to Sydney owing to immense bodies of ice in all directions Saw six schooners and shallops in the ice after seals today

May 23. The schooner Seaflour *of Sydney Captain Florian arrived at Trinity Cove with coal and provisions for myself and keepers*

May 24. Strong breezes from the northeast heavy surf on the north side of the island. The schooner (Seaflour) I am sorry to record drifted on the rocks and was stranded at once. Our flour and provisions was soon at the mercy of the sea We got some barrels of the flour after being washed out of her but some was dashed to pieces against the rocks Our potatoes bread oats Indian meal salt and coal were totally lost and the vessel became a total wreck. *This is the first loss of the kind that I met with since I became connected with St. Paul's, and although the amount is not large yet situated as I am it is a serious loss.*

Worried about his deaf and dumb children, Superintend-

ent Campbell left the island on May 30, 1844, for the mainland. His son Malcolm kept up the journal:

> *May 30. The schooner left with my father and two of
> the children aboard.*
> *June 15. The shallop* John Henry *of Halifax Captain
> Myers arrived here from Sydney C. B. today for to take
> away the anchors and chains of the* Seaflour.
> *June 20. A great sea round the island today several sail
> in flight homeward bound All hand employed at plant-
> ing potatoes.*

John Campbell returned to the island on July 6, 1844,
and resumed his record of events:

> *July 6, 1844 I arrived in the shallop* Adamant *Captain
> Barrington in the afternoon and found everything on
> the island in good order. The light's doing very well.
> I have been absent from the island 36 days. During
> that time I visited every place of note in two of the
> states of America. Landed in the city of Boston.
> Traveled by railroad to Spring Field hence by steam
> boat on the Connecticut River to the city of Hartford.
> Placed two of my children in the Deaf & Dumb asylum
> there and really that asylum is not only a credit to the
> state which supports it but is also such as every citizen
> of America should be proud of.*
> *July 16. The shallop* Adamant *arrived from Bay St.
> Lawrence. The object is to raise by means of diving
> dress some iron of the bottome part of the cargo of the
> Bark* Brunette. *It must be a losing concern. They are
> now 10 days about the island and as yet have not suc-
> ceeded in raising even one bar.*

One spring day Malcolm Campbell and four men from
the island boarded a vessel stranded on the coast, and found
her to be the schooner *Joseph,* with not a living soul aboard.

They brought her back to the cove, where Campbell examined her log book.

> *There is nothing of any value in her. There is a quantity of cord wood in her hold. The log book has been so stupidly kept that I cannot learn from it where she left or where bound to.*
>
> *January 16, 1846. Dyall McPhadain who had charge of the Southwest Light for some time back has gone to Sydney by boat. I have every occasion to be dissatisfied with his conduct as a keeper and also with his moral character which is evidently infamous I will not allow him to remain on St. Paul's while I have charge.*

I have already mentioned Donald Moon, who took White's place at Saint Paul's Trinity Cove Humane Station in 1833. When the Northwest Light was built, Moon became its keeper, a position he held for several years.

The islanders earned extra revenue by catching seals from the ice floes which smashed against the cliffs, and on the evening of February 6, 1844, Donald Moon's two assistants at the lighthouse went out on the ice during a high wind in pursuit of two seals. When the men did not return after a reasonable time, Moon set out to rescue them. But we will let John Campbell tell the story:

> *February 12. High winds from the North Remarkably keen frost The open water for the last four days smoking like boiling water for the last four days impossible to visit the lights which I am most anxious to do This is my eighth winter on the island but never saw or experienced any weather at all like this The whole ocean seems like a boiling cauldron.*
>
> *February 13. Strong breezes from the North Immense fields of ice round the Island but the weather more moderate frost not near so intense Visited the N. E. light today but alas, found only poor Mrs. Moon and*

*her child there and it becomes my painful duty to
record the melancholy fate of D. Moon his two servant
men and his servant girl (as far as this can be learned
from his wife the only one left to tell the direful tale)
I visited Moon's lighthouse on the fifth last and that
night a gale commenced from the north accompanied
by the most intense frost I ever experienced so that for
a whole week it was out of my power to visit poor Moon
either by land or by sea This circumstance did not
trouble me much as I had every confidence in Moon's
prudence, skill and care and he was well supplied with
all necessaries It appears that on the evening of the
6th Inst, Moon's men went on the ice and will never
return With that he took his mittens and ran to the
landing place The servant girl followed him They
launched the boat went off and was neither seen nor
heard of more. Poor Mrs. Moon was left alone on the
island with her child on the breast her only companion
in her awful situation for seven days and seven nights
On the eighth day I found the poor woman in an awful
condition Her lamentations will never be effaced from
my mind what an awful calamity! Four souls swept
away in a moment and launched into eternity. May God
bless this dispensation of his Providence to the others on
the Island and to my own soul and may He accord to
his word comfort the poor widow and the orphan My
own feelings have been much tried by this fatal catastrophe The number of hands now left me are scarcely
competent for the public duties of the island I have
discontinued the N. W. Light until some time in March
or until the shipping will be expected I make no apol-
ogy for this It is indeed a case of Necessity. I have lost
poor Moon my right hand man and my friend for near
eight years on the Island Also William McLeod a
favorite servant for near two years. Oh William I indeed miss you but I will say no more They have run*

> *their race. They have gone to that* Bourn *from whence
> no traveller returns—*

Parts of the journal reflect Mr. Campbell's deep appreciation of beauty. One day in 1858 he writes of the many large ships which were bound up the gulf. It was "really beautiful to see them plunging from the summit of a mighty wave down into the trough of the sea below, and then again mounting high up and leaving a broad white sheet of foam in their wake."

The great masses of ice always impressed Campbell with their awesome splendor. Once, in January, 1860, he watched the ice close in around North Light. It was a "grand and terrific sight to see a sheet of ice about three miles square rising up into the air, one layer upon another, until it becomes a vast mountain of ice upon a precipice of rock."

On April 28, 1856, the Irish emigrant ship *Pallas* sailed from Cork, bound for Quebec. Aboard were 136 passengers and sixteen members of the crew. On May 30, the *Pallas* was approaching the coast of Cape Breton, when a heavy fog set in. At eight o'clock the passengers heard the distant sound of a cannon being fired,[1] but the fog was so thick they could not tell from which direction it came, and the *Pallas* continued at a speed of four and a half knots. Two hours later another cannon-shot was heard, this time from close at hand. The captain ordered the ship veered to the southeast, but it was too late, and the *Pallas* crashed against the granite ledges of Saint Paul's Island.

Superintendent Campbell soon heard shouts and the ringing of a ship's bell. Going to the edge of the cliff with his wife, he tried to peer across the darkness toward the ship, but the fog was too thick. He saw, however, that the waves were dashing forty and fifty feet up against the cliffs. He could do nothing to help the survivors on the wreck, but he

---

[1] In the days before the mechanical foghorn, a cannon was fired to warn away ships at sea.

remained on the rocks all that night, waving lanterns and shouting encouragement. Finally, the surf went down a little.

We carried a boat with great difficulty from Atlantic Cove to the rocks. The ship launched one of her own lifeboats but she filled at once and all in her drowned but three men. With my boat I got the three who were clinging to a sunken rock, having with great difficulty launched my own little lifeboat. It was one of the darkest nights I ever beheld, with rain and snowsqualls.

Later the next day Campbell rescued all the remaining passengers and crew members, most of them "quite naked, having lost everything they had in the world." Eighty-two of the passengers and crew had drowned, seventy were rescued by Campbell and his men. The captain of the *Pallas* went to Sydney several days later and hired the schooner *Nazaire* to transport the survivors to Grosse Island. From there they were taken by regular steamer to their destination, Quebec.

There are many ghost stories at the island. First, there is the legend of the beautiful woman spirit which has great similarity to the famous Sable Island ghost story I told in my *Mysteries and Adventures Along the Atlantic Coast.* Saint Paul's ghost is said to be that of a woman who froze to death after a shipwreck over a century and a half ago. Salvagers who landed on the island the following spring found the frozen bodies but didn't trust each other's honesty and buried the woman with her jewelry. One of her rings held a large, dazzlingly beautiful ruby, and two of the wreckers swore to themselves that they'd return, uncover the grave and pull the valuable ring from the dead woman's finger.

The wreckers did return—separately but simultaneously! In the fight which followed, one murdered the other, took the ruby and fled the island forever. Some time later other sailors landed on the island, found the bodies of the woman and the murdered man, buried them and went their way. But according to former Superintendent John M. Campbell, the ghost of the woman still haunts the vicinity of her grave, appearing in the dark of the moon to demand the return of her ruby.

Another more or less active ghost is that of a woman who was drowned aboard the *Irishman*. Her body never came ashore, and those who have seen her claim that she wanders the island on the anniversary of the wreck. This particular ghost can be identified by a white luminous shroud, always clearly visible, which floats about her in the darkness. Another member of the spirit population is the ghost of Martin Power, a fisherman who chose to settle on the island. Power's ghost is said to still appear near his old home, and there is today a cove on Saint Paul's which bears his name.

But John M. Campbell told me the most remarkable ghost story I have ever heard—remarkable because of its amazing mixture of realism and mysticism.

When he was a boy Campbell had often heard the story of the Negro sailor who had been wrecked on the island long before the lights and the main station were built. Details of the story were never written down, but it is known that the man's body was dug up and moved, not once but several times. One time as it was being moved, the head of the dead sailor fell off. It was recovered later and reburied elsewhere. According to legend, this unfortunate separation caused the dead man's spirit to grow uneasy, and his decapitated ghost often roamed the island, trying to find his lost head.

When John Campbell first heard this story as a very young boy, he paid little attention to it. But one night as he performed one of his regular chores and went down to the cellar of the house to bring up potatoes, he noticed the Negro's headless form standing near the potato barrel. It frightened the lad terribly, and he stumbled up the cellar steps and into the kitchen. Ten minutes later he gathered up his courage to go down again. This time he succeeded in getting his potatoes, for the ghost had vanished.

On another occasion the headless ghost again appeared in the cellar to challenge young John, planting itself directly in front of the potatoes. John Campbell rushed at the ghost, but it easily eluded him and vanished. Time and again the creature would appear to the boy in the cellar until he wondered if its head were not buried there.

Finally, one night John Campbell decided to attack the ghost. He felt that he might better die once and for all than be frightened to death gradually. When the ghost next appeared in the cellar, John pretended to ignore it. He went over to the barrel and began filling his pan with potatoes for the evening meal. Out of the corner of his eye he saw the headless form slowly approaching. Then, just as it came close, John twisted about and grabbed it around the waist.

"Now that I had caught him," John Campbell told me later, "I was determined to find out the truth. It was horrible, for when my hands slid over his soft body and reached his neck—why there was no head at all! That panicked me and I must confess that I ran upstairs.

"We all saw the ghost from time to time after that and came to accept him as one of the things at the island that could not be avoided, like the fog and the storms. I bumped into him quite often but I never had the least desire to grab him again. I left the island in 1890 and came back twelve years later as superintendent, but I didn't see the ghost again. Make no mistake, I saw him that night and when I grabbed him I felt his chest and shoulders and the hollow where his head should have been. Believe me, it was a frightful experience!"

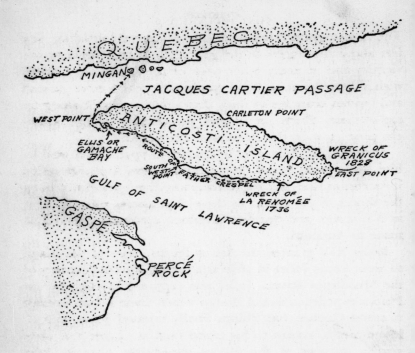

VI. ANTICOSTI

ON CHARTS and maps Anticosti Island resembles a huge seal swimming through the gulf toward the St. Lawrence River. Situated directly in the mouth of the river, the island lies entirely between the forty-ninth and fiftieth degrees of latitude and covers an area 136 miles long and thirty-five miles wide.

A large part of the island coast has a belt of limestone reefs which are bare at low water, making it difficult for the mariner to reach a safe harbor in time of storm. The only suitable harbor is at Gamache Bay, also called Ellis Bay, and it is there that Port Menier is located.

The southern part of the island is fairly low-lying, but on the north, cliffs rise to heights of four and five hundred feet.

The highest point is believed to be at Cape Observation, 625 feet above the waters of the gulf. The coastal rocks in the vicinity and in many other parts of the island are covered with a dense forest of dwarf spruce trees which have gnarled and twisted branches so thick that a man can walk along on top of them. Birch, spruce and, surprisingly enough, southern pine grow in the interior of the island.

Anticosti was discovered by Cartier in 1534, and named by him Assumption Island. In 1542 pilot Jean Alphonse called it Ascension Isle. But the Indians who lived peacefully along the shores of the island in those days always referred to it as Natiscotee, and Spanish fishermen corrupted the Indian name to Anticosti.

Louis XIV granted the fief or feudal estate of the island to Sieur Louis Joliet in 1680 as a reward for his discovery of the Mississippi River. Joliet was captured in 1690 by the Phipps expedition out of Boston which made a vain attempt to storm Quebec, but Phipps finally released Joliet, and allowed him to return to his island fastness. Later that same year, a member of the Phipps expedition, Captain John Rainsford of Boston, was wrecked at Anticosti, but we shall hear more of his story further on in this chapter.

Eventually, members of the Forsyth family acquired possession of Anticosti. In 1825 it was annexed to Lower Canada by an act of Parliament, and in 1895 Henri Meunier, the chocolate king of France, purchased the island for the sum of $125,000.

Anticosti presented many transportation problems to me, but finally I was able to arrange for the trip in successive stages by plane, car and boat.

Landing at the airport in Moncton, New Brunswick, I went overland by car until I reached the Gaspé Peninsula. It was a rough and bumpy ride over roads which time and again showed evidences that their best days had passed. But at last I arrived at a little fishing village and asked one of the natives to take me to the home of a fisherman who had a boat I could charter. Soon I was introduced to Pierre Gaudette and had inspected his fishing craft. It seemed quite suitable for my projected journey and I decided to make arrangements with its owner.

When Pierre Gaudette learned that I merely planned to sail out around Cape Gaspé, cross over to Anticosti and cruise along the shore beyond East Cape to Fox Bay, he could hardly believe his ears. He was certain that I must have some ulterior motive for the trip—perhaps smuggling dope or contraband arms. But he agreed to make the voyage as I outlined it on my chart.

Seven hours later, as we approached Heath Point Light, we ran into a thick fog. Just beyond the lighthouse is Wreck Bay, the scene of the amazing story of the barque *Granicus,* and it was there I wished to land. An hour later we could see the shore at Merrimack Point, and the fog cleared enough for us to distinguish the beacon at Reef Point, marking the southern entrance to Fox Bay. In the distance was a tiny river, with another beacon on a small headland which jutted out into the bay to the northeast of the stream. Luckily, the tide was coming in, and my escort decided to maneuver up the bay as far as he dared.

Now the engine began to skip, and Pierre finally stopped the craft altogether and let it drift slowly toward the beach.

"You take small boat and go ashore?" Gaudette suggested.

I thrilled at the chance. Anticosti laws are very strict, and anyone who goes ashore without permission will be in trouble, but if a shipwrecked mariner finds himself off the shore, he is able to use the island in the emergency. So, being stranded, I was perfectly entitled to go ashore and look for help.

My real reason for landing on the island was that I wished to see the little enclosure where the victims from the barque *Granicus* had been buried and to try to find the old house of refuge nearby where their terrible fate had been perpetrated.

I landed on the beach, pulled the dory high above the reach of the water and had soon climbed up to Fox Point headland, a cliff about fifty feet high. When I found a small enclosed cemetery plot, I realized that I had accomplished half of my objective: here were the *Granicus* graves.

But I still wanted to visit the old house of refuge. On and on I trudged, but there were no buildings in sight. Then, as I came out into a clearing, in the distance I could see Table Head Lighthouse, just to the right of a headland 260 feet high. I began to walk in its direction.

Before I could reach the lighthouse, however, a foghorn blast sounded behind me. It was Pierre's signal that we must be starting back to the Gaspé. I knew that I had already gone too far from Fox Bay and that the fog might come in again so I hurried back to the beach and the dory. It was not long before Pierre Gaudette and I started for Gaspé.

Pierre, still suspicious of my motives, was ready with his queries. "What you do on island? Tell me truth!" he began. "Why you take so long to come back?"

Pierre understood English fairly well, and I decided to tell him the entire fiendish story of the *Granicus,* my chief reason for visiting Anticosti.

While I talked, the fog first drifted in and across us and then cleared intermittently for a minute or two. I shall never forget recounting the story of the *Granicus* to the accompaniment of waves splashing over the bow, ejaculations of amazement from Pierre and fog banks sweeping in across the bay. One develops a feeling of intimacy more quickly than usual on journeys such as we were making, and Pierre and I were better friends because of this unusual voyage than if we had been acquainted for years under other and more normal conditions. Before we had reached Cape Gaspé, we were both deeply under the spell of the strange, fearsome account of the unfortunate barque *Granicus.*

THE "GRANICUS"

ON MAY 8, 1829, Captain Basile Giasson, a sealer of renown on the St. Lawrence, was sailing just off Anticosti Island at a location then known as Belle Baie and now as Fox Bay. Since the wind was unfavorable and the ship's water supply completely exhausted, he dropped anchor there for the night.

Coming out on deck later, he noticed a ship's boat floating on the tide, and he decided to row in and investigate. By the condition of the boat he guessed that it must have been there for months. In examining it, Captain Giasson noticed that the oars were placed neatly together and that clothing and other personal effects were scattered around the bottom of the craft. He decided to go ashore and investigate further.

A house of refuge stood on the nearby cliff, and Giasson, with three members of the crew, landed his own boat and walked up toward the building. The men shouted to attract the attention of anyone who might be near, but once the echo of their own voices had died away, a deathlike silence fell on the bay. The place was so lonely and dreary that the men were seized with sudden fear. They decided to go back to the ship for guns and other weapons before exploring any further.

Returning to the clearing around the house, they found a woman's silk gown and the dress of a baby apparently about a year old. Captain Giasson picked up the garments and examined them. To his horror, he saw that they were covered with bloodstains and that both were torn as if by stabbing.

The four men were more terrified than before. They had seen evidence of murder, and, for all they knew, whoever was responsible might be hiding in the nearby woods, ready to kill them. But Jacques Bourgeois, a stout-hearted sealer who feared nothing, prevented them from running away. "We should not leave," he said. "We are armed, and if anyone tries to attack us he will get a good shower of lead."

Somewhat abashed, the other men now advanced cautiously with him toward the hut, guns in hand. As they entered the outer storm door of the building, a frightful sight greeted their eyes. More than a dozen partly dismembered human bodies were strewn on the floor and hung from the beams in the ceiling!

The four men were stunned. Captain Giasson shook his head as if to clear his senses and then led the way into the inner part of the house.

When the men reached the center of the next room, as their eyes gradually became accustomed to the darkness, they realized that they had left one horror only to find another equally gruesome.

Above the burnt-out logs in the enormous fireplace at one end of the room hung two huge iron pots filled with human fragments. This second horror was too much for Captain Giasson and his men, and they broke down and sobbed bitterly.

Finally, they steeled their nerves to explore the rest of the house.

In the next room they discovered three huge trunks. Shaking with fear, the men opened the lids and found that the trunks were crammed with dismembered human bodies which had been carefully preserved in salt.

In still another room they saw what they believed to be the first live person in this house of horrors. Lying in a hammock at one corner of the room, apparently asleep, was an enormous mulatto, a man with huge shoulders and what seemed the strength of Hercules. On the floor nearby was a pan of soup.

Captain Giasson, suppressing his repugnance, walked up to the man in the hammock and spoke to him. When there was no response, he touched the giant on the hand and found that he was dead.

The group continued to search the grounds and soon discovered a small outhouse. Inside was another pile of human remains, these too terrible to describe. In all, the captain guessed that at least twenty-four persons had been murdered at the house on the cliff. Captain Giasson decided that all the remains would have to be buried that night. Although it was May 8, the ground was still fairly hard with frost, and the four men worked long and hard to dig a pit big enough for the remains of the giant and the twenty-four other dead. Before they had finished, they were digging by lantern-light. It was a ghastly scene as the last of the victims was buried in the impromptu cemetery at Anticosti Island.

When they had finished their grim task, the men quickly returned to the sealing vessel and spent the night there. The next morning they went ashore again for a more thorough inspection. They found a note left by the giant mulatto, asking whoever discovered it to send the money he had left in the hammock to his mother, Mary Harrington, of Barrick Street Cove, Liverpool.

The next discovery was the ship's log or journal. Here the men read of how the *Granicus* had been wrecked and of how Harrington had killed the others. He felt, he wrote, that they would all probably die anyway and that he could prolong his own life by taking theirs. He had lived to write in the log book until just a few days before the sealers landed.

That afternoon the sealers carried aboard their vessel six trunk-loads of clothing in good condition and four other boxes of merchandise of all description. At seven o'clock that night, with the wind from the north, Captain Giasson set sail from Anticosti. Two days later he reached the Magdalen Islands and turned all of his evidence over to Monsieur Colbach, a representative of Admiral Coffin, the Governor of the Magdalens.

Captain Giasson often sailed past Anticosti Island in later years, but he never went by it without a renewed sense of horror at the discovery he had made back in 1829.

When Pierre Gaudette had returned me to the mainland I went at once to Quebec. Here I pieced together all available information about the ghastly story of the *Granicus*. I drew on sources which included Monsieur Placide Vigneau, lighthouse keeper at Parrott Island, J. M. LeMoine of Spencer Grange and Frederick William Wallace, the chronicler of St. Lawrence shipping. I believe I learned as much of the weird story as it is possible to learn so long after the event. The full details are so revolting that I have spared the reader a good deal, but the complete account is available for anyone with a lively curiosity and particularly strong nerves.

The Irish barque *Granicus* sailed from Quebec on October 29, 1828, homeward bound with a load of lumber for the Cove of Cork. Early in November she was caught in a terrible blow. When she grounded on a shoal and a sailor in the mizzenmast was slow in carrying out an order, the captain blew out the sailor's brains. This seems now like a foretaste of what was to come.

In the same storm over a dozen vessels in that area either sank or were wrecked on shore. The *Granicus* eventually piled up near East Point, Anticosti, and it seemed unusually good fortune that every passenger and crew member reached shore safely. On the island they found a sign indicating that a hut of refuge stood a few miles to the northwest along the coast.

Unfortunately, however, when the survivors reached the hut they discovered that every particle of food had disappeared from the building. It was later learned that the old keeper of the hut had taken the food away because it had spoiled, and no replacements had been sent by the authorities.

With all twenty-five of the ship's company assembled in the hut, the captain divided the food he had saved from the wreck. The survivors were able to live on it for several weeks. Then one night, justifying himself with the inhuman excuse that all would die sooner or later, Harrington, the giant member of the crew, decided to act for himself.

Actually, Harrington must have gone insane. The evidence indicates that he committed the wholesale murders some time in February, 1829. After carrying out the acts which could only be born of a hopelessly disordered mind, he methodically preserved the remains as best he could.

Harrington managed to stay alive for weeks on his horrible diet. But as the weather grew warmer, he found himself getting weaker and weaker. Finally, he became violently ill and was confined a good deal to his hammock. He was able to get up for a few hours a day for a while, but on April 28, 1829, he climbed into his hammock for the last time. His logbook record indicated that he never got up again. It is probable that he was killed by either scurvy or a poisoned stomach.

Anticosti Island has been the scene of countless tragic shipwrecks. Its weird history of spectacular disasters begins with the first records of navigation in the area. Situated as it is in the center of the Gulf of Saint Lawrence, it was once the dread of all sailing masters during fog or stormy weather. Authorities were slow to erect lighthouses on its desolate shores, but by 1872 four towers were built to guide the luckless mariner. They were located at Heath Point, on the east, Southwest Point, West Point, and South Point near Bagota Bluff. Since then, four other lighthouses have been built at Table Head, Carleton Point, Cap de Rebast and Port Meunier. In addition, there are two range lights to assist the navigator making his way into Ellis Bay at Port Meunier.

Two famous expeditions from Boston met with grief on the shores of Anticosti. The first was that of Sir William Phipps, who in 1690 was chosen to lead a fleet of thirty-two vessels against the citadel of Quebec. He failed in his purpose, and one of his warships, the brigantine *Mary*, commanded by Captain John Rainsford, was wrecked on Anticosti Island.

Rainsford and his sixty-six crew members were able to get safely ashore on the island, but the subarctic winter took a terrible toll. By spring, only twenty-two, including Rainsford, were alive. On March 25, 1691, Rainsford and four of his men launched a rebuilt boat and sailed all the way to Boston, arriving there May 9. This trip was one of the great unwritten sagas of the period. Rainsford later returned to Anticosti and rescued the seventeen remaining survivors, landing with them at Boston, June 28, 1691.

A second Boston expedition against Quebec was organized by Sir Hovendon Walker, who planned a surprise campaign against the Canadian stronghold in 1711. The fifty-five ships which he assembled in Boston Harbor that summer constituted the largest fleet of warships ever seen in the New World.

On July 20, 1711, Sir Hovendon Walker's fleet left Nantasket Road in Boston, bound for the capture of Quebec. Walker carried Phipps' diary with him, believing that he would profit by the latter's mistakes. In this he was mistaken. On August 22 eight of his transports crashed to their doom in a terrible fog at Egg Island in Saint Lawrence Bay.

Walker sighted the grim shores of Anticosti in the distance and was forced to turn back. His mission was not only unsuccessful but he had suffered the loss of eight heavily laden transports and 884 human lives.

One of the most remarkable events in the year 1736 was the wreck of the French sloop-of-war *La Renommé*. Armed with fourteen guns, she sailed from Quebec with fifty-four men on November 3, 1736, bound for Rochelle, France. Eleven days later she struck heavily on Anticosti during a dreary rainstorm.

Terrible confusion took possession of all on board except Captain de Freneuse and the gunner's mate, who rushed below and gathered provisions and firearms before the rising water engulfed them. Then the ship's rudder was wrenched off by the mighty waves, and *La Renommé* went over on her side. Captain de Freneuse ordered the long-boat hung to the davits. Twenty seamen climbed in, but the forward block gave way and over half of the men were lost in the sea. The others clung desperately to the sides of the boat dangling in midair. When the remaining tackle let go, the boat hit the water. Two waves swept entirely over her, but the men were able to shove her off and row toward land.

As they neared the shores of Anticosti, the men in the long-boat heard the ominous roar of breakers hitting the rocky beach. Then a great wave broke over the boat, capsized it and swept it on toward the shore. The men jumped for safety and were later able to pull the boat up above the surf. They found that they were stranded on a tidal island which would be submerged at high water, and that Anticosti itself was across the mouth of the Pavillion River, which emptied into the gulf at this point. They patched up the worst of the leaks in the long-boat and started for Anticosti. They were nearly capsized several times but eventually they reached the shore.

Soon they could see the jolly-boat making its way through the surf, and in a few minutes six more sailors landed safely on the beach. "Captain de Freneuse is still on the ship," said one of the men. "He won't leave, and he has the rest of the crew with him."

The survivors on the shore were in little better situation, for they were stranded on the rugged island of Anticosti without fire or shelter of any type. The storm reached its height at midnight, and the sailors on shore abandoned all hope for the men on the warship.

On board *La Renommé*, Captain de Freneuse believed that the ship would hold together until dawn. He hoped then to be able to take supplies and food ashore. His gamble succeeded, for when morning came, *La Renommé* could still be seen by the survivors on shore.

During a lull in the storm the captain ordered provisions, tools, tar and canvas placed in the third lifeboat. Then he sadly rolled up his ship's flag and jumped from the quarterdeck into the boat, the last to leave the shattered vessel.

When he reached shore Captain de Freneuse quickly took charge and ordered a lean-to constructed. Just as the men were placing the canvas on top of the shelter, another great storm started. Now it was snow instead of rain. By morning two feet of snow surrounded the survivors' camp. Without the lean-to, Captain de Freneuse believed that they all would have frozen to death.

The captain wisely realized that if the men began to feel sorry for themselves, they would soon despair of leaving the island alive. And he knew that their chances for surviving the terrible winter ahead were very slender. Several months would elapse before they could hope for escape, and unless they were kept occupied, melancholia and worse would soon seize the minds of the survivors.

The captain therefore divided the men into groups, and each group was assigned specific tasks. The mizzenmast of the vessel had drifted ashore, and one group of men cut it up to make a keel for the damaged jolly-boat. They succeeded in caulking the boat and making it seaworthy again. Another group busily cut wood and still another melted snow for drinking water in a giant caldron.

Provisions were apportioned, enough to last each man forty days. Ice soon formed offshore, preventing any return to the ship for further supplies. Shortly, the incessant snowstorms piled up drifts ten and twelve feet deep around the camp. But still worse was the fever which attacked almost every survivor.

Captain de Freneuse now saw that he would have to make an effort to reach the nearest settlement on Mingan Island across Jacques Cartier Passage in northern Saint Lawrence

Bay. His party must skirt the shores of Anticosti for over one hundred miles, and then attempt crossing the open sea to reach Mingan, thirty-six miles to the north, near the Romaine River on the mainland. The captain realized that there was not room for the entire ship's company in the two boats then available and that he would have to leave some of the men behind. When he called for volunteers, however, none would consent to remain at the camp.

In the emergency Father Emmanuel Crespel, the ship's priest, suggested that they "seek counsel and succor from God." He celebrated Mass, and that day twenty-four of the crew resigned themselves "to the Divine Will" to winter at Pavillion River. The others made plans to start their long journey.

Father Crespel heard confessions all through that long night. Early the next morning, with a favoring wind, the captain, the priest and thirty-nine of the crew made final preparations for their long, hazardous journey in the two open boats. At ten o'clock on November 27, 1736, farewells were taken, for many men their last, and the two boats started northwest up the southern coast of Anticosti.

At first luck was with them. Taking turns at the oars, the sailors rowed eight or nine miles each day, pulling their boats high on the shore when the tide came in and sleeping on the snow each night. Their meal was apportioned daily. It consisted of a few crumbs of dried codfish and two teaspoons of flour which they mixed with melted snow. Once a week, on Sunday, Father Crespel gave each sailor a spoonful of peas. "This was our best meal," he commented later.

By December 2 they had covered about fifty miles. When they awoke that morning the weather was bright and balmy, with a gentle breeze favoring their plans. Their objective was to round the southwestern point of the island that afternoon. When they reached the point, the long-boat met with a strong cross sea and a heavy storm set in. At the height of the gale, the sailors in the long-boat lost sight of the jolly-boat.

At dusk Captain de Freneuse landed on shore and had a great bonfire lit to guide the missing jolly-boat ashore. But it failed to appear, and they never saw the boat nor any of its occupants again.

The storm grew worse that night and damaged the long-boat. Early the next day Captain de Freneuse divided his men into two groups, one to set snares for foxes and the other to repair the long-boat. By the time it was finished, two foxes had been trapped, and the entire party enjoyed its first real food in weeks.

On December 7, when they set out again, the survivors ran into heavy weather almost at once. The waves were so high that no landing could be attempted that night. By the next morning, the storm had gone down, and when they sighted a suitable landing beach, the men in the long-boat went ashore to rest from their night on the open water. Before they could launch again that afternoon an intense cold hit the area, and within a few hours massive blocks of ice were pushing up on the beach.

Finally, the bay froze over completely, and the boat had to be abandoned. The men carried the stores ashore and built a number of huts from spruce boughs. They placed a shelter for provisions in a clearing so that no one could enter it without being seen by the others.

Fox snares yielded enough to furnish more than adequate provisions of meat. The rules were amended so that each of the seventeen survivors could have four ounces of codfish, two portions of flour and two pounds of fox meat daily. A spoonful of peas was continued as a special treat every Sunday.

A type of communal or help-thy-neighbor government was instituted whereby each man did some work each day. One group cut branches for fuel, another carried wood into the huts, a third kept the forest paths open and a fourth set snares for foxes and other wild animals.

But in spite of careful planning, conditions in camp soon became serious. First, lice and vermin preyed on the men because they had no change of clothes. Second, the smoke in the huts and the brilliant whiteness of the snow brought on ophthalmia. Moreover, the limited diet gave the men intestinal complaints and, what was more serious, diabetes.

On December 24, Father Crespel made arrangements for a Christmas service. He thawed a small portion of wine for sacred purposes and celebrated Midnight Mass. The priest recalled later that it was a touching spectacle as the shipwrecked castaways wafted "their tearful adoration to the Saviour at Bethlehem."

Trouble soon began again. On January 1, 1737, the longboat was carried away by the ice. The effect of this discovery on the little group of discouraged men was startling. For five days they did nothing but grieve over their new misfortune. Several of them decided to commit suicide, for they thought that there was no hope at all.

Father Crespel saw the desperate need for spiritual guidance and solemnized the Mass DE SPIRITU SANCTO on Epiphany Day, January 6. That afternoon, their faith renewed, two men agreed to go out and search the shores for the lost longboat. Toward dusk they returned with the startling information that they had located an Indian wigwam and two canoes less than a mile away. This bit of good news was immensely cheering to the men. When the very next day the missing long-boat was located and a chest of clothes was found on the beach, hope revived strongly. But these events created only a brief moment of happiness before disaster struck the camp again. On January 23 the master carpenter died. Within a few days every man at the camp began to suffer from swollen legs. One by one the sailors died. Their brave captain was buried on February 16.

On March 6 a blizzard overwhelmed the survivors and five

more men died before the storm ended. When the sufferers tried to go outdoors, they found that the entire camp, including, of course, the provision hut, was under a gigantic snowdrift thirty feet high. By the time they had tunneled their way out through the snow, several had frozen hands and feet and still they had not reached their supplies. Again and again the men tunneled through the snow to get to their food until finally their efforts succeeded. They had been without anything to eat for five days.

When the weather improved, Seaman Furst went with Father Crespel into the woods for fuel. They brought back huge loads of wood and piled it up on the floor of their hut. That night the cold hit again with terrible penetration. Father Crespel and Furst were able to keep a fire going all night long, but the next morning they found a sailor in another hut frozen to death on his bed of spruce bows. Others in the camp froze their fingers and toes and a few days later the affected parts began to drop off.

On April 1 Seaman Leger, hiking in the woods, discovered an Indian and his squaw living in a wigwam. Father Crespel, with tears in his eyes, went to the Indians and asked for help. They agreed to aid the white men, but that night they carried one of their canoes to the water and fled the vicinity. When the survivors saw what had happened, Father Crespel and Seaman Leger took the remaining canoe and tied it firmly to their own door.

A week later only four men of the seventeen survivors from the long-boat were alive. The next casualty was de Senneville, who in his youth had been a page of Madame La Dauphine of France. His death left only Father Crespel, Leger and Furst. These three decided to attempt the rest of the journey by canoe.

On April 21 they arose early, boiled a freshly caught fox and prepared to drink the juice. But their appetites carried them away and they ate the meat as well. They soon became violently ill. Two days later, when they were still recovering from the effects of their gorging, they heard the sound of gun-fire. Father Crespel and Leger discovered that the shot had been fired by the faithless Indian who had returned with his seven-year-old son to take the last canoe away with him. But Father Crespel forced them to agree to transport him to a settlement in the canoe and Leger and Furst would follow their course hiking along the beach.

That night, as the party from the canoe gathered on the shore and Father Crespel was occupied in starting a fire, the Indian and his son fled into the woods. When he learned of their desertion, it was a trying moment for the priest. Leaning against his musket and bowing his head in bitter despair, he sought solace in the Bible. Recalling the trials of the man from Uz, he began reciting aloud verses from the Book of Job. As he spoke, Leger strode into view. He and Furst had, of course, been hiking along the shore, but now Leger appeared alone. He explained that Furst had fainted in the snow and could not be revived. Leger had been forced to leave him on the beach.

Just then Father Crespel and Leger heard a shot in the forest. They went into the woods to investigate and discovered an Indian chieftain standing by his wigwam. Cowering in the back of the wigwam was the Indian who had run away from Father Crespel.

The chief explained that the Indian had fled to him, frightened that he would catch the white man's smallpox, scurvy and what he called "bad air." Father Crespel accepted the chieftain's explanation but implored the Indians to go in search of Furst. They refused.

The next morning Leger and Father Crespel started out together to find their companion. Before they had gone a mile they saw him walking toward them. He had slept in the woods that night and had not awakened until the sun came up. It is amazing that he did not freeze to death in the bitter cold.

The next day Father Crespel discovered a small sailboat

pulled up on the shore. The Indian chief explained that it had come ashore some months before. The Indians agreed to let the priest take the boat and sail for help. On May 1 Father Crespel, his two companions and several Indians started for the island of Mingan in the sailboat. The priest was anxious to bring relief to those who might still be alive back at the Pavillion River.

A few days later, less than eighteen miles from their goal, the wind failed them completely. The Indians were anxious to turn back, but Father Crespel was equal to the occasion. There was a small canoe on board the sailboat, and he volunteered to paddle it alone across the Jacques Cartier Passage to Mingan. The Indians agreed not to turn back to Anticosti and promised that if the wind came up, they would follow him to Mingan. After a sad farewell with Leger and Furst, Father Crespel paddled away.

Late that night the priest arrived at Mingan and went directly to the head of the post, M. Volant. Although he was in a terribly weakened condition, Father Crespel insisted that an expedition be organized immediately to find the shipwrecked survivors. While the relief craft was being outfitted, the sailboat with Furst, Leger and the Indians arrived at Mingan. That very night, in the light of a full moon, the rescue expedition set out.

Three days later the relief vessel neared the site of the original camp on the Pavillion River. A small deck cannon was discharged. The men on board watched anxiously for signs of survivors, and at last they were gratified to notice four men crawling out from the forest onto the beach. Reduced to living skeletons and so weak that they were unable to wave a greeting, the four sailors knelt on the beach in helpless confusion, apparently unable to comprehend that help had arrived. The rescuers brought them out to the ship and gave them food, but they took great pains to prevent the starving men from overloading their shrunken stomachs.

At the camp on the Pavillion River, twenty corpses

were buried and a cross erected to show the site of the graves. M. Volant dispatched his men down the shore in each direction. Three hours later the searchers to the northwest discovered two dead bodies and the remains of the jolly-boat. Without question, all thirteen men in the jolly-boat had perished in that sudden December storm when they were separated from the long-boat.

The sufferings and deaths of the survivors were not at an end, however. In the cabin of the relief ship, two days later, it was decided to revive sailor Tenguy of Brittany with a small glass of brandy. As he brought the glass to his lips, Tenguy drank deeply with great pleasure. Suddenly his eyes glassed over, the brandy crashed to the deck and Tenguy was dead. The excitement of the drink had been too much for him.

The following morning Tourillet, another sailor, went stark mad with joy. He never recovered, and was later confined ashore in an institution.

Father Crespel and the five other survivors were taken back to Quebec. There they were hospitalized for several weeks. Of course, none of them fully recovered for many months.

Father Crespel returned to Paris after a brief pastorate at Soulanges. Finally, he was sent to Quebec, where he died in 1775. His brave fight against terrible odds is one of the greatest epics of the Saint Lawrence River.

LOUIS GAMACHE

ONE OF the most remarkable characters in Anticosti history was Louis Olivier Gamache. Born in 1784 at Islet, fifty miles to the east of Quebec on the Saint Lawrence River, Gamache left home as a boy and enlisted aboard an English frigate. He spent the next twenty years of his life sailing around the world and participating in the Napoleonic Wars.

With the defeat of Napoleon, he returned home to find his parents dead and himself penniless.

Gamache then went to the little port of Rimouski, 110 miles from Islet, and established himself in business. But eventually he failed and, disgusted with people in general and with life itself, he determined to sail across to the lonely island of Anticosti and settle there.

He chose Ellis Bay as his headquarters and, living in a wigwam for several months, he built himself a comfortable cabin there. The building was half a fort and half a home. Twelve double-barreled firelocks ornamented the walls, and a moderate-sized cannon stood in front of the house. There were loopholes in the walls, and the building could have withstood a siege for a long period of time.

Industriously hunting, fishing, trading and sailing, Gamache soon acquired a comfortable little fortune and left the island temporarily to find a wife. He was a well-built man, six feet tall, with bristling black eyebrows and a full beard slightly graying around the edges, and apparently he did not have much difficulty in persuading a lady of his choice to become Madame Gamache.

The bride wasted away, however, in the wilderness of Anticosti. Its loneliness and intense cold were more than she could stand. She died just as spring came to the island, ten months after her marriage.

With the advent of summer, Gamache took refuge from his unhappiness by sailing on a sealing expedition. He came back with many pelts of walrus and gray seal. It had been a profitable venture, and Gamache erected new and stronger buildings with his money. He also stocked the island with cows, sheep and horses, and had built up a fine farm before the next summer ended. Near Quebec, he courted and won his second wife and brought her back to the island that fall.

The next seven years were the happiest of Gamache's life. He and his wife were blessed with four children. Not wishing to lose the second Mrs. Gamache, he had an Eskimo squaw-suit made for her by the Indians from the skins of several of giant bears on the island. This remarkably warm and efficient garment, which Madame Gamache wore from October to May, proved to be the wonderment of all who visited the Gamache stronghold.

One wintry day Gamache found that his money and provisions were running low and decided that he must set out on one of his long seal hunts. His wife became ill and died during his absence, and later his two daughters and a son also died. Only one son was alive when Gamache returned.

Gamache lost his reason when he learned of this tragedy. He discharged his servants and the sailors in his crew, keeping with him only his trusty man Goudreau. Then he sailed away for the mainland to place his son in the home of a friend.

Returning to Anticosti, Gamache brooded for several months before he determined on a plan of action which eventually made him dreaded up and down the Saint Lawrence. Since he was all alone on the island with his companion Goudreau, in danger of capture at any time either by roving bands of Indians or pirates, he decided to make such marauders fear to go ashore at Anticosti.

His first measure was to anchor in Griffon Cove on the mainland and go ashore to the local inn, leaving Goudreau aboard ship. There he ordered two gigantic meals, one for himself and the other for a friend who, he said, would soon arrive. He engaged the entire dining room, and after the meals had been served, locked all doors. The servants could hear voices coming from the room, but two hours later when Gamache ordered the dishes removed, he was still the only person there. The plates were completely empty. But the servants declared that the meals had been far too much for one mortal man! Gamache in this way successfully started the rumor that he had entertained the Devil himself at a feast. Soon his friendship with the Evil One was discussed up and down the Saint Lawrence River and Gamache became known as the Wizard of Anticosti.

Gamache had been guilty, at least in the eyes of the government men at Quebec, of several infractions of the laws, and the authorities were anxious to enforce justice. Late one autumn day when Gamache moored his craft to a water-front pier, the government quickly sent a constable aboard the vessel to collect fines. Gamache was ready for trouble, however. He invited the constable below into his warm cabin, where the fierce winds of late autumn could not reach them as they discussed their business. Then he opened a bottle of his finest wine, and soon the two were drinking as old friends. When the constable finally grew befuddled, Gamache rushed up on deck, ordered Goudreau to cast off and soon they were sailing down the river toward Anticosti.

When the constable awoke the next morning, the vessel was a hundred miles from Quebec. The following night the anchor rattled down in Ellis Bay at Anticosti. The unhappy officer stayed on the island for the entire winter. When spring came, a fishing vessel took him ashore at Rimouski.

For several years after this event the government gave Gamache a wide berth. Eventually, however, he was suspected of forbidden bartering with the Labrador Indians, and the officials decided to make an example of him.

One peaceful summer afternoon when Gamache left a small port on the Labrador coast, he saw an armed sloop lying in wait three miles away. The government ship hoisted sail in close chase, but after a few hours, night overtook both pursued and pursuer. Just before dawn Gamache slid his vessel into the harbor of Mingan. When morning came, however, he saw the armed sloop on the horizon. He fled to sea again, and all that long day the chase continued. Finally, Gamache tired of the sport and went below, leaving Goudreau at the tiller. In the cabin he built a makeshift raft, and, bringing it up on deck, he placed three tar barrels aboard and set them afire. He then let the raft go adrift **and** changed his course.

The sloop soon came alongside the burning raft **and** discovered the hoax, but by then Gamache had made his escape.

Then there was the time when a drunken Indian, knowing that Gamache was alone at his home, went ashore and stole up to the house. The Frenchman was ready for him and warned the Indian that if he took another step he would fire. The Indian took the step and Gamache fired. The bullet shattered the Indian's thigh bone, and Gamache carried the helpless man inside and nursed him for several weeks. When the Indian recovered Gamache turned him loose with the final warning that the next time his premises were invaded, the intruder would get a bullet through his head. Never again was he bothered by the Anticosti Indians.

On another occasion a young ship's pilot was driven by a gale into the harbor at Gamache Bay. He knew Gamache's reputation, and when he saw the Wizard of Anticosti approaching in a small skiff, he tried to conceal his uneasiness. Realizing that the pilot was afraid of him, Gamache invited the man into his home and decided to have some fun.

As he was shown around the house, the pilot noticed wall after wall covered with pistols, shotguns, derringers, hatchets, harpoons and cutlasses. His terror grew by leaps and bounds, and he began to wonder whether he would ever be allowed to leave the island alive. The crafty Gamache watched the pilot closely and enjoyed his discomfort.

The two entered the dining room, where Goudreau served a steaming hot meal which included such delicacies as moofle and beaver's tail. The pilot seemed to have lost his appetite, however. He even suggested that since the storm was going down, perhaps he could sail back to Quebec that very night.

"I would not think of it," replied Gamache. "The sea is rough, the night is dark and wet and you cannot leave the bay. I have, instead, a comfortable bed upstairs, and tomorrow you can leave—if you are still alive," he added smilingly.

The frightened young pilot ascended the steps to his bedroom with Gamache at his side, carrying a lantern.

"Here is your room," the smiling host explained. "Your bed is soft, for it is made from the down of birds which I have killed. I am a good shot, and never miss my game. Goodnight for the time being."

The pilot glanced around the room. Over the mantelpiece a gun hung on two pegs. Thinking about the gun, he undressed and tumbled into bed, but his sleep was troubled.

At midnight a knocking on the door awakened the young pilot. His host had returned.

"I suppose," began Gamache, taking down the gun from the pegs, "that you heard that I murder everyone who tarries at my house. And you've probably heard that I bury my victims out in the forest." The Wizard of Anticosti put back the gun, reached into the closet and withdrew a bottle and two glasses.

"Here," he said, "take a good pull in case I come in to attack you during the night. If I do, leap from your bed and grab the gun which I have placed back on the pegs."

Both men took a quick drink, and Gamache left the room. The pilot finally fell into an uneasy, troubled sleep.

The morning sun announced to him both the end of the storm and the fact that he had lived through the night. He dressed and came downstairs to be greeted by Louis Gamache, smiling as usual. An hour later the pilot hoisted sail and was on the way to Quebec, bewildered but elated to think that he was still alive. Gamache had had his fun!

When Louis Olivier Gamache, the Wizard of Anticosti, went hunting in the vast reaches of his forest domain one day in 1854, at the age of seventy, he caught a bad cold. A severe freezing spell had sent the temperature suddenly far below zero. He was barely able to reach his home before he collapsed into the arms of his faithful Goudreau.

Gamache was confined to bed, but he insisted on a strong drink of rum every morning when he awakened. The wise

Goudreau, however, diluted it with water, since the Gamache brand of rum was of terrific potency. One morning this scheme went awry. We shall let Goudreau himself tell of the incident:

"One day in the month of September, 1854, I forgot to put the water in his rum, and at ten o'clock, when I returned to his bed, I found poor Louis dead. He had taken the clear rum and it had finished him!"

The loyal Goudreau buried the Wizard of Anticosti near his home, and a rude tombstone sheltered by a hemlock still stands to mark the site where the unusual Frenchman lived and died.

Henri Meunier, the chocolate manufacturer, bought Anticosti Island in 1895, paying $125,000 for the title. Before long he had established a remarkable island kingdom which he ruled as if he were indeed a king. He established farms, built roads and railways, drained swamps and brought hundreds of French-Canadians to work there. He had geologists and naturalists explore the island and report their findings. His law was absolute, and there were many severe clauses in the rules he arbitrarily set down. For example, all dogs were outlawed by Meunier's rules:

The possession or introduction of any dog, of no matter what species, is formally prohibited, dogs having been recognized as essentially harmful to the island, to persons as well as to wild and domestic animals.

There were other more stringent rules. No visitor was allowed to land on the island unless shipwrecked; the possession of alcohol was forbidden; no workman could leave his camp and seek employment at another camp.

Henri Meunier died in 1914, and his brother Gaston took over Anticosti Island. In 1927 Gaston sold out to a lumber corporation for an estimated six million dollars. Anticosti became a vast lumber camp.

But in spite of all their activity, the owners of the island never forgot their obligations to shipwrecked mariners, and up and down the three hundred miles of Anticosti's coastline huts of refuge are strategically placed and well-stocked with provisions.

THE "EMPRESS OF IRELAND"

THE SECOND greatest passenger ship disaster in peacetime history occurred in 1914 when the steamer *Empress of Ireland* went down almost in sight of Anticosti Island. Few people today have ever heard of the *Ireland*, for it has been overshadowed by the more spectacular disaster of the steamer *Titanic* two years earlier.

The *Ireland* left Quebec for Liverpool late in the afternoon of May 29, 1914, carrying 1477 passengers and crew. She was scheduled to pass West Point Light on Anticosti Island around four o'clock the next morning. For the first eight hours of the trip, the weather was clear and the sea smooth. At one-thirty in the morning she dropped her pilot off Father Point, Rimouski, and picked up mail from the steamers *Eureka* and *Lady Evelyn*. Out of Rimouski, patches of fog appeared, and soon the ship encountered impenetrable masses half a mile thick.

Steaming out of a fog bank, Captain Kendall sighted a collier about five miles away, approaching up-river toward the *Ireland*. Then another fog bank hit the ship and this time it did not disperse. To be safe, Captain Kendall rang for full speed astern and gave three loud blasts on his whistle to indicate to the oncoming collier that he was going astern. Captain Kendall always claimed that he received an answer to this signal, though those aboard the collier later denied it.

Suddenly the fog lifted a trifle, and every man on the *Ireland's* bridge saw with horror the lights of the collier less than a hundred yards away. The collier *Storstad* was coming at right angles to the *Ireland*. A collison seemed inevitable.

Captain Kendall ordered his helm hard aport. At the same time he shouted "Full speed ahead" to the bridge of the collier, hoping that the maneuver would bring the *Ireland* and the *Storstad* together starboard to starboard in a glancing blow.

It was too late for this plan, and before the maneuver could be executed the *Storstad,* loaded with eleven thousand tons of Cape Breton coal, struck the *Ireland* squarely between her two funnels and tore a gaping hole through the liner's side. Water began to pour into the ship at the amazing rate of 260 tons a second.

Wireless operator Ronald Ferguson had sent out a call to stand by for distress signals and flashed the SOS as soon as the captain ordered it. Across the bay at Father Point, Wireless Operator Whiteside signaled that he would send assistance at once. Then the dynamos aboard the *Ireland* went under water and all communication stopped.

Captain Kendall shouted across to the collier to go full speed ahead into the hole she had made. He hoped this might prevent the water from pouring into the gap and sinking the *Ireland,* but the injured bow of the *Storstad* had been bent completely out of shape and could not re-enter the torn side of the great liner. Steam on the *Ireland* had failed almost immediately after the collision, so no attempt could be made at beaching her.

Back at Father Point, Wireless Operator Whiteside ran down to the village pier, where Captain Berlanger was still aboard his steamer, the *Eureka.* "For God's sake, get down stream at once," Whiteside shouted. "The *Empress of Ireland* has gone down!" A moment later he reached the *Lady Evelyn* and repeated his stunning news. Both vessels had steam up and left at once for the scene of the disaster.

Out on the fast-sinking *Ireland* the experiences of the passengers were many and varied. One of the most unusual adventures was that of Dr. J. F. Grant. He was thrown out of bed by the collision and reached for the cabin light. The liner gave a lurch, and the floor tilted down and away from him. The ship heeled far over in a few minutes, and in the darkness he couldn't find his cabin door. When he eventually located the door, he couldn't open it at first, but finally he managed to squeeze out into the corridor.

The *Ireland* was now almost over on the side, and Dr. Grant discovered that he could walk much more easily on the wall of the passageway than on the floor. Fighting his way to a porthole, he glanced out and was amazed to find other passengers walking along the side of the *Ireland* as though it were the deck. He shouted for help and was pulled through the porthole to the comparative safety of the *Ireland's* side. He saw a lifeboat floating some distance away and leaped into the water and swam to it. A few moments later he helped rescue over a score of others floundering in the water.

Those who reached the deck of the *Ireland* before the ship sank climbed over the rail as the *Ireland* rolled over and stood on the side of the ship. As the liner settled lower and lower, scores walked off her side into the water, hoping to stay afloat away from the *Ireland* and avoid being pulled down by her mighty suction.

Finally, the *Eureka* and the *Lady Evelyn* arrived on the scene. Assisted by the *Storstad*, they saved 463 persons from the 1477 aboard the *Empress of Ireland*. Over one thousand lives were lost.

Actually the greater number of those who died on the *Ireland* never had a chance to leave the staterooms, corridors and cabins of the doomed liner. Over eight hundred bodies were later removed by divers from inside the sunken vessel.

Two famous passengers aboard the *Ireland* were the actor Laurence Irving and his wife. They reached the deck but clung to the rail, choosing to die together rather than attempt to swim away from the vessel. They went down with the *Ireland,* and their deaths were far more dramatic than any deaths they had ever enacted on the stage.

One man aboard the *Ireland* who was fortunate enough to be saved had also survived the sinking of the *Titanic* two years earlier. Fireman William Clarke had an apt comment on the two disasters: "The *Titanic* went down like a little baby going to sleep, while the *Empress of Ireland*, much as I hate to admit it, rolled over like a hog in a ditch!"

Indeed, the *Ireland* disaster in many ways surpassed the horror of the loss of the *Titanic* with 1500 persons aboard. The *Titanic* stayed afloat two hours and forty minutes, but the *Empress of Ireland* sank less than ten minutes after the collision. Everyone aboard the *Titanic* had time to get up on deck; more than half the passengers aboard the *Ireland* never even reached the corridors from their staterooms.

Aboard the ship for just a few hours, the *Ireland's* passengers were awakened by the terrific impact of the crash. A moment later, as they struggled to leave their staterooms, they heard the terrible rush of tons of water entering the ship. Their efforts must have become desperate as the ship began to roll over on her side, but they were absolutely helpless. Finally, the solid mass of water invaded their staterooms, and they died with the cries of their shipmates and the roar of the ocean torrents mingling in their ears.

Without question, the outstanding historian and enthusiast for Anticosti is an American, Eugene E. Wilson, who has written an article on it for the *National Geographic* Magazine and also recently published a book, "Slipstream."

I talked with Mr. Wilson in February, 1950, and there was much he had to tell me. I learned that until recently the great lumber combine had failed to make money out of the pulpwood enterprise at Anticosti. With the rise in demand for paper, however, the Consolidated Paper Company inaugurated a new system of operation under the direction of a Mr. Wilcox. Wilcox did away with the old railroad and put in truck routes which penetrated the western part of the island. He brought in several of the lake steamer type of craft which were used with success in the enterprise. But only the future can tell whether or not Anticosti will be profitably worked.

But, Mr. Wilson told me, the old on-island feeling of friendliness seems to have vanished with the introduction of outside, off-island lumberjacks. Another thing that has been unfortunate is partial destruction of the natural beauty of the western end of the island, which has been spoiled considerably for fishermen and hunters by the inroads of the pulp men.

I asked Eugene Wilson about the grave of Anticosti's Wizard, Louis Olivier Gamache. "It is still to be seen about halfway between Port Meunier and the old château," Mr. Wilson explained. "The old château has been closed and its furniture removed and sold to provide equipment for large tourist hotels along the Saint Lawrence."

I asked him if there was to be an airport at Anticosti. "Yes, there is an airport there and a service is operated between Port Meunier and Rimouski." Steamship service with Quebec still continues, and small craft are often seen coasting along the Anticosti shore.

In Meunier's famous château there was a spiral staircase which led to an observatory where formerly a long telescope allowed a view of the great domain of the chocolate king. Nearby was the master's bedchamber, with a secret staircase leading to the floor above. It is unfortunate that such a delightful old landmark has been stripped of its trappings and closed to visitors.

To quote from Eugene E. Wilson's words, the island's "wild and barbaric charm has attracted ardent fishermen from all over the world. No salmon fisherman visits Anticosti without coming under its magic spell. Here indeed is the Enchanted Isle. Anticosti's spell is that of the primeval north woods, almost unchanged since Jacques Cartier trod its shores. But, superimposed upon it is the almost legendary spirit of Meunier, le Grand Seigneur."

Anticosti Island lies silent and remote awaiting the dictates of the market place to determine further destruction of its wonderful natural resources. Jacques Cartier, Louis Joliet, Louis Olivier Gamache and Henri Meunier have all trod its soil and gloried in its beauty. It is one of the few remaining isolated places which seem to offer so much to the civilization-weary individual. Let us hope that it is allowed to retain part of its primeval splendor as an outpost of the better things of life.

ELLSWORTH
THE MAINLAND

UNION BAY

AIRPORT

THE NARROWS

FRENCHMAN BAY

BAR HARBOR

MOUNT DESERT

MOUNT CADILLAC
1532 FEET

SOUTHWEST HARBOR

MANSET

SHIP HARBOR
WRECK OF
GRAND DESIGN
1741

BASS HARBOR

GREAT GOTT

BLACK

VII. MOUNT DESERT ISLAND

MOUNT Desert Island, located just off the coast of Maine about forty miles southeast of Bangor, was my next objective. I planned to fly to the Bar Harbor Airport, which in spite of the name, is actually on the mainland and not at the town of Bar Harbor on Mount Desert. When I telephoned my friend Keeper Howard R. Gray of West Quoddy Head Light, who was visiting his daughter at Manset on Mount Desert, he promised to meet my plane at the airport.

There was a terrific tail wind as we took off from Boston

and it pushed us up the coast so fast that in what seemed less time than it takes to tell it I could see the outlines of several Maine islands below me. When Portland Head Light appeared, we veered to starboard for the journey down east. Owl's Head, Vinalhaven, and Deer Isle slid by below us in rapid succession, and in exactly sixty-nine minutes after we left Boston we circled Bar Harbor Airport, landed and taxied up beside a huge flying boat which was on skids for the winter. It had been a rough but incredibly fast journey.

Keeper Howard Gray had brought quite a delegation to meet the plane, and once old acquaintances were renewed, we went over the bridge to Mount Desert Island and Manset. After a fine dinner, Howard Gray and I left the women folk to do the dishes and started out on our tour of exploration.

On several previous trips to Mount Desert I had learned quite a little of the island's history. I had also read a score of books which discuss the island in some detail. I knew that Henry Hudson himself had stopped at Mount Desert in 1609, but more than any other event except the wreck of the *Grand Design* in 1741, Champlain's visit to the island intrigued me. Elsewhere in this book I tell of Champlain's settlement of Saint Croix Island, and since he is one of the most interesting explorers ever to visit our coast, I include a little of his history and background here.

American children have listened time and again to the story of the Pilgrims who landed at Provincetown and Plymouth in 1620 and have heard extolled the virtues of the staid Puritans who settled Boston in 1630. But history books and schoolteachers have little to say about Samuel de Champlain, a man who combined his love for the sea with a feeling for adventure seldom equaled among explorers of this coast. Champlain sailed into both Boston Harbor and Plymouth fifteen years before the Pilgrims left Leyden and twenty-five years before the eleven ships of John Winthrop's fleet appeared in Massachusetts Bay.

One has only to read the dedication of a book written by Champlain to realize his love of adventure on the sea. It might be said that in spirit he was a combination of Byron and Columbus:

Among the most useful and excellent arts navigation has always seemed to me to take the first place. In the measure that it is dangerous and accompanied by a thousand perils, by so much is it honorable and lifted above all other arts, being in no wise suitable for those who lack courage and confidence. By this art we acquire knowledge of various lands, countries and kingdoms. It is this art that has from my childhood lured me to love it, and has caused me to expose myself almost all my life to the rude waves of the ocean.

Born in 1567 at Brouage, France, on the Bay of Biscay, Champlain was interested in the sea and ships from earliest childhood, for his father was a captain in the royal navy and his uncle a pilot. Champlain grew up during the civil and religious wars of the period and Brouage was captured and recaptured during his youth.

Finally, in 1598, Champlain sailed with his uncle in the fleet which visited Cadiz and Seville, and he then seized an opportunity to visit the West Indies, Mexico, Panama and Cuba. Wherever he went, he wrote careful notes and made excellent sketches of what he saw. On his return to France, he presented his work to King Henry IV. Although the king studied appreciatively Champlain's fine sketches and the copious notes he had made, the records of that particular voyage were not published until two centuries after Champlain's death.

Henry IV, to reward Champlain for his outstanding services, made him Royal Geographer and gave him a pension. But Champlain had little interest in the affairs of the court and in 1603 he embarked on a trip to North

America with his friend Pontgravé. Their object was to explore and examine the possibilities for trading and colonization. When they reached the St. Lawrence, they sailed on to the site of Montreal.

After his return in September, Champlain published an account of this voyage and his story attracted the attention of a Huguenot named De Monts who had been granted the land of Acadia by the King. De Monts lost no time in inviting Champlain to join him on an expedition to his domain, which included Nova Scotia, New Brunswick and most of what is now New England.

De Monts and Champlain left Havre in April, 1604, with 120 men, and reached Nova Scotia at what is now Saint Mary's Bay. Champlain and De Monts left their ships in a *patache* or "barque of eight tons" for a voyage up and down the coast. Champlain was in his glory for the next few weeks, sketching and writing as the tiny barque cruised along the unexplored shores.

The two adventurers visited and explored the sites of Annapolis Basin, Saint John's and Passamaquoddy Bay. Finally, they reached a swift tidal river. Both men decided that an island which lay in this river was ideal for their purposes. They named it Saint Croix and called the river by the same name. On September 2nd Champlain left Saint Croix in the *patache,* accompanied by twelve sailors and two Indian guides. Let us translate Champlain's account of this trip:

> Continuing our course along the coast, we made the same day some twenty-five leagues, and passed by a large number of islands, banks, reefs, and rocks, which in places extended more than four leagues out to sea. We called these islands the Ranges, most of which are covered with pines, firs, and other trees of an inferior sort. Among these islands are many fine harbors, but undesirable for a permanent settlement. The same day

(September 5, 1604) we passed also near an island about four or five leagues long, in the neighborhood of which we just escaped being lost on a little rock on a level with the water, which made an opening in the barque near our keel.

From this island to the mainland on the north, the distance is not more than one hundred paces. The island is high and notched in places; so that from the sea it gives the appearance of a range of seven or eight mountains extending along the other side. The summits are all bare and rocky. The slopes are covered with fir, pine and birches. I named it Isles de. Mont Deserts.[1]

From Champlain's description of his visit to Mount Desert it would seem that he sailed up Frenchman's Bay to Mount Desert Narrows, the waterway connecting Frenchman's Bay to Bluehill Bay, between Mount Desert and Long Island.

The next day Champlain sailed two leagues to reach a point on the island now known as Hull's Cove, where he saw smoke in a cave at the foot of the mountains. He sent out his two Indians for a good-will visit, but the natives fled into the woods. The following day, however, another attempt to establish contact succeeded and biscuits, tobacco "and other trifles" were presented to the Indians of the island. The natives agreed to guide the expedition down to Pentagoet, and Champlain sailed with them from Mount Desert.

Champlain's brief visit to Mount Desert has been commemorated by a fine tablet placed on the island near Seal Harbor.

Another interesting person who figures in the history of Mount Desert is the Marquise de Guercheville, a lady-in-waiting to the Queen of France, who was responsible for the

---

[1] The Anglicized version, Mount Desert, should be pronounced "dessert."

establishment of the first Jesuit Mission in the northern part of the North American continent. Madame de Guercheville had long been intensely interested in the Jesuit missions in Asia and South America and when, in 1610, Henry IV was assassinated, she realized that Sieur De Monts, then Viceroy of Acadia, would lose his monopoly.

When De Monts returned to France, Madame de Guercheville sought him out and offered to buy his rights to Acadia, a vast area extending from Nova Scotia southward and westward and embracing half the continent. De Monts was in need of funds and sold his domain to the Marquise, reserving his rights at Port Royal.

In the summer of 1611 several Jesuits, sponsored by Madame de Guercheville, crossed from France to Port Royal. There was friction between the adventurous ship's company and the Jesuits from the very start. During the winter another Jesuit arrived, announcing that the Dowager Queen of France, Marie de Medicis, had been won over to the plan of Christianizing the heathen Indians and would soon send a strong expedition to New France to supplement the colony.

On March 12, 1613, the ship *Jonas* left Honfleur, under Captain Charles Flory and the Sieur de la Saussaye. Father Quentin and forty-nine other Jesuits made up the passenger list, bringing with them horses, goats and abundant supplies. After touching at Port Royal, they were caught in a bad fog off Mount Desert and when the fog lifted, they found themselves in the vicinity of what is now Bar Harbor. They soon entered the roadstead and anchored.

Again there were differences between the ship's company and the Jesuit colonists. The Jesuits wanted to go on to Pentagoet as they had originally planned and the captain of the *Jonas* wanted them to stay at Mount Desert. But since the Indians on the island were intensely anxious to have the priests settle there, they eventually capitulated.

The Jesuit Mission was established at Fernald's Point at the entrance to Somes Sound. More disputes now arose among the Jesuits themselves as to whether they should begin by erecting fortifications or tilling the land. Before they could get under way with either project, a marauding Englishman appeared off the coast and doomed the colony to early extinction.

Sir Samuel Argall, little better than a pirate, had sailed into northern waters from his Virginia stronghold. When he discovered the Jesuit settlement on Mount Desert he tried to frighten the men there by having drums beaten and trumpets sounded aboard his ship. Then, reaching the Western Way at the approach to Somes Sound, Argall opened fire on the Jesuits. After two volleys the Frenchmen surrendered. Father Gilbert du Thet and several other Jesuits were killed and the remaining members of the mission were either captured or dispersed. This was ostensibly the end of the Jesuit settlement at Mount Desert.

Three-quarters of a century after the Jesuits had attempted to settle there, the island still slumbered on. John Smith, in 1617, and the Puritans in 1630, mention using Mount Desert as their landfall and in 1689 Governor Andros of New England records "Cadolick and wife" living on Mount Desert.

This last reference was to Antoine de la Mothe Cadillac, who moved to Mount Desert in 1688 with his bride, but when, the very next year, Port Royal fell to the English, Cadillac moved westward. He later went to Michillimackinac where he founded Detroit, and then on down to Louisiana, where he ruled as governor from 1712 to 1717. Cadillac never returned to Mount Desert, but his granddaughter appeared years later to claim half the island.

On September 13, 1759, Wolfe's triumph over the French at Quebec gave England a clear-cut victory after a century and a half of conflict. By this time many New England towns had become overpopulated, and when the war ended, hundreds of Massachusetts and Connecticut families left their homes for the northeast. Before the close of the year 1759, two hundred immigrants had left Boston, bound for Nova

Scotia. Another 180 went from Plymouth and one hundred from New London. By 1762 the bays and coves of Maine were explored and settled all the way from Pemaquid Point to Saint Croix Island. This great exodus from the older towns and villages of New England has never been given the importance it deserves. It was the first great migration in New England history and the only one which went eastward rather than to the west.

During the spring and summer of 1760 and 1761 hundreds of men journeyed to Maine by every means at their disposal. Usually the men went alone the first year, chose their sites and made their clearings. The following summer they brought their families and lived aboard ship until houses were ready for occupancy. In this manner almost every town and hamlet east of Pemaquid was settled.

Governor Francis Bernard, of Massachusetts, who had been living beyond his means in Boston, saw in the eastward movement a chance to recoup his fortune. On February 27, 1762, he received a grant of one half of Mount Desert Island and decided to visit his new domain as soon as possible. An account of Bernard's journey is still preserved at Harvard College in the Sparks Collection of Manuscripts. Here is a part of it:

September 28th 1762. I went on board the sloop Massachusetts *lying off Castle Island in Boston Bay at* 5 P.M., *weighed anchor, and with wind southeast passed Deer Island on the left.*

September 29. Morning hazy. Passed Cape Ann by reckoning at 5 A.M., *stood for Portsmouth, looked for Isles of Shoals. A thick fog arose, bore out to sea, keeping a good offing to avoid rock called Boone Island Ledge. Saw it two miles distant at 2* P.M. *Weather cleared up, a fresh gale arose from south to east, bore for Cape Porpoise with all the sail we could set, passed into harbour in narrow channel with frightful rocks and came to anchor at four o'clock.*

Sept. 30. Course East, Northeast, passed Wood Island, Cape Elizabeth, Segwin Island, wind fair.

Oct. 1. At daybreak entered Penobscot Bay; passed the Musselridges and the Owl's Head on the left, and Fox Island on the right. Between Fox Island saw Mt. Desert hills at near 30 miles distant. Passed Long Island on the left.

Oct. 2. Came to Neskeag Point, found several vessels there, among which was a schooner with my surveyors on board. Took them on board and with a pilot proceeded for Mount Desert. We anchored about the middle of Southwest Harbour about 5 P.M.

Governor Bernard chose Southwest Harbor as the site for his proposed settlement. In a relatively short time he had a prospective town laid out in lots and several houses built. With such an auspicious beginning, it seemed that the governor would soon attain his objective.

However, because of his arrogance toward them, the people of Boston grew to hate Governor Bernard and complained of him to the mother government in England. With the Stamp Act Riots, followed by Bernard's seizure of John Hancock's sloop, *Liberty,* the people were up in arms. Complaints against the governor finally reached the king himself who eventually announced that he was "graciously pleased to condescend" to allow Bernard's return to England.

Governor Bernard sailed away from Massachusetts in August, 1769. Two years before his son, Shute, had died[1] and another son, John, chose to remain behind when his father left for England.

After the Revolution, John Bernard, then living in Bath, Maine, petitioned for the Bernard share of Mount Desert.

---

[1] Shute Bernard was buried in the walls under the arch at the fort on Castle Island, Boston Harbor.

When his father died in 1779, he had willed John the property. Governor James Bowdoin of Massachusetts, on June 23, 1785, approved a settlement which gave John Bernard half of the island. Less than two weeks later John had mortgaged his property on Mount Desert and left the country for England. As far as we know, he never returned to the island.

The other half of Mount Desert was awarded in 1787 to the granddaughter of Cadillac, Madame Therese de Gregoire. She received the property not so much because she was legally entitled to it, but more as a token of gratitude from the American Government to the French allies of the late Revolution.

A curious and long-delayed consequence of the Jesuit settlement on Somes Sound was discovered by Benjamin Franklin De Costa on his exploration of Mount Desert in 1866. Hiking near Somes Sound with his friends Amarinta and Aureole, De Costa came upon the hut of a Jesuit who was living in solitude not more than a few rods from the site of the original mission in 1613.

De Costa, who in 1903 was ordained as a Catholic priest himself, was fascinated to find such a far-removed follower of the ill-fated Jesuits who had lived on the island for such a brief time two and a half centuries before. We quote from De Costa:

> *Hearing by accident of his existence, we resolved to pay him a visit, expecting to find one of those venerable characters in old pictures, with flowing robes, sandaled feet and a snowy beard sweeping down to his breast.*
> *"Like Barbarossa, who sits in his cave,*
> *Taciturn, sombre, sedate and grave."*
> *But instead, he proved a short, red-faced individual clad in a flannel shirt and patched sordid trousers, with the remnant of a greasy felt hat on his head. His house was a mere hut, about twenty feet square and eight feet*

high, the flat roof having just enough inclination to shed water. The only mode of ingress was through a latticed hen-coop, the roof of which was partially formed of an old boat turned bottom up. On invitation, we entered by this porch, and when the pupils of our eyes had accommodated themselves to the feeble light struggling through a single pane of glass, the situation became apparent. Of floor there was none, save the mother earth. On one side was a bunk for sleeping, and in the corner a bin for potatoes, with an old broken stove in the middle. All was wretched and unclean to the last degree, yet he seemed to feel very comfortable. He was also in good spirits, having just received five dollars from an artist for sitting for his portrait.

A glance into the bin discovered a sitting hen spreading herself, as the hermit said, over a dozen and a half of eggs, while in the corner another venerable fowl clucked proudly in the midst of fourteen offspring that had just walked out of their shells. When we begged for a little more light on the subject, he drew back a shingle slide underneath the pane of glass and revealed a hole which he said was for the accommodation of his cat. Looking into a corner, the eyes of Felix appeared flashing in the twilight like a couple of balls of green fire. Getting out again we sat down on a bench, and listened to the hermit as he told the manner of his life, passed so democratically in his dingy den with his chickens and cat. He was weary of the world, and liked to be with himself. His summer work secured the winter's simple fare. What wood he wanted the sympathizing waves tossed up at his door, and as for candles he had none. The long evenings were especially consecrated to meditation, spiritual songs and prayer. All this was for the good of his soul.

Amarinto hinted that cleanliness was next to godliness, which sentiment gave this disciple of St. Francis

*so little concern, that it was followed up with a point-
ed homily on dirt. For this likewise the holy man did
not seem to care either, and when bringing some water
he still had the courage to present a cup which Amarinta
vainly turned around once and again in the endeavor to
find the clean side.*

*In striking contrast with his hut and person was his
"garden," yclept a potato patch, without weeds, fault-
lessly neat, inclosed by a brushwood fence, and extending to the edge of the beach. From thence he
volunteered to bring Amarinta a "nosegay," but finally
presented only a sprig of mint of which he planted a
little for "sickness." Aureole, who is a judge, afterwards
vowed it was for juleps, and cited in proof the hermit's
red nose. We bade the hermit of Mount Desert good
day, persuaded that we had at least found a character.*

It was not until after the Civil War that the population
of Mount Desert began to increase substantially. About that
time the island gained a reputation as a desirable summer
resort. Local industries were declining, with the herring
fisheries losing money, the lumber business falling off and
the coasting trade slackening, but when the summer visitors
began to arrive, new avenues of revenue were opened.
Mount Desert prospered from that time on.

In the early days Mount Desert could only be reached
from Bangor or by steamboat twice a week from Portland.
But soon daily steamers began calling at the island. By the
time the advent of the automobile had removed the pretty
little steamers from the scene, a fine bridge was completed
from the mainland, and Mount Desert is now firmly en-
trenched as a dignified summer resort. Many families who
came for the summer have remained to live the year round.

The great Bar Harbor fire of October 23, 1947, the worst
in the history of Maine, caused a property damage which
ran into the millions. Many famous homes were destroyed.

At the height of the disaster residents of Bar Harbor crowded onto the pier to await rescue, but the exodus was not necessary and those whose homes were not touched by fire were allowed to return to them.

To me, the most interesting historical event at Mount Desert was the wreck of the immigrant ship *Grand Design*, which I mentioned in my last book. There is still considerable discussion and even mystery connected with the vessel and the subsequent history of those who survived the wreck. I was anxious to locate the old cemetery of the *Grand Design*, containing the graves of those who died near the little brook at Ship Harbor. Most of all, I wanted to find the grave of the famous "Widow of Mount Desert" of whose ten thousand descendents I am one.

The *Grand Design* was an Irish immigrant ship wrecked July 28, 1741, with two hundred passengers aboard. The shipwrecked men, with the exception of two or three who were sick, went to find help and were never heard from again.

Many of the women survivors died. Eventually Indians visited the camp and promised to notify the white people at Saint George's, Maine, that the group had been wrecked at Mount Desert. Before the men of Saint George's reached the starving women and children, however, all but a few were dead.

Two of those who survived were Mrs. Isabella Asbell Galloway and Mrs. Sarah Sherrer. Both were now widows and they seemed desirable to two of the rescuers from Saint George's. Mrs. Galloway attracted the interest of Archibald Gamble; and John McCarter of McCarter's Point paid court to Mrs. Sherrer. Both couples were married the following spring and, as I have said, the Gambles' descendents now number over ten thousand. Mrs. Gamble is justly famous as the "Widow of Mount Desert."

On the afternoon of my airplane visit to Mount Desert, Howard Gray took me over to Ship Harbor, where the

Grand Design was wrecked. There we interviewed eighty-year-old Captain Herman Farley, who remembered visiting the ancient wreck of the *Grand Design* seventy years before when it was still visible in the mud of East Cove, Ship Harbor. Captain Farley agreed to guide us to the spot and an hour later we were wading knee-deep in the mud, searching for timbers from the old immigrant vessel. Finally, Captain Farley discovered the keel of the *Grand Design* and we later picked up several muddy fragments of the ship. Captain Farley took us to the tiny cemetery where the women of the *Grand Design* had buried their dead.

Now I wanted to find the grave of Isabella Asbell Galloway Gamble. I had been told to search in Warren, Maine, formerly Saint George's, and had been given an introduction to Miss Lulu French in that town. Miss French recalled a cemetery down by the river which she had visited some years before and which she thought might contain the grave of "The Widow."

Soon I was pushing my way through the deep forest. I found a creek bed and followed it until I saw a clearing ahead. The clearing proved to be the lost cemetery of Warren, Maine. The path which led to it had not been used for years and heavy tree branches blocked my entry. But I finally stood inside the wire-fenced enclosure situated at the top of a small rise above the Saint George's River.

Although I found several ancient stones, neither Mrs. Isabella Gamble nor her husband Archibald were remembered on any of them. I knew that Archibald Gamble had drowned in 1779 while hauling a load of hay across the Saint George's River and that his wife had followed him in 1783. All documentary evidence indicated that they had been buried there but still I could find no trace of their graves. I noticed a long granite slab lying flat on the ground but since there were no inscriptions on it, I did not pay much attention to it.

I returned to Warren and announced my failure to Miss

French. She suggested that I visit a Charles Dillaway near Rockland who now owned the house of the Mr. Spear who had been in charge of the old cemetery.

I went to see Mr. Dillaway and learned that Mr. Spear was believed to have moved several of the old cemetery stones to make a floor for his cellar.[1] I visited the cellar with Mr. Dillaway and we did find eight stones which might have been gravestones but none that were identified with my ancestors. Only one stone bore any inscription at all. As the illustrious progenitors of at least ten thousand descendants, surely the Gambles had been given a tombstone over their graves. But where was it?

A few months ago I received a clue indicating that there was a gravestone and that it was shaped in the form of a sidewalk curbstone. I remembered that the long prone granite stone in the cemetery fitted that description. But it had not carried any inscription! Could someone have overturned the slab to hide information? And if so, why would they do such a thing?

There was only one way to settle my doubts—visit the old cemetery again and examine the other side of the granite slab. Late in January, 1950, because of the relatively mild winter, I was able to motor to Warren with Mrs. Snow.

We hiked across the fields and into the forest, following the creek bed until finally we reached the clearing. Ten minutes later we found the granite slab, frozen solidly into the ground. It was then late afternoon, and the dense forest growth had allowed very little daylight to seep through.

A more careful examination still did not reveal any inscription so we were faced with the problem of prying the heavy stone from the frozen ground and turning it over. First we jammed a dozen birch branches down around one side of the stone. Soon I had leverage with a stout tree limb and was able to loosen the stone and raise it an inch or two. Each time I lifted the slab Mrs. Snow shoved a small branch

---

[1] Mr. Spear's daughter later told me that this was incorrect.

underneath. Finally, one corner was raised six inches above the ground.

We kept at it for another twenty minutes, until finally, with a lusty shove, we overturned the heavy slab of granite. And there, before our astonished eyes, were two inscriptions side by side on the bottom of the stone. They announced that our long search was over:

ISABELLA
WIFE OF
A. G.
D. 1783

A. GAMBLE
D. 1779

Though I had achieved two of my objectives by finding the ancient timbers of the *Grand Design* and discovering, at last, the gravestone, I wondered whether there was another interesting story at Mount Desert which I would never learn.

Why should anyone visit an abandoned cemetery to turn over the gravestone of the "Widow of Mount Desert?" Could there be some strange unknown twist in her story which would explain it? As we drove back to Boston I realized that those were questions which would probably never be answered.

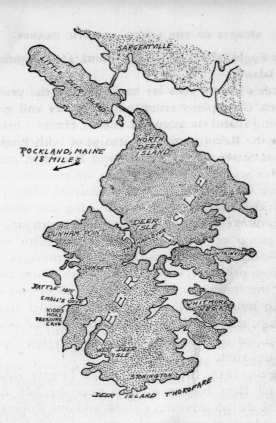

SARGENTVILLE

LITTLE DEER ISLAND

NORTH DEER ISLAND

ROCKLAND, MAINE
18 MILES

DEER ISLE

DUNHAM POINT

DEER ISLE

THE HAULOVER

SUNSET

MOUNTAINY

BATTLE 1815
SMALL'S COVE

KIDD'S HOAX
TREASURE
CAVE

WHITMORE NECK

WEST DEER ISLE

STONINGTON

DEER ISLAND THOROFARE

VIII. CAPTAIN KIDD AND DEER ISLE

I NEXT journeyed to Deer Isle, Maine, in a small plane
from Rockland. This sleepy Maine Island, located across
the Penobscot from Rockland, was settled in 1762 by William Eaton of Haverhill, John Billings of Boston and five
Greenlaw brothers from Scotland. In 1897 the town of
Stonington was incorporated on the southern part of the
island. It had often been my privilege as the Flying Santa
to drop presents at Christmastime to the lighthouse keepers

165

at nearby Eagle Island and Deer Island Thoroughfare Light at Mark Island.

Deer Isle's history goes far back through the years to the time when Champlain sailed off its shores and gave to a neighboring island the name of Isle au Haut.

During the Revolution the warships of both England and the United States were active around Deer Isle, and in the war of 1812 several naval skirmishes are recorded as having taken place there. The first battle occurred when a heavily-loaded British transport got lost in a fog and anchored off the shores of Webb's Cove, on the southeastern side of Deer Isle. A group of Deer Islanders, armed with makeshift weapons—cudgels, pitchforks, knives and muskets—boarded an American privateer, sailed her to Webb's Cove and began to attack the transport. The battle was short and decisive. Within an hour after the Americans swarmed aboard the British ship, she was theirs. The spoils of war were quite substantial, for the transport had been carrying flour, beef, molasses and rum.

In August, 1814, the United States Frigate *Adams* ran aground off Deer Isle on a ledge near the Isle au Haut. There were British prisoners aboard, and one Robert Knowlton and his brother transferred them onto their fishing sloop and started for what is now Rockland, Maine. During the voyage, the prisoners rebelled and tried to take over the vessel, but the two Knowltons soon demonstrated their knowledge of warfare on the high seas and put down the disturbance, landing the next morning at Thomaston, Maine.

Captain Morris of the *Adams* eventually floated the frigate off the ledge and brought her up the river into Hampden. Here the Americans blew her to pieces a short time later so that the British, who had captured Castine, could not take possession.

Early in January, 1815, an English brig bound from Castine to the West Indies was chased by an American privateer, the *Paul Jones,* into Small's Cove on the southwestern side of Deer Isle. There the brig was grounded on a bar. Heavily loaded with beef, pork, salmon and lumber, she was an important prize. Unknown to the Americans, the mate of the brig came from Deer Isle, where many British sympathizers lived. On shore, a Yankee named Ebenezer Small realized that the *Paul Jones* was unable to navigate near enough to fire on the brig. He rowed out and offered to pilot the *Paul Jones* to a position within cannon-shot. The battle between the brig and the privateer began with an exchange of cannon fire,[1] but as the brig was closer to the shore, the privateer could maneuver more easily and soon disabled the enemy vessel. An American lieutenant climbed into the rigging to watch the progress of the battle, and a Deer Islander on shore aimed his musket at the officer and fired, missing his mark. Years later that Islander was to regret firing at the American lieutenant.

The British brig soon surrendered, and the Americans put a prize-master aboard and anchored offshore. During the night the British sympathizers on the island boarded the prize and took command of the vessel. The prize-master had been forewarned and fled through the woods to the home of an American, and the Yankee sailors on the privateer quickly rowed in and recaptured the prize. The American captain learned the names of those Deer Islanders who had attempted to seize the brig again and give it back to the British. He intended to sail across and retaliate for the Deer Islanders' disloyalty, but the war ended before he accomplished his purpose.

Thirty years afterwards, the Islander who had shot at the American lieutenant was running for a Deer Isle town office against a Yankee veteran of the War of 1812. The charge of active participation in the British cause was brought against

---

[1] Gordon MacKay of the Stonington Ad-Vantages has one of the cannon-balls fired by the *Paul Jones.*

him, and when he admitted its truth, he was defeated in the election which followed.

Deer Isle was a great shipbuilding center for many years. A century ago Joseph Sellers launched the schooner *Franklin* at Deer Isle, and the following year, 1851, the *Sunbeam* and the *A. Fifield* slid down the ways there. Today, however, many of its shipyards, stone piers and wharves have gone to ruin, unnoticed and forgotten in the general decadence of Maine maritime activity.

But Deer Isle maritime traditions are continued whenever the great international yacht races are held, for the sailors from this island are always eagerly sought to take over the intricate details of sailing the beautiful yachts in the defense of the *America's* Cup.

Shipwrecks have played an important part in Deer Isle history. The wreck of the *Shakespeare* in 1818, the *Lingan* in 1822, the *Huntress* in 1830, the *Georgiana* in 1839 and the *Commodore Perry* in 1845 carried Deer Islanders to their deaths. Between 1846 and 1879 the *Lincoln, Tamerlane, Sarah, Lion, Mary Moulton, R.S. Warren* and *Anna N. Torrey* went down with sailors from Deer Isle aboard.[1]

Deer Isle began to be recognized as a beautiful summer location at about the time that schooners and ships started to disappear from the builders' yards. With the coming of the summer visitors, there were many new houses erected in the vicinity of Small's Cove, where the battle between the American privateer and the British brig occurred in 1815.

One of the summer visitors who came to Deer Isle at about this time was Frederick L. Olmsted, prominent landscape architect of Brookline, Massachusetts. He settled on the

---

[1] A strange drowning was that of Mr. Francis Haskell, mate aboard a Deer Isle schooner tied up at Boston Harbor. He disappeared and the schooner sailed without him. Several days later his body was found. He was standing under water, his feet stuck in the mud at the edge of the pier and his hat still on his head. Evidently he had attempted boarding the schooner at night, missed his step and landed in the water. He was unable to extricate himself from the thick mud at the bottom.

peninsula south of Small's Cove where he became acquainted with another summer resident, Franklin H. Head of Chicago. In 1894, for the purpose of amusing the Olmsted family, Mr. Head wrote a story which was so clever and interesting that it has been copied and reprinted all over the United States. Millions have seen and read the story, and believed it to be true. It is, of course, merely a pleasant hoax.

My particular copy of this story was printed in Helena, Montana, where it fell into the hands of my father-in-law, the late Louis Vernon Haegg, to whom I have dedicated this book. Other copies were printed all over the country.

As the years went by, more and more people wrote to the Olmsteds with questions, until the family printed a circular, explaining the story and how it was written. *Forum* Magazine in 1931, printed both the story and the commentary issued by the Olmsted family.

I repeat: the account which you are about to read is not a true story.

A NOTABLE LAWSUIT
SUMMARIZED BY FRANKLIN H. HEAD

THE SUIT commenced some three years since by Mr. Frederick Law Olmsted against the various members of the Astor family, in the New York Superior Court, attracted considerable attention at the time, both from the prominence of the parties to the litigation and the large amount claimed by Mr. Olmsted, something over $5,000,000. The case has not yet come to a hearing, owing to the delays at law; the matter has, in a measure, passed from notice, scarcely anything connected with it having appeared in the newspapers.

Through the courtesy of Mr. Olmsted, I spent several days as a guest at his summer residence on Deer Isle, which lies in Penobscot Bay off the mouth of the Penobscot River, on the coast of Maine; and having heard in detail the history of the cause of action, which seemed to me to prove the maxim

169

that truth is stranger than fiction, I take pleasure in giving the story as told me by Mr. Olmsted and the members of his family.

An ancestor of Mr. Olmsted, seven generations back, whose name was Cotton Mather Olmsted, was an Indian trader and spent a part of each year, from 1696 to 1705, in what is now the State of Maine. His treatment of the Indians was always fair and honorable, whereby he won their confidence and esteem. Winnepesaukee, then the head sachem of the Penobscot tribe, was at one time severely wounded by a bear, and because Mr. Olmsted cared for him, dressed his wounds and aided greatly in his recovery, the chief, as a token of gratitude, presented him with Deer Isle, before named, a portion of which has ever since remained in the possession of his descendants, and is now the property and summer home of Mr. Frederick Law Olmsted. The original deed of gift, written on a piece of birch bark, and bearing the date of January 24, 1699, is still in the possession of Mr. Olmsted. After the independence of the United States was acknowledged, the validity of the transfer was recognized and affirmed, and a formal patent issued by the Secretary of the Treasury during the second term of President Washington's administration.

Upon the rocky shore near the residence of Mr. Olmsted, and at the extreme south end of the island, is a cave, the opening of which is on the sea. The cave is about ten feet wide and ten feet high, of irregular shape, and extends back into the rock formation some twenty-five feet. It has evidently been excavated by the ceaseless action of the waves upon a portion of the rock somewhat softer than its surroundings. At high tide the entire cave is under water, but at low tide it can be entered dry-shod, being entirely above the sea level. The bottom of the cave is covered with coarse sand, five or six inches deep, below which is a compact bed of hard blue clay. At low tide the cave is often visited by the family of Mr. Olmsted and the other residents of the island. On one such visit Mr. Olmsted observed upon the rock at the inner end of the cave some marks or indentations, something in the form of a rude cross, which seemed to him possibly of artificial origin. If so, it was of ancient date, as its edges were not well defined—were rounded and worn, as by the action of the waves and ice. Still, it appeared more regular in form than the other markings upon the walls of the cave, and one day when in the cave, Mr. Olmsted suggested to his family that as stories of Captain Kidd's buried treasures had sometimes located them upon the Maine coast, they should dig at the place below the cross for such hidden wealth.

Purely as a matter of sport, the excavation was commenced; the sand was cleared away, and, to their surprise, a rectangular hole in the clay was discovered, about fifteen by thirty inches on the surface and about fifteen inches deep. This was filled with sand, and when the sand had been carefully removed, there, plainly to be seen upon the bottom of the hole, were the marks of a row of boltheads some three or four inches apart, and extending around the bottom about one inch from its edge. The appearance was precisely as if an iron box heavily bolted at its joints had been buried on the compact clay for a period long enough to have left a perfect impress of itself in the clay, and after its removal, the excavation having been filled with sand, the impression had been permanently preserved. After a perfect facsimile of the bottom of the hole had been taken in plaster of Paris, the excavation was again filled with sand. The clay was so hard that the taking of the cast did not in the least mar its surface. As there were various legends relative to the presence of Captain Kidd upon the Maine coast, the discovery of the excavation was sufficient to awaken eager interest in the question of the iron box and the person who had carried it away.

About the year 1801, a French-Canadian named Jacques Cartier, who was one of the employees of John Jacob Astor in his fur trade, and who had for several winters traded with the Indians and hunters along the upper waters of the Penobscot River, returned from New York, where he had gone to deliver the season's collection of furs, and expressed a desire to purchase from Oliver Cromwell Olmsted, who was then the owner, by inheritance, of Deer Isle, either the whole island or the south end, where the cave before described was located. Mr. Olmsted refused both requests, but finally sold him a few acres near the center of the island, where Cartier built a log house and lived for many years with an Indian wife, hunting and fishing occasionally as a diversion, but giving up entirely his former method of gaining a livelihood. This trader had for several years previous to 1801 camped upon the south end of Deer Isle when collecting his furs, passing up the Penobscot River and its tributaries in a small canoe, and storing his furs in a hut at his camping place until the end of his season, when he sailed with his little cargo for New York.

He had always seemed extremely poor, having but a meager salary from Mr. Astor; but when he purchased a portion of the island, he seemed to have an abundance of money, sufficient in fact to meet his wants for many years. Occasionally, when under the influence of whisky, he would speak vaguely of some sudden good fortune which had befallen him; but when sober he always denied ever having made the statement, and seemed much disturbed when asked about the source of his wealth; this led to various suspicions among the few inhabitants of the island as to the honesty of his methods in acquiring it. These suspicions ultimately became so pointed that Cartier suddenly disappeared from the island and never returned. On searching his cabin, some fragments of paper were found, torn and partially burned, so that no connected meaning could be determined from them. On one fragment was the signature of John Jacob Astor, and on another, in the same handwriting, the words: "absolute secrecy must be observed because . . ."

These fragments were preserved, however, and are now in the possession of Mr. Frederick Law Olmsted. From the story of the trader and from the fragmentary papers, Mr. Olmsted fancied that there might be some connection between the mysterious box and the newly acquired wealth of the trader, and that the secret, if one there was, was shared by Mr. Astor. As the trader for many years previous to his sudden good fortune had camped upon the end of the island immediately adjoining the cave, it might readily be conceived that a heavy storm had washed the sand away so as to make the top of the box visible, and that he had found it and taken it with him to New York to Mr. Astor, with his boatload of furs. His desire to purchase this particular location in the island harmonized with this suggestion.

Various questions presented themselves regarding this theory. Had the box contained the long-lost treasures of Captain Kidd? If so, to whom did the box and its contents belong? Mr. William M. Evarts, to whom Mr. Olmsted applied for an opinion as to the legal phase of this question, after careful examination of the evidence, gave his views, in substance, as follows:

1. That Captain Kidd, in the year 1700, had acquired by pillage vast treasures of gold and gems which he had somewhere concealed prior to his execution in 1701.

2. That if such treasure was concealed upon Deer Isle, that island was the absolute property, at that time, of Cotton Mather Olmsted; for while the record title to the island bore date in President Washington's administration, in 1794, yet this, as appeared by its tenor, was in affirmation of the title made in 1699, at the time the island was given to Cotton Mather Olmsted by the Indian chief, Winnepesaukee, and established the ownership of the island in Mr. Olmsted when the box, if concealed by Captain Kidd, was buried; and that Frederick Law Olmsted, by inheritance and purchase, had acquired all the rights originally held by his ancestor in that part of the island where the treasure was concealed.

3. That, as owner of such real estate, the treasure would belong to him, as affixed to the land, as against the whole world, except possibly the lineal descendants of Captain Kidd, if any there were.

Mr. Olmsted learned that in his early life Mr. Astor kept for many years his first and only bank account with the Manhattan Bank, and as the books of the bank are all preserved, he was enabled, by a plausible pretext, to secure an examination of Mr. Astor's financial transactions from the beginning. His idea in this search was to learn if Mr. Astor's fortune had increased at the same time as that of the French-Canadian.

The business of both Mr. Astor and the bank was small in those early days, and the entries of the customers' accounts were much more in detail than in our time, when, as a rule, only accounts are recorded. The account commenced in 1798, being one of the first accounts opened after the picturesque organization of the bank by Aaron Burr, and for several years the total deposits for an entire year did not exceed $4,000. Mr. Astor shipped some of his furs abroad, and others were sold to dealers and manufacturers, and whenever he drew on a customer with the bill of lading, the books of the bank showed virtually the whole transaction. Entries like the following are of frequent occurrence:

Cr. J. J. Astor $33, proceeds draft for sale of 40 Muskrat, 4 Bear, 3 Deer, and 12 Mink Skins.

Credit John J. Astor $49.50, proceeds of draft for sale of 400 Skunk Skins.

Cr. John Jacob Astor $131, proceeds of draft on London for £26.10s for sale of 87 Otter Skins, 46 Mink, and 30 Beaver Pelts.

Each year showed a modest increase in the volume of business of the thrifty furrier, but the aggregates were only moderate until the year 1801, being the same year the Canadian trader bought of Mr. Olmsted a portion of Deer Isle, when the volume of bank transactions reached, for the time, enormous dimensions, springing from an aggregate for the year 1799 of $4,011 to over $500,000 for the year 1801. Among the entries in the latter year are two of the same date for checks to Jacques Cartier, the French-Canadian: one for $133.40, drawn "In settlement to date." Inasmuch as in each previous year the aggregate fur transactions with Mr. Cartier had never exceeded $500, the entry of $5,000 seemed inexplicable on any ordinary grounds.

The enormous growth of Mr. Astor's own transactions also seemed equally mysterious. Mr. Astor had evidently visited England in the year 1801, as the bank entries are filled with credits to him of drafts remitted by him from a Roderick Streeter, varying from £10,000 to £40,000, and aggregating during the year nearly $495,000. Credits of the same Streeter drafts are also made during the two following years to the amount of over $800,000, or a total of over $1,300,000, when the Streeter remittances abruptly cease.

Edwin W. Streeter of London is at the present time one of the largest dealers in precious stones in the world; and as in England the same business is often continued in a family for many generations, it occurred to Mr. Frederick Law Olmsted, who, from the facts already given, had become greatly interested in following the matter to a conclusion, that the Streeter who had made the vast remittances to Mr. Astor might be an ancestor of the present London merchant. An inquiry by mail developed the fact that the present Mr. Streeter is a great-grandson of Roderick Streeter, and that the business had been continued in the family for five generations. Mr. Olmsted sent a confidential agent to London, who succeeded in getting access to the books of the Streeter firm for the years 1798 to 1803, inclusive. Here was found a detailed statement of the transactions with Mr. Astor.

The first item was for £40,000, entered as "Advances on ancient French and Spanish gold coins" deposited by Mr. Astor, and later another of £4,213.8s for "Balance due for

French and Spanish gold coins." All other entries were for the sale of precious stones, mostly diamonds, rubies and pearls which, in all, with the sums paid for the French and Spanish gold, reached the enormous aggregate heretofore given. Certain of the gems were purchased outright by Mr. Streeter, and others were sold by him, as a broker, for the account of Mr. Astor and the proceeds duly remitted during the years 1801-02. The whole account corresponded exactly, item for item, with the various entries of Streeter remittances shown on the books of the Manhattan Bank.

The facts gathered thus far enabled Mr. Olmsted to formulate a theory in substance as follows: That Jacques Cartier had found the box containing the buried treasures of Captain Kidd; that he had taken it to New York and delivered it to Mr. Astor; that Mr. Astor had bought the contents of the box, or his interest in them, for the check of $5,000; that he had taken the contents to England, and from their sale had realized the vast sums paid him by Mr. Streeter.

Many links in the chain of evidence, however, were still missing, and a great point would be gained if the mysterious box could be traced to the custody of Mr. Astor. It seemed reasonable that this box, if ever in the possession of Mr. Astor, and if its contents were of such great value, would be retained by him with scrupulous care, and that if he had imparted the secret to his children, the box would still be in their possession. If not, it might have been sold as a piece of worthless scrap-iron and lost sight of after the death of the first Mr. Astor. Mr. Olmsted learned that the last house in which the original John Jacob Astor had lived had been torn down in the year 1893, to be replaced by a superb modern building, and that the old building had been sold to a well-known house-wrecking firm for an insignificant sum, as the material was worth but little above the cost of tearing down and removal. In the hope that the rusty box had been sold with other rubbish about the premises, Mr. Olmsted inserted the following advertisement in the New York *Tribune*:

> A rusty iron box, strongly made and bolted, was by mistake sold in 1893 to a dealer in junk, supposedly in New York or Brooklyn. The dimensions were 15 x 30 x 15 inches. A person, for sentimental reasons, wishes to reclaim this box, and will pay to its present owner for the same several times its value as scrap-iron. Address F. L., Box 74, New York Tribune.

Within a few days Mr. Olmsted received a letter from Mr. Bronson B. Tuttle of Naugatuck, Connecticut, an iron manufacturer, stating that in a car of scrap-iron bought by him from Melchisedec Jacobs of Brooklyn, was an iron box answering the description given in the *Tribune*; that if it was of any value to the advertiser, it would be forwarded on receipt of eighty cents, which was its cost to him at $11 per ton, the price paid for the carload of scrap.

Mr. Olmsted at once procured the box and shipped it to Deer Isle, where the bolts upon its bottom and the box itself were found to fit perfectly the print in the clay bottom of the cave. The plaster cast of the bottom of the cavity, taken when it was first discovered, matched the bottom of the box as perfectly as ever a casting fitted the mold in which it was made. Every peculiarity in the shape of a bolthead, every hammer mark made in riveting the bolts, as shown in the clay, was reproduced in the iron box. There was no possible question but that the box was the identical one which had long before been buried in the cave. On the top of the box, too, was distinguishable, despite the heavy coating of rust, in rude and irregularly formed characters, as if made by strokes of a cold-chisel or some similar tool, the letters "W.K."—the initials of the veritable and eminent pirate, Captain William Kidd.

Further inquiry developed the fact that Melchisedec Jacobs,

the Brooklyn junk dealer, had purchased the box in a large drayload of scrap-iron, mostly made up of cooking ranges, sashweights, gas, steam and water pipes, etc., from the wrecking firm of Jones & Company; and that Jones & Company had taken such material from the family mansion occupied by the original John Jacob Astor at the time of his death, when tearing it down to make room for the new buildings. The indications thickened that the mysterious box contained the long-lost and widely sought treasures of Captain Kidd. One peculiarity of the box that there had apparently been no way to open it except by cutting it apart. The top had been firmly riveted in its place, and this fact possibly indicated the reason of its purchase by Mr. Astor at the moderate price of $5,000, since the trader who found it had been unable to open it before his arrival in New York. However, as we have no information on the contract between Mr. Astor and Jacques Cartier, the amount named, $5,000, may have been precisely the percentage agreed upon, which he received upon the profits of his season's business in addition to a salary.

Mr. Olmsted had an accurate copy made of all entries in the books of the Manhattan Bank as to the transactions of Mr. Astor shown by such books, from 1798 to 1803, and his English agent had similar copies of many letters passing between the parties. The agent also looked up and reported everything available relative to the career of Captain Kidd, the substance of which was as follows:

Captain Kidd had won an enviable reputation in the English and American merchant marine as a brave and intelligent officer. For many years the English merchant vessels had been preyed upon by pirates, numerous vessels were captured and destroyed and others robbed of all their treasure. These depredations were largely along the coast of Madagascar and Mozambique, on the route of the English vessels in the India trade, and off the coasts of South America, where the Spanish galleons bore great treasure from the

Peruvian gold fields. The depredations of the pirates became so great that the English merchants finally bought and equipped a stanch war vessel, placed the same under the command of Captain Kidd, and sent him out expressly to chastise and destroy the pirates. As these pirates were known to have secured vast amounts of gold and gems, it was expected that Captain Kidd might not only clear the infested seas of the piratical craft, but capture from them enough treasure to make the operation a profitable one.

After reaching the coast of East Africa, news was received of the destruction by him of sundry piratical vessels containing much treasure, but the capture of this treasure seemed to excite his own cupidity and he decided to engage himself in the occupation of being a malefactor. For some two years thereafter he was literally the scourge of the seas. He plundered alike other pirates and the merchant vessels of every nation. Finally, after a cruise along the eastern coast of the United States, as far north as the port of Halifax, he, for some reason, decided boldly to make an entry at the port of Boston as an English merchant vessel, under the papers originally furnished him in England. Before entering Boston Harbor, he put ashore and concealed on Gardiner's Island a considerable quantity of merchandise, consisting largely of bales of valuable silks and velvets, with a small amount of gold and silver and precious stones. These articles were afterwards discovered and reclaimed by the owners of the vessel, and sold for some £14,000.

From the great number of vessels which he had destroyed and plundered, with their ascertained cargoes, it was known that the treasure thus discovered was but an insignificant fraction of what he had captured—it was known that gold and gems of vast value were somewhere concealed—and thence came the endless searches from Key West and Jekyl Island to Halifax, for the treasure which had thus far seemingly escaped human vision and utterly disappeared. In fact, from the little care taken by Captain Kidd as to the plunder

179

hidden on Gardiner's Island, the owners of his ship concluded that to be merely a blind to divert their attention from the vastly greater wealth he had appropriated.

A short time after his arrival in Boston he was arrested and sent to England, and at once put on trial for piracy. In two days he was tried, convicted and hanged. This illustrates the great progress in civilization since that benighted age, for now the most red-handed and popular murderers are allowed months for preparation and trial, are feted, garlanded and made the heroes of the day, and assigned with all priestly assurance to the mansions of the blest. Captain Kidd's wife was not allowed to see him, except for a half hour after the death sentence had been pronounced. They had a whispered conference, and at its close he was seen to hand her a card, upon which he had written the figures, 44106818. This card was taken from her by the guards and never restored, and even claimed not herself to know. The paper was preserved among the proceedings of the trial, and a photographed copy was secured by Mr. Olmsted.

From the records of the trial, it appeared that Captain Kidd was the only child of his parents; that he had been married for several years; that two children had been born to him, a daughter who died while yet a child and before the trial, and a son who survived both his father and his mother. It also appeared that this son, ten years after his father's execution, enlisted as a private soldier in the English army, and was killed in the battle near Stirling in 1715. The records of the English War Office showed that the widow of this son applied for a pension under the then existing law, and her affidavit and marriage certificate showed her to have been married to the son of Captain Kidd, and that no child had been born to them, and the usual pension was awarded to her and paid until her death in 1744. These facts settled the question as to any claim upon the treasure by descendants of Captain Kidd.

The records of the trial also contained a report by experts

upon the card given by Kidd to his wife, to the effect that they had applied to the figures upon it the usual tests for the reading of cipher writings without avail, and that if the figures ever had a meaning, it was undiscoverable. The same conclusion was reached by several people to whom Mr. Olmsted showed the copy of the card. Shortly afterwards, when Professor David P. Todd, the astronomer of Amherst College, was visiting the family of Mr. Olmsted at Deer Isle, he one day amused himself by calculating the latitude and longitude of the home near the cave, and gave the results to Miss Marion Olmsted. As she was entering these results in her journal, she was struck by the fact that the figures for the latitude, 44° 10′, were the same as the first four figures on the card, 4410, and that the other four figures, 6818, were almost the exact longitude west from Greenwich, which was 68° 17′, a difference easily accounted for by a moderate variation in Captain Kidd's chronometer. The latitude, taken by observation of the pole star, was absolutely accurate. It appeared as though Captain Kidd had told his wife in this manner where to find the hidden treasure, but that, inasmuch as the government authorities had seized the card, she preferred silence toward those who had pursued her husband to his death, and the total loss to everyone of the treasure, rather than, by a confession, to give it into the hands of his enemies. The very simplicity of the supposed cipher writing had been its safeguard, since all the experts had sought for some abstruse and occult meaning in the combination of the figures.

By the happy thought of Miss Olmsted, another link was thus added to the chain of evidence. With the facts given, the only point seemingly needed to show that the Kidd treasure had come into the possession of Mr. Astor was to show that some of the money or gems sold by him had been actually seized by Captain Kidd. Even this, by a happy chance, became possible through the correspondence secured from Mr. Streeter in London.

It appeared that, in the year 1700, Lord and Lady Dunmore were returning to England from India, when the vessel upon which they had taken passage was fired upon and captured by Captain Kidd. His first order was that every person on board should walk the plank into the sea, but several ladies who were passengers pleaded so earnestly for their lives that Kidd finally decided to plunder the cargo and passengers and let the vessel proceed on her voyage. The ladies were compelled, on peril of their lives, to surrender all their jewelry, and among the articles taken from Lady Dunmore was a pair of superb pearl bracelets, the pearls being set in a somewhat peculiar fashion. Another pair, an exact duplicate of those possessed by Lady Dunmore, had been purchased by Lord Dunmore as a wedding present to his sister, and the story of the two pairs of pearls, which were of great value, and of her pleading for her life to Captain Kidd, is a matter of history, as well as one of the cherished family traditions.

In 1801, Roderick Streeter wrote to Mr. Astor that the then Lady Dunmore, in looking over some gems which he was offering her, had seen a pair of exquisite pearl bracelets which were a part of the Astor consignment, and had at once recognized them as the identical pair taken by Kidd nearly one hundred years before. She returned the following day with the family solicitor, bringing the duplicate bracelets; told and verified the story of the loss of one pair by Lady Dunmore; compared the two pairs, showing their almost perfect identity, showing certain private marks upon each and demonstrating beyond question that the pearls offered by Mr. Streeter were the identical gems seized by Captain Kidd. The solicitor demanded their surrender to Lady Dunmore on the ground that, having been stolen, no property rights in them could pass even to to an innocent purchaser.

Mr. Streeter then stated that he had asked for delay until he could communicate with the owner of the gems, and had asked Mr. Astor for instructions. Mr. Astor replied, authorizing the delivery of the bracelets to Lady Dunmore, and asking Mr. Streeter to assure her that the supposed owner was guiltless of wrong in the matter and was an entirely innocent holder. He repeated the caution, given also in sundry other letters, that to no one was the ownership of the gems sold by Mr. Streeter to be revealed. They were to be sold as the property of Streeter, acquired in the regular course of business. Lady Dunmore afterward sat to Sir Thomas Lawrence for her portrait, and was painted wearing upon her arms the pearl bracelets thus curiously reclaimed. This portrait is considered one of the masterpieces of Lawrence.

By the discovery of the hole in a cave in Maine, after a lapse of two hundred years, was thus curiously brought to light the apparent origin of the colossal Astor fortune. Prior to the acquisition of the Kidd treasures by the first American Astor, he was simply a modest trader, earning each year, by frugality and thrift, two or three hundred dollars above his living expenses, with a fair prospect of accumulating, by an industrious life, a fortune of twenty or thirty thousand dollars. When he became possessed of the Kidd plunder, he handled it with the skill of a great general. He expanded his fur trade until it embraced the continent. The record of his checks given during the three years when he received the $1,300,000 shows that he expended over $700,000 of the amount in the purchase of real estate in the city of New York. The entries of the various checks are recorded as "Payment for the Wall Street property," the "Bond Street land," the "Broadway corner," etc., the descriptions being sufficiently accurate, when verified by comparison with the titles of record, to locate at this date every parcel of land bought, all of which is still in the possession of the Astor family. Some twenty different tracts of land in what is now the very heart of the business and residence portion of New York were thus purchased, each one of which is now probably of more value than the price originally paid for the whole.

In obtaining a knowledge of the various details already given, over two years had been spent by Mr. Olmsted and his agents. The results seemingly reached may be summarized as follows:

1. Captain Kidd had sailed along the Maine coast shortly before his arrest, and an iron box marked with his initials was afterward taken from the cave into Mr. Astor's possession.

2. Jacques Cartier had camped for many years, while employed by Mr. Astor, immediately adjoining the cave where the box was concealed, and his rapid increase in wealth and that of Mr. Astor were simultaneous.

3. Mr. Astor's great wealth came from the sale, through Mr. Streeter, of ancient Spanish and French gold, and of gems, some of which were proved to have been a part of the spoils of Captain Kidd, which made it a reasonable presumption that all of such property was of the same character.

4. Captain Kidd was known to have captured and somewhere concealed gold and gems of vast value, and the card given his wife before his execution indicated, by a plausible reading, the cave upon Mr. Olmsted's land as the place of concealment.

5. The family of Captain Kidd had long been extinct, and no one could successfully contest with Mr. Olmsted the ownership of the property concealed upon his land.

Having his evidence thus formulated, Mr. Olmsted called upon the descendants of Mr. Astor, accompanied by his attorney, Mr. William M. Evarts, and demanded of them: 1. A payment by them to him of the sum of $1,300,000, the amount received of Mr. Streeter, with interest from the date of its receipt. The total amount, computed according to the laws of New York in force since 1796, was $5,112,234.80; and Mr. Olmsted offered, on condition of immediate cash payment, to deduct the item of $34.80. This demand was refused. 2. Mr. Olmsted then demanded that the Astor family should convey to him all the real estate in New York City purchased by their ancestor with the money received from

Mr. Streeter, with the accrued rents and profits from the date of its purchase, and this demand was likewise refused.

These refusals left to Mr. Olmsted no alternative except to resort to the courts for the establishment of his rights, and an action was accordingly commenced. The declaration filed by his attorneys, Joseph H. Choate, Steward L. Woodford and Frederick W. Holls, set out in full the history of the claim from the beginning, as has been detailed herein, and petitions the court for alternative relief; either that the descendants of John Jacob Astor pay to Mr. Olmsted the sum of $1,300,000 with interest from the time of its receipt by Mr. Astor; or, failing in this, that Mr. Astor be adjudged a trustee for the rightful owner of the money thus received, and that the property purchased with such funds be ordered conveyed to Mr. Olmsted.

To this declaration the Astor family, by their solicitors, Elihu Root and Edward S. Isham, answered, denying all liability, upon the ground that the cause of action, if ever valid, was barred by the statute of limitations. To this answer the plaintiffs demurred, alleging for grounds thereof that it appeared clearly from the pleadings that Mr. Olmsted had been vigilant in the assertion of his claim as soon as reasonable proof of its existence came to his knowledge, and further, that the statute of limitations did not run as against a trust. The demurrer was sustained by the court upon both grounds, the court intimating, however, that when the case came to a hearing the plaintiff must select and rest his case on one or the other form of relief demanded, and could not, in the same action, secure the alternative relief sought. After this decision the defendants filed a general denial of all the claims of Mr. Olmsted.

This is the present status of litigation, and it is expected that the case will be brought to a final trial during the present year.

Should the judgment upon the trial be in favor of Mr. Olmsted, or even against him upon some technical ground, it would, in either event, be a great boon to the people along our Atlantic seaboard, in that it will reveal the actual fate of the Kidd treasures. The publicity upon this point will stop the ceaseless and fruitless expenditure of money in digging for such hidden wealth, as well as the exactions of clairvoyants, Indian spiritual mediums, rappers, professional ghosts and witch-hazel experts, who have yearly preyed on the credulity of their victims in locating the Kidd deposits.

From the dramatic character of the claim, from the eminent ability of the counsel for each contestant and from the large amount involved, it is needless to add that the trial will be watched with intense interest, and that it will stand as the cause celebre of our century.

COMMENTARY UPON "A NOTABLE LAWSUIT"
BY FREDERICK L. OLMSTED

This interesting and amusing yarn has been in private circulation and has appeared from time to time in the newspapers in garbled form since 1894. In that year it was written for the amusement of the author, Mr. Franklin H. Head, and Miss Olmsted, and was subsequently read before a small literary club in Chicago of which the author was a member. Intended as a burlesque hoax, it was so written as to carry a pervading atmosphere of serious verisimilitude, interwoven with enough of the preposterous to let the reader gradually catch on to the joke. It is a delightful example of this type of yarn.

Unfortunately, in passing from hand to hand, and especially from mouth to mouth, it has often lost its delightful humorous quality and becomes a bald hoax story, arousing various degrees either of credulity or of speculation as to what possible basis in fact was a dinner conversation between the author and Miss Olmsted, in Chicago, during which they talked about legends of Captain Kidd, about Penobscot Bay and the land which her father had then recently pur-

*chased there, and about a sort of hollow in the rocks on the
shore of that land almost big enough to call a cave and almost
fit to weave some kind of romantic legend about. Miss Olmsted may even have said that a chest of buried treasure would
be indispensable for the proper sort of legend, and may have
indicated her willingness to stretch the size of the cave as
much as might be necessary to make room for a chest of suitable dimensions.*

*The seed was planted, and in the fertile soil of the author's
imagination soon produced the full-grown story, bristling
with apparent facts. It is hardly surpassed by his pseudo-
scientific monograph, in the manner of the higher criticism,
"Shakespeare's Insomnia."*

*It has been pleasing and amusing to explain all this to my
many friends, but it is getting to be something of a bore to
explain it individually to unnumbered eager inquirers.*

In March of 1950, I talked with Miss Carolyn Olmsted, who,
with her sister, owns the "Binnical" cottage on that part of
Deer Isle located to the southwest of Small's Cove. It was
believed that the original cave was under the porch of the
old Falsted home, which first was a private house, then an
inn and now again a private house. Miss Olmsted assured
me that this belief was incorrect, and gave me particulars
about the actual cave which Mr. Franklin H. Head chose as
the scene of his fictitious story about Captain Kidd and the
Astor fortune.

"The cave is all solid rock, of course," Miss Olmsted began, "and when the tide is half in, the bow of your boat can
be inserted into the mouth of the cave. At low tide the cave
is about five feet high, and nine or ten feet wide. I have
stood inside the cave with two others and there was room for
all three of us and a little bit more. Our cottage is quite a
distance from the cave, about a mile or more through the
woods, and there is no residence or building near the cave
and never has been in my memory. Incidentally, Mr. Head

never intended that his story should be published, as it was just for the reading pleasure of Mr. Head, Miss Marion Olmsted and a small literary club."

In June, 1950, I visited the cave and found it essentially as described by Miss Carolyn Olmsted.

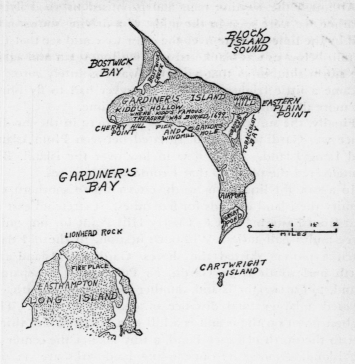

IX. GARDINER'S ISLAND,
WHERE KIDD BURIED TREASURE

IN APRIL, 1950, we took off from Norwood, Massachusetts, for a flight across Long Island Sound to Gardiner's Island in New York State. My pilot, Bill Ashton, proved to be as interested in visiting the island as I. When he realized that we were heading for the spot where Captain William Kidd, the privateer, had actually buried treasure, he told me that one of his ancestors, Philip Ashton, had been captured by pirates back in 1722.

Although the weather man had promised us good flying weather, we were soon in the midst of a driving snowstorm, and by the time we were over the coast we could see that the terrain below us was blanketed with white. Again and again the storm shut in so that visibility was absolutely zero. It became a little frightening, but we never had to fly blind for more than three or four minutes at a time.

Finally, the sun came out briefly and there in the far distance was Gardiner's Island, situated between Plum Island and Long Island. As we flew in low over the island, Bill maneuvered the plane so that I could take pictures.

In a straight line from northwestern tip to southern extremity the island extends for five miles. It stretches east to west from Eastern Point to Cherry Hill Point for not quite three and a half miles. Without question, in the old days when explorers skirted the shores, Gardiner's Island ran north and south from Gardiner's Point, now a separate island, to Cartwright Island, another island to the south. It covered a larger total distance of over seven miles. The highest point on the island is a hill of a hundred and thirty feet to the north of Casey Pond, a tiny lake at the center of the island. Among its outstanding landmarks are an old windmill near the pier and Kidd's Hollow, where the famous Captain Kidd buried his treasure near Cherry Hill Point.

Soon after we had landed at the island airport which consists of more or less rolling meadows, we were met by the island keeper who introduced himself as Charles A. Raynor. After securing the plane, we jumped aboard his truck and started for his house. As we drove along, we passed hundreds of osprey nests. Mr. Raynor told us about these interesting birds. There are about two thousand of them every spring, he said, and, though they are "monogamous," keeping the same mate year after year, they always return to the island singly.

"We watch the osprey for our seasons," he said. "Their arrival is a pretty sure sign that spring is around the corner, and when they leave—well, autumn is about over. They were very late getting here this year, arriving on the twenty-eighth of March. Usually they arrive between the seventeenth and the twenty-third of March."

I learned later that the ospreys or fish hawks had lived on the island for hundreds of years. In his diary, John Lyon Gardiner, who lived on the island in 1791, mentions seeing blackbirds, robins, meadow-larks, eagles, crows, owls, wild gulls and black ducks by March 10. "I have observed," he continues in his diary, "that fish hawks come on the 21 of March and go on the 21 of Sept. at the time of the Equinoxes. They are very regular in coming and going and seldom vary more than 48 hours. They wage war with the eagle as soon as they come, and numbers together overcome that large bird." Gardiner didn't care much for the eagles, because he had found that they often fix their claws "in the back of a lamb and bear him away from his helpless mother."

We soon arrived at Charles Raynor's home and met his wife, Elizabeth. Later we made the acquaintance of the only other person who lives on the island, Jack Finch, and the three dogs which were very much in evidence.

Before visiting the place, I had talked with Miss Sarah D. Gardiner of East Hampton, Long Island, who owns Gardiner's Island. Miss Gardiner has written a delightful book entitled *Early Memories of Gardiner's Island* in which she tells of the many generations of Gardiners who have lived there.

It was obtained from the Indians by Lion Gardiner in 1639. The founder of the Gardiner family had originally gone to Connecticut from the old world to build and command the Saybrook Fort at the mouth of the Connecticut River. He was an engineer, the first of his profession ever to arrive in New England. He tells the story in his family Bible:

In the year of our Lord 1635 July the 10 Came I,

Lion Gardiner, and Mary,[1] my wife, from Woerden, a town in Holland where my wife was born. We ... dwelt at Saybrook Fort foure years of which I was Commander ... then went to an island of mine owne which I bought of the Indians called by them Manchonake by us the Isle of Wight.

John Lion Gardiner built a comfortable house on the island and brought his wife and children there soon afterwards. Gardiner showed great courage in building over thirty miles from the nearest settlement, but as the years elapsed, he and his descendents found that the island was almost too accessible from the sea to pirates, privateers and other ocean-wanderers.

The early history of Gardiner's Island is full of blood and sacrifice. In fact, the Indian name of the island, Manchonat, stands for "the place where many have died." There is a tradition that the island was sold to Lion Gardiner by the sachem of Wyandanch in gratitude for his attempt to rescue Wyandanch's daughter from Ninigret during the Indian warfare on Long Island. Gardiner had been the one person who had kept the Connecticut and Massachusetts colonies from total destruction during the terrible Pequot Wars,[2] and he felt perfectly equal to living on an island called "the place where many have died." He was tired of the gross mismanagement of government on both sides of the ocean.

Gardiner's Island and the eastern end of Long Island at Montauk Point, where the sachem Wyandanch ruled, were never really affected by Indian warfare after Lion Gardiner came to the island which still bears his name. He seems to

---

[1] Mary's last name was Deureant, and not Willemsen, as is erroneously believed.

[2] At the height of the war Sir Harry Vane wrote from Boston asking for the best method of quelling Pequots. To show what the English were faced with, Gardiner sent along with his advice a human rib pierced completely by an arrow.

have had the personality and diplomacy which other English leaders lacked in dealing with the red man, and the Long Island Indians were free to come and go as they wished on his island.

In 1649 the settlement at Southampton was infuriated when an English woman was murdered and the Indians feared there would be a general reprisal against them. The settlers sent for Wyandanch. At the time Gardiner was visiting Sachem Wyandanch at his Montauk castle, and he offered to stay at Montauk as a hostage against Wyandanch's safe return. Fortunately, Wyandanch caught the murderers on his way to Southampton. They were Pequots from the mainland who were subsequently sent to Hartford to be tried and executed by the authorities there.

As the years elapsed, Gardiner's Island became a thing of beauty, with the lords of the manor employing from eighty to ninety servants who kept the fields rich in oats, wheat and other staple commodities. Each year more than two thousand tons of hay were gathered, and from three to five hundred cattle grazed on the hillsides. Almost two thousand sheep fed on the pleasant meadows and pastures, yielding from ten thousand to twelve thousand pounds of wool. There were butter and cheese in abundance and over a hundred pigs and hogs. Wild turkeys and deer roamed the island, and from fifty to eighty horses were accommodated in the stables.

Indeed, the island was a little kingdom of its own, and its only disadvantage was its previously mentioned accessibility to marauders of the sea.

Lion Gardiner died in 1663, aged sixty-four. His widow, Mary, died two years later, and it was her will which settled the disposition of Gardiner's Island:

> *I give my island called the Isle of Wight to my son David, wholly to be his during his life and after his de-*

cease to his next heire maile begotten by him . . . Never to be sold from then and to be a continuous to the heires of me and my husband forever . . .

David Gardiner, only son of the founder of the island, and the first white child born in Connecticut, received a patent from Governor Dongan of New York whereby the island became a lordship and manor with courts *leet* and *baron*. The yearly fee was to be "one lamb on the first of May." David Gardiner died in 1689 while visiting in Hartford, Connecticut, and is buried there in the Old Center Church cemetery. I copied the inscription on his tomb telling the visitor that he was: *Well, Sick, Dead, in one hour's time.*

John Gardiner, David's oldest son, succeeded him as owner of the island. It is interesting to note that for eight generations the John-David variation continued, as in the old rhyme about the Kings of England. After Lion Gardiner's death in 1663 there were the following proprietors of Gardiner's Island: David, John, David, John, David, John, David, John. This succession began in 1665 and ended in 1861, extending over a period of almost two centuries.

Charles Raynor, Bill Ashton, and I started out in a jeep to explore the island. Deer flashed by us with apparent nonchalance. Finally, we reached Kidd's Hollow, where a small granite marker tells us that Captain Kidd's treasure was "buried and recovered" in that hollow. Raynor and Ashton drove on ahead and I got out and walked around with the double intention of photographing ospreys close at hand and studying the famous hollow where Captain William Kidd himself had buried golden doubloons and pieces of eight.

Kidd's was quite a story, and after taking a few pictures of the ospreys in various attitudes of flight and nest-watching, I sat down in the hollow and leaned against a tree trunk to think it over.

When William Kidd anchored off Gardiner's Island in June, 1699, John Gardiner, whose proprietorship extended from 1689 to 1738, was lord and master of the island. He was the eldest of the four children of David Gardiner, the second proprietor, and was known as a "hardy, active, robust man, generous and upright, rough in his manner, plain, agreeable to the manner of his time." Captain Kidd called on John Gardiner with an unusual request. In order to explain the reasons for this peculiar call it is necessary to explain William Kidd's background and how he became one of the most wronged men in maritime history.

At the back of every great misunderstanding or legend there is always an event of real dramatic interest which has been warped by incorrect retelling until it no longer even faintly resembles the truth. Such a misunderstanding is the current and common belief that Captain Kidd was a bloodthirsty buccaneer, killing men, women and children and scuttling ships wherever he went. He is known as the very symbol of piracy, and there is scarcely a cove or an island along the Atlantic coast which is not said to contain a part of his "fabulous treasure." Falsehoods seem to prosper far more often than the truth, and I hope that by telling the real story of Captain Kidd I will help to balance the scales on the side of truth.

William Kidd was born in Scotland around 1654. Following the sea until 1691, he amassed a respectable fortune which allowed him to retire that same year. He was then known as William Kidd, gentleman. In May, 1691, Kidd married a New York widow, Sarah Bradley Cort, and in 1695 traveled to London.

At that time Richard Coote, the Earl of Bellomont, was preparing to leave England as Governor of both New England and New York. King William III was short of money, and Lord Bellomont suggested that a privateering expedition with broad powers granted and sponsored in part by the king himself would be a very lucrative venture. At that time privateering and piracy had little in common. Privateering was the capture of enemy ships in wartime, and piracy was the capture of anyone's ships at any time.

Lord Bellomont suggested that a privateering expedition to the Red Sea would be especially profitable. There ships of the Great Mogul were sailing under passes given them by France, and they were easy prey. Captain William Kidd was suggested as the suitable leader of the expedition. When summoned before the King, Kidd showed little interest in the plan at first, but finally, because of Bellomont's persuasive manner, Kidd gave in and accepted the commission as the King's privateer against England's enemy, France. Eventually, the King, Bellomont, Kidd and six other high government officials were included in the plan. Kidd set forth under the Great Seal of England, on a partnership basis with the King himself!

The *Adventure Galley* was selected to serve as the ship for Kidd's adventure. Kidd sailed her to New York to augment his English crew and then headed for the Red Sea.

During the summer of 1697 a third of Kidd's crew of 155 died of cholera. The remainder were anxious to turn pirate but Kidd held them off and refused to board a friendly vessel which carried rich spoils. The crew was disgusted and would have mutinied if Kidd had not attacked their ringleader, Moore, the ship's gunner. The gunner later died of his injuries.

Soon after this misadventure, Kidd captured the *Novembre,* a Moorish vessel sailing under letters of marque from France. Kidd as a privateer demanded and received the French pass, thus exonerating himself from any charge of piracy.

In the winter of 1698, privateering Captain Kidd captured a rich prize, the *Quedah Merchant.* It proved to carry about $500,000 worth of rare silks, silver plate, jewels, pieces of eight and gold. After obtaining the captain's French pass,

Kidd transferred his crew and goods to the *Quedah Merchant* and scuttled the *Adventure Galley*.

Meanwhile, in England, King William and the Whigs were forced to declare Kidd a pirate when the Tories exposed the secret partition treaty of 1698 which Kidd's partner, Lord Somers, had negotiated and revealed the use of the Great Seal of England for a personal privateering enterprise sponsored by the King. The Tories implicated Kidd and the King and the others in the affair, until finally the King and his Whig adherents, to save themselves politically, sacrificed for all time Kidd's good name by declaring him a pirate.

As Captain Kidd made his triumphant return trip to Boston, he stopped at several West Indian Islands, including Nevis, Saint Thomas and Antigua. At each port he learned that he had been declared a pirate. He sailed desperately from port to port like a hunted animal before he finally found a friend in Henry Bolton, an English trader who agreed to help him. Kidd's ship had begun to leak, and so for this and other reasons he decided to sail to Boston in a smaller vessel. After an exchange of goods, Bolton allowed Kidd to sail with the spoils from the *Quedah Merchant* aboard Bolton's six-gun sloop *Saint Antonio*.

And thus it was that Lord John Gardiner had a visit from Captain William Kidd in June, 1699. On or about the 28th of June, Gardiner noticed the *Saint Antonio* riding at anchor off the island, and when the sloop was still there two days later Gardiner rowed out to investigate.

When Gardiner came aboard, Kidd explained that he was on his way to meet Lord Bellomont in Boston, and asked Gardiner if he could put ashore two Negro boys and a girl. The proprietor agreed. He had had previous experience with privateers and knew that it was useless to object. Two hours later, after the Negroes were on the island, Kidd sent two bales of goods and a fourth Negro ashore.

The next morning the privateer requested and received a barrel of cider and six sheep and, in return, presented Gardiner with some damaged muslin and Bengal silk as a present for his wife. Soon afterwards the sloop sailed away, firing four guns in salute.

Three days later Kidd returned and sent in to shore "a Chest and a box of Gold and a bundle of Quilts and four bales of Goods,[1] which box of Gold the said Kidd told the Narrator was intended for Lord Bellomont." Two thirty-pound bags of silver and a small bundle of gold and gold dust were also put into Gardiner's keeping. The treasure was buried in Kidd's Hollow, and the *Saint Antonio* sailed away again. Later Kidd transferred two more treasure chests to his friend "Whisking" Clarke, leaving himself only enough gold and gold dust for expenses in Boston.

Meanwhile, a Mr. Emmott of New York was dispatched to Boston to discover what reception Kidd was likely to receive there. Bellomont, the man who had urged Kidd to undertake the expedition, was now to turn Judas and trick Kidd into going to Boston. He wrote a fine letter, assuring Kidd, among other things, that he would get him the King's pardon and pledging that "on my word and on my honor I will performe nicely what I have now promised."

Kidd, greatly relieved, went to Boston and roamed the streets freely for a week. At the end of the week, Governor Bellomont ordered him thrust into jail and later sent back to England. Bellomont kept Kidd's French passes from the Moorish vessels—Kidd's only proof that he was a privateer and not a pirate.

In England, Captain William Kidd was convicted of piracy and sentenced to be hanged.

Until the very end, Kidd expected a reprieve. But on Friday, May 23, 1701, he was taken to Wapping-on-Thames and hung from the scaffolding. The scaffolding broke as well as the rope and half an hour later his executioners had used a nearby tree for their grim purpose. Kidd's body was later cut down and preserved with tar so that the mortal remains

---

[1] There is still preserved a pitcher which Kidd also gave Mrs. Gardiner.

of the "wicked pirate" could be taken to a point near Tilbury Fort and suspended in public view.

In America, authorities soon confiscated all of the hoard Kidd had left on Gardiner's Island, as well as the chests in Whisking Clarke's custody and what few valuables had been found in Kidd's bedroom after his arrest. They even took Sarah Kidd's silver spoons, though she later recovered them. So the fabulous treasure which Kidd is alleged to have buried was reclaimed a few weeks after it was brought to Gardiner's Island, New York. The official list appears on the following pages. As the reader will see by looking at it closely, every bit of treasure of every sort was carefully itemized and listed by a committee of six leading citizens. The spoils include the Gardiner's Island booty, what was found in Kidd's lodgings at Boston and what was still aboard the sloop *Saint Antonio*. This most interesting document completely destroys the century-old myth concerning Captain Kidd— that his treasure is still to be found somewhere along the Atlantic Coast.

One reason why many people are confused as to the character of William Kidd and the nature of his visit to Gardiner's Island is that eighty genuine pirates visited the island on September 2, 1728, causing great damage and much sorrow. The *Boston News-Letter* of September 19, 1728, tells us that owner John Gardiner was tied to a mulberry tree and severely cut; the family's beds were ripped open and the house was rifled of all silver except the famous Kidd tankard which Mrs. Gardiner carried as she fled. She and several other women were able to escape the island with the help of a faithful Indian who took them to Accabonack by canoe. An armed expedition was sent to Gardiner's Island at once, and the pirates fled the scene when their lookout sounded the alarm. They were Spanish and French pirates, high-seas desperadoes who roamed from Cuba to Maine, attacking both houses ashore and ships at sea.

Another pirate visitor to Gardiner's Island was Captain

BOSTON NEW ENGLAND JULY 29TH 1699

True Accompt of all such Gold, Silver, Jewells, and Merchandizes, late in the Possession of Capt: William Kid, Which have been Seized and secured by us under written Pursuant to an Order from his Excellency . . . . Earle of Bellomont Capt. Generall & Governor in Chief, in & over, his Majesties Provinces of . . . : Massathusets Bay . . . : bearing date July . . . . 1699 Viz:

	Gold Ounces	Silver Ounces	Precious Stones or Jewels	Baggs of Sugar	Canvis Peices	Bailes of Merchandize
..Capt: William Kid's Box—						
One Bag-qt. Fifty three Sillver Barrs		357				
One Bag-qt. Seventy nine Bars & pieces of Silver		442½				
One Bag-qt. Seventy four Barrs Silver		421				
One Enameld Silver Box, in which are		....	4 diamonds set in Gold Lockets one diamond loose; one large Diamond set in a Gold Ring			
Found in Mr: Duncan Campbel's House—						
No 1—One Bag-qt. Gold	58½					
2—One Bag-qt.	94					
3—One Handkerchiefe qt:	50					
4—One Bag-qt.	103					
5—One Bag-qt.	38½					
6—One Bag-qt.	19¼					
7—One Bag-qt.		203				

Also Twenty Dollers, one half and one quart: & ps of eight, Nine English–Crowns, one small Barr of Silver, one smal lump Silver, a small Chaine, a Corral bottle a Corral Necklace, one ps white, & . . . . of Chequered Silk ......

In Capt. William Kid's Chest:

	Gold Ounces	Silver Ounces	Precious Stones or Jewels	Baggs of Sugar	Canvis Peices	Bailes of Merchandize
Two Silver B . . , Two Silver Candlesticks, One Silver Porriger & som Small things of Silver-qt.		82				
Rubies small and great, sixty seven, Green Stones two, One large Large Loadstone			69			

Landed from on board the sloop Antonio, Capt: Wm:
Kid late Command

dize, Where of one he had Opened Getting much Damaged by Water:

Eighty five ps. Silk............

Sixty ps.....& Muzlins............

Received the 17th instant of Mr. John Gardner:

No 1—One Bag dust Gold-qt:	60¼
2—One Bag ... Gold-qt.	11
and in it Silver-qt.	
3—One peck dust Gold-qt.	24¾
4—One Bag qt. & Three Silver Rings and Sundry precious stones	47/8 ounces
—one bag unpolished stones	
—one ps. of Cristol & ....Two cornelian	
—Rings, two small agats, Two omathests	
—All in same bag	
5—One Bag Silver Buttons & a Lamp	29
6—One bag broken Silver-qt:	173½
7—One bag Gold Barrs-qt:	353¼
8—One bag Gold Barrs-qt:	238½
9—One bag Dust Gold-qt:	59½
10—One bag silver Barrs-qt:	212
11—One bag silver Barrs-qt:	309
	2353

The Whole of the Gold above Mentioned is a Eleven hundred and Three
Eleven ounces, Troy Weight
The Silver is Two Thousand three hundred and Fifty/ounces
The Jewels .... Precious .... Weighed one ....
....
The Sugar is Contained in Fifty Seven Baggs
The Merchandize is contained in Forty one Bailes
The Canvis in Seventeen Peices

(Signed)

Sam Sewall	Laur. Hammond
Natha'l Byfield	L. Colt
Jos. Dumer	Andr. Belcher

Paulsgrave Williams, former associate of the notorious buccaneer, Captain Samuel Bellamy, whose fabulous treasure is still aboard his sunken galleon off Cape Cod. When Williams anchored off Whaling Hill on Gardiner's Island, David Gardiner, the fourth proprietor, and his wife went aboard to greet the visiting captain. Only after they had taken dinner on the ship did they realize that their host was a pirate. They were allowed to go ashore in safety.

In addition to visits from pirates, many other interesting events have taken place in the history of the Gardiner family.

Religious services were something of a problem to the early Gardiners, but when a chaplain agreed to live there, they were able to attend church on Sunday. All went well until Mary, daughter of the fifth proprietor, eloped with a Mr. Blague, then the island chaplain. Formal religious services were dispensed with after this episode. However, after the death of John Gardiner in 1764, it was revealed that he had forgiven his daughter's elopement, for in his will he left her twenty pounds of "New York money."

This same Mary Gardiner, as a schoolgirl, had embroidered the family coat of arms, adding her own variations, and for years afterwards the embroidery was on exhibition in the manor house.

David, the Sixth Lord of the Manor, married Jerusha, the daughter of Dr. Samuel Buell, Easthampton's Revolutionary War minister. Jerusha Buell was named after little Jerusha Williams who had been tomahawked by the Indians during the terrible Deerfield massacre a half century before.

It was David, the Sixth Lord, who built the manor house which stood until its destruction by fire in 1947.[1] His diary tells us that he "raised the house" on May 25, 1774, with the help of forty-eight others. But David never saw the completion of his home, for he died September 8, 1774, and was buried on the island. His son John, who was born four years

---

[1] The original manor house built by Lion Gardiner in 1639 was also destroyed by fire at some unrecorded date before 1774.

before his father's death, was taken to Connecticut when the Revolution broke in full force in 1775, and Colonel Abraham Gardiner, as the boy's guardian, presided at the island. When the British Commander tried to purchase cattle and swine from the boy's guardian, the colonel refused and dealt instead with General Gage in Boston.

During the Revolution, Major André, later executed by the Americans as a British spy, made frequent trips to Gardiner's Island, which he found a delightful spot for hunting and fishing. During stormy weather he and his British friends took over the manor house and played quoits with Spanish pieces of eight. The oaken floors of the manor still bore the marks of those quoit games when the manor was destroyed by fire over a century and a half later.

In 1791 John Gardiner came into possession of the island as the seventh proprietor and proved an able and methodical administrator. His order of life was written inside the cover of one of his carefully kept notebooks: *Undertake coldly, but pursue with vigor.* His plans and business notes are interesting and include an item declaring his intentions "to see those I owe and pay them," and "to buy a suit of clothes and a great coat, 1 green hat now fashionable." The most unusual item follows: "To get me a good wife."

Soon John Lyon Gardiner's last intention was realized in the person of Sarah Griswold, twenty-one year old daughter of Deacon John Griswold of Connecticut.

One pleasant day Sarah Griswold and a group of her friends sailed across from Connecticut to see close at hand both the island and the handsome bachelor proprietor they had heard so much about. They were eager to go ashore and visit the manor, the old windmill and the hollow where Kidd's treasure had been buried. They received their wish sooner than they had bargained for.

The party of young ladies, sailing near the island to get a glimpse of its proprietor, was suddenly caught in a bad gale and forced to steer for the island landing, moor their craft and go ashore for shelter. The storm continued through the evening, and the lord of the manor, John Lyon Gardiner, made arrangements for the girls to spend the night. After a fine supper, music and dancing were in order. The next morning the party was able to sail away. But perhaps it was shortly after this visit that John Gardiner wrote in his notebook that he was going to get himself a "good wife."

At any rate, within two weeks the master of Gardiner's Island had visited Connecticut and the home of Miss Sarah; before the summer came to a close they had made plans for a winter wedding. They were married at Black Hall, near Lyme, Connecticut, and soon returned to the island.

During the War of 1812 the Gardiners had several narrow escapes as a result of skirmishes between the British and a group of men under Decatur. Because of its isolation, the island was really neutral territory, but when a party of British officers came ashore, Decatur's men, who had been hiding in a thicket near the manor, captured the officers and took them across the Sound to Connecticut. When British Commodore Thomas Hardy heard of this incident, he went ashore with a company of marines to arrest proprietor John Gardiner for collaboration with the Yankees. Warned of this danger, Mrs. Gardiner forced her husband to go to bed in the so-called green room, where everything took on a greenish tinge. The British demanded to see John Gardiner and were escorted into his bedroom. They admitted that the proprietor did indeed look deathly pale and agreed with his wife that such a sick man could have had no part in the trap by which the British officers were captured.

On Christmas Day, 1812, a French schooner, the *Marie Louise,* was wrecked off the island. It was an intensely cold day, and several of the French crew froze to death before help from the island reached them. The others were hurried to the lower kitchen in the Gardiner manor house and soon recovered.

Mr. Gardiner noticed a beautiful Maltese cat clinging to a fragment of wreckage, and gave the order to have it saved. When it had been brought ashore, he wrapped it in a large silk handkerchief and carried it home. The cat had many descendants through generation after generation of the Gardiner family.

When the bay froze over the Gardiners were often tempted to go across Long Island Sound on the ice. Once, during a severe winter, Mrs. John Gardiner decided to attempt the crossing to a spot known as the Fire Place.[1] Her family wrapped her in cloaks and enclosed her feet in a foot-muff made of red morocco leather, lined and trimmed with rabbit fur. Then with buffalo robes tucked around her, she started out in the sleigh pulled by her servants. Two men went on ahead to test the ice with axes. The long trip was negotiated successfully up to the last minute. But, just as the party was going ashore, the ice broke and a basket of eggs sank into the water. It was rescued later with crab nets.[2]

In 1825 David, John and Sarah Gardiner's oldest son, graduated from Yale and on the death of his father became the eighth proprietor of the island. He died four years later at twenty-four, the last Gardiner to receive the island by entail, for the law of primogeniture, establishing the oldest son's inheritance of all family property, had been abrogated by the state. From this time forth the island would be inherited equally by all children of the owner.

John, Sarah Gardiner's second son, came of age in 1833 and bought out his brother's and sister's shares to become the ninth proprietor. He never married. Sarah Griswold Gardiner, the widow of John Lyon, was, therefore, the lady of the manor for many years. One winter she wrote friends

---

[1] So named because it was there that those who wished to reach Gardiner's Island always lit a fire to attract attention of the family, who would send a boat across to pick them up.

[2] Then there is the story of Miss Lucretia Gardiner of New London, Connecticut, who came for a visit of three weeks to Gardiner's Island and liked it so well that she didn't leave for eighteen years!

that she was shut inside for a fortnight and would "feel very lonely if it were not for letters I receive. I had better remain at home by my airtight stove."

Sarah Gardiner's beloved son John died in June, 1861, and the island fell to Samuel Buell Gardiner, her younger son. On August 12, 1861, when Sarah was eighty years of age, she moved to East Hampton on Long Island. Early in 1863 she died, and her children and grandchildren buried her in the island family hillside cemetery February 10, 1863, by the side of her long-dead husband.

I stood there looking down at their tombs. Here was buried the girl who came for a sail to Gardiner's Island, later fell in love with its proprietor, and returned to rule as the lady of the manor for almost sixty years. Her gay girlhood, her happy married years and her long widowhood gave her a full life. Indeed, Sarah Griswold Gardiner was worthy of the epitaph which I read on her tombstone, *"Precious in the sight of the Lord."*

With the death of Sarah Gardiner in 1863 the island entered a new period of absentee ownership. Samuel, the tenth proprietor, died in 1882, and was succeeded by his son David, a bachelor, whose interests were elsewhere. He sold the island to his brother John Lyon, who became the eleventh master of the island. A colonel in the Civil War, John became an active lawyer in New York. At his death, his son Lion became the twelfth proprietor. In 1920 he leased the island to Clarence Mackay as a game preserve. Later the island was purchased by the son of Samuel Buell Gardiner, Jonathan Thompson Gardiner, the genealogist, who became the thirteenth proprietor. At his death in 1933 he willed Gardiner's Island to Winthrop Gardiner, son of Lion's younger brother, and Winthrop became the fourteenth proprietor of the isle.

Miss Sarah Diodati Gardiner, author of *Early Memories of Gardiner's Island*, whose book proved invaluable in my research, bought the island in 1937 to keep it in the family.

In 1938 she leased the island to Winston Guest, famous polo player, and an airport was completed in 1939, so that Mr. Guest could land there in his two-engined Cessna.

Miss Sarah D. Gardiner is a worthy successor to her namesake, Sarah Griswold Gardiner, the girl who married the seventh proprietor in 1803. Although Sarah D. Gardiner has lived well beyond her allotted Biblical span of years, her spirit is strong in the inherited family traditions. Founder Lion Gardiner has lived again and again in his descendants through the centuries, and it has been said, "some may weary of planting, some may elope with the chaplain, but always one comes to renew the courage, to redeem the harvest."

Where else in America can we find a family which has kept an island in its possession for more than three centuries, an island which no person has been able to call his own unless he bore the name of Gardiner?

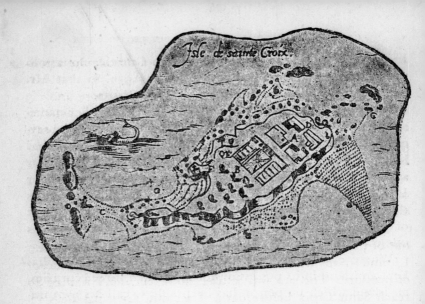

Isle de sainte Croix

X. DOCHET OR SAINT CROIX ISLAND

LOCATED on the Saint Croix River downstream from Calais, Maine, and Saint Stephen, New Brunswick, Dochet Island, or Saint Croix Island, has a history which few other places in the vicinity can equal. Before either the Virginia Colony at Jamestown or the Pilgrim Colony at Plymouth had been established, the first religious services ever held in this part of the country were observed by a group of Huguenots and French Catholics on Saint Croix Island in 1604. The first Christmas service north of Florida was shared by Protestant ministers and Catholic priests on this tiny island. For some time afterwards, the island of Saint Croix was the very center of the French Province of Acadia.

After stopping in Red Beach, Maine, I received directions from the proprietor of the general store on how to get across to Saint Croix. I was told to go down to the point of land where a few small boats were tied up and attract the attention of the lighthouse keeper on the island.

It was almost sundown when I reached the shore and no amount of waving or shouting seemed to arouse any activity on the island. Nearby I saw a decrepit-looking dinghy with two badly mismated oars and about seven inches of water in her. It seemed my only means of getting to Saint Croix, so with payment of a small fee to her owner, I took possession of this dubious vehicle of transportation until noon the next day.

With steady bailing I managed to get most of the water out of the skiff. But when I fitted the oars into the rowlocks, I found, to my dismay, that one gave way under a minimum of pressure. The sun was setting, however, and I wanted to reach Saint Croix before dark. I set out, favoring the starboard rowlock at every stroke.

A friendly seal soon poked his head from under the water, possibly wondering where I was going so late in the day, and followed me from a distance of forty yards. Before I knew it, I had neared the landing pier on Saint Croix and the keeper's home with the lighthouse built up through its roof. Resting on my oars, I gave several rousing "halloos," but there was no response. Just as I was about to row back to Red Beach, a woman came out of the house and waved at me. I rowed in fifty yards closer to shore and asked permission to land.

"Why, yes," the woman shouted. "My husband will be right down."

I rowed on into the lighthouse landing slip, where I met Keeper Everett W. Quinn. Soon we had the skiff pulled up high on the slip and were walking toward the house. I told him that I wanted to explore the island and he invited me to stay the night. I went with him as he illuminated the lighthouse and then we were called downstairs for supper.

After Mrs. Corice Quinn's fine meal, we sat around the oil lamp and exchanged stories of the lighthouse service.

Only the occasional activity of the dog or the cat intruded on our conversation.

Keeper Quinn told me that he had been at many lighthouses where I had dropped Christmas presents. He entered the service in 1930 and began lighthouse duty at one of the loneliest beacons of all, Mount Desert Rock. "When I landed there in May, 1930, George W. York was head keeper and Vinal W. Beal first assistant. Beal retired and I became first assistant, and then in 1936 I became head keeper. I transferred to the Cuckolds, and was head keeper there, but we didn't like it after Mount Desert. We all liked it at Mount Desert Rock even though it is so far away."

"Yes," Mrs. Quinn volunteered, "it seems strange to say it, but I've been a lot more lonesome down at Sabine Point Light in Rhode Island."

Quinn went on to tell me of his experiences at other stations. After two years at the Cuckolds he went to Manana Island Fog Signal Station across from Monhegan. From Manana he transferred to Sabine Point, Rhode Island, and then to Whaleback Ledge Light in Portsmouth Harbor. He and his wife had been at Saint Croix since April, 1949.

Keeper Quinn told me he had heard that Saint Croix was half in Canada and half in the United States and said he believed that the boundary line ran right through the kitchen where we were sitting. However, even though we read in the State Street Trust's excellent pamphlet [1] that the island "forms the boundary line between Maine and New Brunswick," I was later told by the accurate historian, Mr. H. Edgar Lamb of Milltown, Maine, in no uncertain terms that the boundary does *not* go through Saint Croix Island.

Keeper Quinn told me of the big celebration held on the island in July, 1949, when the local owners of different parts of Saint Croix presented their shares to the government for a national park. Most of the distinguished visitors came on a Navy destroyer and were ferried over to the island. Senator

---

[1] *France and New England*, Volume III, page 63.

Brewster of Maine and Consul Albert Chambon of France were among those who spoke at the island on the occasion.

After saying good night to the Quinns I went upstairs and soon fell asleep, dreaming of Champlain and his men who suffered so terribly here at Saint Croix that hard winter back in 1605.

Early the next morning I awakened to the steady patter of rain against the window pane. It was only quarter of six but I got up, dressed and went outside without disturbing the Quinns. There was enough light to take a hike around the island and the rain had settled down to a fine drizzle so I was able to visit all the interesting places on Saint Croix.

It was to this tiny island, less than half a mile in length, that Sieur De Monts and Champlain traveled in the summer of 1604. They had sighted Sable Island in May and a week later reached what is now Liverpool, Nova Scotia. On either June 26 or 27 they reached two islands in the Saint Croix River. The larger island is now known as Saint Croix [1] or Dochet Island and the smaller Little Dochet Isle.

Here is Champlain's description of the trip:

> We found two islands; one very small near the western bank; and the other in mid-river, having a circumference of perhaps eight or nine hundred paces with rocky sides three or four fathoms high all around, except in one small place, where there is a sandy point and earthy clay adapted for making brick and other useful articles. . . . The island is covered with firs, birches, maples, and oaks. It is by nature very well situated, except in one place, where for about forty paces it is lower than elsewhere; this, however, is easily fortified. . . . This place was named by Sieur De Monts the Island of Saint Croix. . . . Here seemed to be a paradise, for the weather was

---

[1] The island is so named because the river forms a cross some distance above Saint Croix Island.

warm, fish and deer were plentiful, and the location was convenient for shipping. . . .

Having found no more suitable place than this island we commenced making a barricade on a little islet a short distance from the island, which served as a station for placing our cannon. The mosquitoes annoyed us excessively in our work. There were several of the men whose faces were so badly swollen that they could hardly see. . . .

For the next few weeks the men worked to build houses and storage sheds on the island. Then they moved ashore to Red Beach, where De Monts built a grain mill on Beaver Brook, on the site of the plaster mill which stood there until a few years ago.[1]

By late fall all the buildings were completed. Unfortunately, the following winter was probably the severest in years. Snow began to fall on October 6, 1604; on December 3 the unhappy men watched great bodies of ice sweep down the river and out to sea; the snow on the island was still three and four feet deep in April. The men were more or less confined to the island by the ice which clogged the Saint Croix River.

All the stores froze solidly during the winter, for the bins had not been set deeply enough into the ground. Spanish wine was the only liquid which did not freeze. Disease seized the camp and only those who remained active escaped death or serious illness. Champlain tells us that those who got the sickness had:

great pieces of superfluous and driveling flesh in their mouths . . . which got the upper hand to such an extent that scarcely anything but liquid could be taken. Their teeth became very loose, and could be pulled out with

---

[1] Probably the first grain in the United States came from a plot of ground at Red Beach sown by De Monts' men in 1604.

*the fingers without it causing them pain. . . . They ex-
perienced pain also in the loins, stomach and bowels,
had a very bad cough and short breath. In a word, they
were in such condition that the majority of them could
not rise nor move and could not even be raised up on
their feet without falling down in a swoon. So that out
of seventy-nine, who composed our party, thirty-five died
and more than twenty were on the point of death.*

Without question, this was scurvy, caused by lack of fresh
fruits and vegetables and an excess of salt in the diet. The
younger men hiked around the island, played games in the
snow and skated on the ponds. They escaped the disease,
but thirty-five victims were buried on the island that winter.[1]

When spring came the survivors were anxious to leave the
island. All during April they hoped that a vessel would come
to rescue them, but none appeared. On May 15 Sieur De
Monts ordered two ships made ready to go in search of help,
but before their departure two French vessels arrived off the
mouth of the Saint Croix.

Sieur De Monts now thought back on the unhappy winter
spent on Saint Croix and decided to search for "a place
better adapted for an abode." On June 17, 1605, the colony
was transferred to Port Royal, Nova Scotia. Two barques
were fitted out with the framework of several of the Saint
Croix houses and the settlement left the island.

Champlain returned there to visit on September 7, 1606,
hoping to find wheat and other crops which he and his men
had planted there. He did find wheat and some garden vegetables which had come up "fair and large." In July of 1607

---

[1] Some years ago the lighthouse keeper noticed that the embankment
where Champlain's men had been buried was caving in. He removed many
of the skeletons to a safer place near the center of the island. When I visited
the island by air with my brother Winthrop in June, 1950, archeologist Wendell S. Hadlock had just uncovered two skeletons and fragments of brick
from the original buildings on the island.

Lescarbot and Poutrincourt went ashore to discover cabbages, sorrel and lettuce. They noticed that the Indians had not touched the wood, salt and other supplies which had been left there.

In 1613 the notorious English privateer, Captain Argall, went ashore and destroyed all buildings which remained on Saint Croix. Not until 1632 do we find further mention of the island. In that year it was granted to Isaac de Razilly.

In 1763 Saint Croix was ceded by France to England, and in 1783 the Treaty of Paris divided Canada and the United States at the Saint Croix River. As late as July 7, 1896 the New Brunswick Legislature listed Dochet's Island as within the bounds of the Parish of Saint Croix in Charlotte County, Canada. In 1899 the Canadians passed a law excluding Dochet's Island from the limits of their country. Since then, officially at least, there has been no claim that half, or any, of what should be called Saint Croix Island is outside of the United States.

An Enoch Arden situation occurred at Saint Croix Island more than a century ago. After living for several years with his wife, Mary, in comparative peacefulness, the island's owner, Mr. Hilliker, suddenly disappeared. As the years went by, everyone assumed that he had probably fallen into the river and that his body had washed out to sea. Mrs. Hilliker now considered a widow, was courted by a neighbor named Dan Post. Finally, Post proposed marriage and since it had been many years since Hilliker's disappearance, Mrs. Hilliker accepted him. They were married and Post became the owner of Saint Croix Island.

One summer day, however, Hilliker reappeared and met the new husband. After a long discussion, it was agreed that the three could get along on the island, and this unusual arrangement lasted for many years. When Hilliker died, he left his property to Mrs. Mary Hilliker, with the admonition in his will that the property should go "at her death to Daniel Post." What the neighbors thought of this comfortable triangle has not been recorded.

Saint Croix Island has had many names through its long career: Bone, Hilliker's, Big, Hunt's, Neutral, Great, Dosia, Doceas, Doucett's and Dochet. The last four are said to be from one source, a girl named Theodosia Millbury who lived nearby in the late eighteenth century and used to row over to the island as often as she had the opportunity.

Historian H. Edgar Lamb tells me that when the commission settled the Saint Croix River boundary they decided that the channel, which ran to the north and west of Saint Croix Island, should be the deciding factor. After it was agreed that the island was United States property, Massachusetts gave a quit-claim deed to Saint Croix to John Brewer of Robbinston for $30. In 1856 Thomas Brewer sold two-thirds and Elizabeth Brewer sold one-third of the six-acre island to the United States Government so that a lighthouse could be built there.

Skirting the shore carefully, I hiked over toward the southern tip of the island where Champlain's cannon and fort had once been located. Not too many years before several cannon-balls had been dug up there, but I could locate nothing except several swallow nests in the bank, a raft in the cove and a gallon jug full of colored liquid with a label which read "Bright Sail."

Finally, I returned to the lighthouse where the Quinns were waiting breakfast for me. After cordial farewells were exchanged and before taking off in my leaky dinghy, I walked over to the memorial plaque on the rock at the north end of the island. It had been placed there in 1904 at the three hundredth anniversary of Champlain's settlement of the island. The inscription read:

1604   1904
TO COMMEMORATE
THE DISCOVERY AND OCCUPATION
OF THIS ISLAND BY
DE MONTS AND CHAMPLAIN
WHO NAMING IT
L'ISLE SAINCTE CROIX
FOUNDED HERE 26 JUNE 1 6 0 4
THE FRENCH COLONY OF ACADIA
THEN THE ONLY SETTLEMENT
OF EUROPEANS NORTH OF FLORIDA
THIS TABLET IS ERECTED BY
RESIDENTS OF THE SAINT CROIX VALLEY
1904

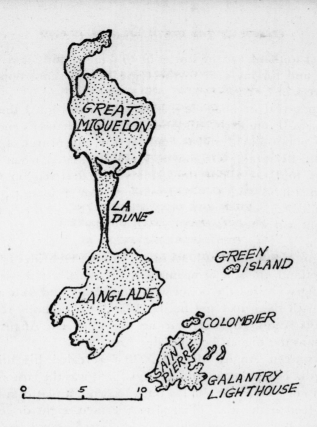

XI. CAPE BRETON AND
SAINT PIERRE

TAKING off on a Trans-Canada Airlines plane from Boston,
I soon arrived at Sydney, Cape Breton Island. From here I
planned to fly to the last remaining possessions of France in
the New World—Saint Pierre and Miquelon, off the coast of
Newfoundland. But the weather soon shut in, and it was
several days before I could leave Cape Breton.

Meanwhile, Jack Stuewe of the airlines did everything he
could to make my stay an agreeable one. I have the bad

weather to thank for the stories he told me about Giant Mac-Askill and for my visit to the Cape Breton shore opposite the wreck of *Le Chameau*.

Giants, real or imaginary, have always intrigued the human race. From early childhood most of us have listened to stories about David and Goliath or the adventures of Jack and the Beanstalk. Of course, I was fascinated when Jack Stuewe told me about the giant who had lived on Cape Breton Island and we soon arranged for a long trip up through Baddeck where the giant had lived and then out to Englishtown where he was buried.

Angus MacAskill was born in 1825 in the Hebrides Islands off Scotland, the son of normal-sized parents. At the age of six, Angus crossed the ocean with his mother and father and went with them to Cape Breton Island. The family settled at Saint Ann's. By the time he was fourteen, Angus was known as the biggest boy in Saint Ann.

At sixteen Angus MacAskill first revealed his mighty strength. Before cutting up a heavy log it was the custom for a group of men to lift the log onto a sawpit, a platform built seven feet in the air. Then after the men, eight or ten in number, had arranged the several-hundred-pound log, two of them began sawing with the whipsaw, one at the top and the other at the bottom. It was a hard task to place the log and an equally hard job to saw it.

One day Angus and his father were sawing away in this manner. It came time for lunch and the father went home, but Angus wasn't hungry and stayed behind. After his father was out of sight, he walked over to the great beam on the sawpit, lifted it onto his shoulder and down to the ground. Then Angus lay under a tree and went to sleep.

An hour later Mr. MacAskill returned, noticed the huge beam lying on the ground and his son asleep nearby, also on the ground. Rushing over to Angus, he berated the boy for getting so many neighbors to help him take down the log.

Angus defended himself, but the father, of course, did not believe his story. Harsh words were passed between them. Then Angus stood up. Already over seven feet tall, he walked over to the massive log and easily lifted it seven feet in the air to put it back on the platform.

Mr. MacAskill was both amazed and ashamed. He apologized for the words which had been spoken. But Angus was equal to the occasion.

"Father," he began, "we have had a quarrel and have both spoken harsh words for which I am sorry. As it was our first quarrel, let it be our last as well. But in a way I'm glad that it was you, for if it had been anyone else, I'd have relieved him of his head with one clip of my hand." The two shook hands in silence, and it is said that they never had an argument again.

Shortly afterwards Angus went to sea as a cabin-boy. When the voyage ended, he returned to North Sydney with the other sailors. As was often the local custom in the summertime, Angus went ashore barefooted and accompanied the others to a dance that night. In the hall was a dandified young man-about-town who decided to have some sport with Angus. Whenever the two met, the young dandy would step on Angus' bare toe. Time and again he would dance over to Angus and deliberately stamp on the giant's foot. The others at the dance thought this was funny, and finally Angus felt that he had stood enough of their laughter. When the dandy next lunged for his toe, Angus pushed the young man into a row of chairs, smashing several of his bones and the chairs as well.

One day a pugilist arrived at North Sydney and, hearing of Angus, decided that he could successfully match his skill against the giant's strength. Angus, not wanting to injure the fighter, refused to meet him. Time and again the pugilist challenged the giant, but on each occasion he was refused. Finally, the stranger charged Angus with cowardice. Now the giant stood up, extended his hand and suggested that they at least part as friends. The fighter, somewhat abashed, put his hand into Angus' mighty grip. Angus gave a slight squeeze and blood oozed from the tips of the fighter's fingers! That closed the incident.

On another occasion a powerfully built American sea captain visited Cape Breton, and when he heard of the mighty MacAskill, determined to challenge the giant to a wrestling match. The captain was nearly seven feet tall and weighed over three hundred pounds, and he had never been beaten at wrestling. But again MacAskill did not want to hurt an opponent and refused to wrestle. The captain then became incensed and rushed at Angus MacAskill.

The giant grabbed the huge captain as though he were a baby and tossed him over a large woodpile standing close at hand. The woodpile was fully ten feet in height and twelve feet in width, but the amazed captain went whistling over it as though he were a projectile fired from a gun.

The captain now determined to take some sort of revenge against the giant. He ordered his crew to gather ballast stones from MacAskill's farm. Angus learned what had happened and asked the captain to return the ballast. The captain retorted that MacAskill could take the stones back himself. The giant promptly picked up a boulder weighting some two hundred pounds and sent it crashing against the deck of the American vessel.

Now the captain readily agreed to have his crew return every last stone. When the final boulder was restored to its original position, the belligerent American hoisted anchor and left the island, completely baffled by Angus MacAskill.

On another occasion MacAskill was invited to a barn raising. Strong drinks were served as the men worked, but because of MacAskill's tremendous capacity no refreshments were offered to him. Before long, Angus noticed that he was being deliberately by-passed. Finally, after seventy men had succeeded in raising the frame of the barn, the dinner bell rang. MacAskill let the others go in to dinner but he was in no mood for food himself. While the others were busy eating, he walked over to the frame, climbed up and lowered down to the ground a beam fifty feet long and eight inches thick. Then, shouldering it, he walked four hundred yards to the ocean and dumped it into the water. It had been one of the side plaits of the building. Angus MacAskill then hiked home, satisfied with his revenge.

On one occasion MacAskill's neighbors thought that they would have sport with him and asked for his assistance in hauling a heavy fishing craft up above the reach of the tide. After he had joined them and begun pulling, they then tugged the boat in the other direction. MacAskill decided that if they wanted a joke he'd give them one. He pulled with his full strength and the boat parted with a ripping sound, leaving Angus in possession of the bow and the others holding the stern. After this, the fishermen of Saint Ann's avoided any further jokes with Angus MacAskill.

In 1849, when MacAskill was twenty-four years of age, his fame had spread so far that a Mr. Dunseath traveled to Saint Ann's, met the young giant and made arrangements for him to be exhibited around Canada, the United States, the West Indies, Great Britain and Europe. Angus had then attained his full height of seven feet nine inches and weighed four hundred and eighty pounds. Although many of the giants known to history were badly proportioned and physically quite weak, Angus MacAskill was as perfectly proportioned as a Greek statue.

Dunseath and MacAskill first stopped at Quebec, in July of 1849, and the giant was an immediate success. For the next few years he traveled far and wide and people who came to see him as a curiosity stayed to admire him as a fine physical specimen. Later, arrangements were made for MacAskill to go on a tour with the midget, Tom Thumb, who, only twenty-five inches tall, was one of the smallest men ever to live. Tom Thumb's tiny body was also well proportioned and, of course, was even more astonishing in contrast with that of the Cape Breton giant.

The two put on an act together. MacAskill would reach down from his towering height with the little finger of his right hand and allow Tom Thumb to grasp the finger with both his tiny hands, swinging on it as one might from a trapeze. Then MacAskill would lift the midget up with his little finger and place him on the palm of his hand, which was fourteen inches long and eight inches wide. There was plenty of room for Tom Thumb to begin his important part of the program. At a signal from the giant, the midget would nod to the musicians in the background to strike up a lively jig and then he would give his interpretation of the Highland Fling on the palm of MacAskill's hand. When the dance was finished MacAskill opened the massive pocket on the right side of his coat and moved his left hand to within a foot of the pocket. Tom Thumb, to the accompaniment of a rolling drum, stood poised at the edge of the giant's palm. Then, with a skillful leap, the midget sprang into the open pocket of Angus MacAskill.

Tom Thumb often challenged the giant to fight but MacAskill always declined with a show of fear. He usually pretended that he was no match for his friend the midget.

It was an exciting existence for the next few years, traveling back and forth across the American continent and down to the West Indies. Later, the giant was called across the ocean to London to appear before Queen Victoria. But finally Angus MacAskill grew tired of being exhibited as a freak. He left the carnivals and became a longshoreman, working on the piers of Boston, New York and Halifax from time to time.

On one occasion, during the lunch hour, while a French vessel was being unloaded at Halifax, the French sailors decided to tease the giant. Walking up to him as he was sitting on the edge of the pier eating his lunch, they told him of a mighty French strong man whose feats of physical prowess were greater than his. "You not so strong," one sailor taunted. "Our French strong man, he lift thousands of pounds. He even lift two thousand pounds."

MacAskill paid no attention until he had downed the last fragment of his lunch. Then he stood up and glanced down at the little group of Frenchmen extolling the abilities of their countryman. Just then their spokesman reached the climax of his description: "Why, our strong man of France can even lift that anchor!" The sailor pointed across the pier to a massive 2100-pound anchor lying on the wharf. MacAskill shrugged his shoulders and walked slowly toward the anchor. Word traveled quickly that something sensational was about to happen and before MacAskill reached the anchor one hundred men were hurrying toward the spot. They quickly formed a circle around the giant. MacAskill took off the jacket he was wearing and placed it on the pier. Then he leaned down over the anchor and read the weight mark. Resting one of the huge flukes over his shoulder, he straightened up and began to walk with the massive anchor on his shoulder. Up and down the pier he went, until he decided to use the anchor as a true Scotsman would and threw it from him as through he were tossing the caber.[1] After telling the men to get back, he balanced the weight against his chest with both hands and threw the 2100-pound anchor away from him. But he forgot to take into consideration the length and curve of the anchor flukes. As the anchor shot out, one of the flukes caught in his shoulder and MacAskill and the great weight came down on the pier together. He was quickly taken to a hospital where he slowly recovered his strength. But never again was he able to straighten his body.

After his recovery, he went back to Cape Breton and spent the remainder of his life there. Having been prudent and thrifty, MacAskill was comparatively wealthy. He opened a store on the island and there he sat by the hour

---

[1] A favorite Scotch athletic event, in which a miniature telegraph pole is thrown for distance.

on his favorite stool, a 180-gallon molasses puncheon. His many friends came to the store to visit him. Once in a great while he would attempt to stand in their presence, but his back had been so severely injured that it took almost ten minutes for him to rise and even then he was unable to stand fully erect. His injury never affected his strength, however, and he continued to amaze his friends by lifting puncheons of molasses over his head.

Angus MacAskill's death came in August, 1863, and was caused by brain fever. His coffin was the largest ever made, of sufficient size to float three men across Saint Ann's Bay! After a funeral which attracted people from all over Cape Breton and Nova Scotia, Angus MacAskill, the Cape Breton giant and strongest man in the world, was buried in the hillside cemetery at Saint Ann's which overlooks the bay.

Jack Stuewe and I fought our way through a blizzard to visit MacAskill's home where his clothes are still preserved and many of his keepsakes are on exhibition.

Next, I decided that I'd have to see his grave and take a picture of it. The blizzard grew worse but still we drove on. Finally, after several misdirections from helpful natives, we reached the cemetery. Of course, every gravestone was covered with thick wet snow, and it was another hour before I found the one for which I searched. The simple inscription reads:

ERECTED TO THE MEMORY OF

ANGUS MacASKILL

THE NOVA SCOTIAN GIANT

WHO DIED AUGUST 8TH, 1863

AGED 38 YEARS

A DUTIFUL SON, A KIND BROTHER

JUST IN ALL HIS DEALINGS

UNIVERSALLY RESPECTED BY FRIENDS AND ACQUAINTANCES

MARK THE PERFECT MAN AND BEHOLD THE UPRIGHT

THE END OF THAT MAN IS PEACE

When the weather continued bad the next day I knew that we still couldn't fly to Saint Pierre. I then decided to visit the Cape Breton shore north of Louisburg, opposite the rock where a great shipwreck occurred in the year 1725.

A terrible southeast gale began in August of that year and reached its height on the night of the 25th, forcing the coastal inhabitants inland. At ten o'clock the following morning, when they dared to return, they found the shore littered with debris from what had been a dreadful disaster at sea, the wreck of the famous French vessel *Le Chameau*. Several identifying fragments of the ship were found and reported. Soon all officials along the coast converged on the area, for there were many important passengers aboard *Le Chameau*.

Evidently the disaster had taken place without warning for most of the bodies which washed ashore were dressed in night clothes. Among the 310 passengers and crew, all of whom drowned, were Monsieur de Chazel, the new Intendant of Canada, Monsieur de Louvigny, the new Governor of Trois Rivieres, and the son of de Ramesay, late Governor of Montreal.

DeMezy, Commissaire Ordonnateur at Louisburg, declared that the gale had been the worst in the thirty-five years he had been on or near the sea. In the language of the day, the storm was so violent and intense that "not even a pig came ashore alive." DeMezy learned that all along the coast from Grand Lorambec to Baleine the shores were strewn with wreckage. In its midst he found a beautiful figurehead which he easily recognized as having come from *Le Chameau*.

I went down on the ledges opposite Chameau Rock, where the ill-fated vessel had smashed to pieces, and speculated as to the treasure which went down with the ship. I was not fooled by much that I had heard. Many claimed that the *Chameau* held millions of dollars in gold when she disappeared beneath the waves but I had learned the real amount of the treasure from the French Archives. I reveal it here for the first time in print: The gold and silver in the strong-boxes aboard *Le Chameau* amounted to 289,696 livres.[1]

When I went with Jack Stuewe to visit the home of Captain John S. Arsenault at Big Harbor, Captain Arsenault presented me with an ancient cannon-ball, which some say was brought up from the wreck of *Le Chameau*. Many divers have spent considerable time at the scene of the wreck, but little of any value has ever been brought to the surface.

Finally, the fog lifted long enough so that we could take off for Saint Pierre, Langlade and Miquelon. When the local paper, the Sydney *Port-Record,* learned that I was going to wear my Flying Santa Claus suit, they decided to cover the event for their readers. They knew what I didn't—that never before in history had a Santa of any sort visited those three lonely isles.

Five of us made the long over-water jump to France's only remaining American possession. There were two pilots which the Maritime Central Airways placed at our disposal, Captain H. S. Jones and Captain Ray Meraghan; Ian MacNeil, staff writer for the *Port-Record;* John Walker, the newspaper's photographer; and, of course, myself.

We soon ran into boisterous winds after our take-off from Sydney, but a glance at the seas raging below us made us very happy to be traveling by air. As we flew past the outer islands with their tiny, lonely lighthouses, we watched the waves sending spray far up the rocky shores.

Finally, Saint Pierre appeared out of the clouds ahead and we circled out over the two other islands before landing. Then, down below us, we saw a single runway and a small collection of people. We landed and taxied across to the outdoor customs office.

Children soon flocked around the plane. I was already wearing my Santa suit and, one by one, the French children

---

[1] A livre is worth from nineteen to fifty cents, depending on the period in which it was minted.

quietly came up for their gifts. It was a strange experience, for the children were so solemn. Soon all my presents were given away except one giant box of five-cent candy bars. I emptied the box into the crowd of youngsters and there was a great deal of squealing and shouting. Well, I thought to myself, I have finally broken the ice! It was only then that I discovered what the others in the plane already knew—there had never been a Santa Claus at Saint Pierre before and the children didn't know what to make of him. With my matter-of-fact toss of the candy, they saw that Santa Claus was just human after all. From then on, Santa and his new converts talked in the best Saint Pierrais French on subjects of mutual interest.

Finally, the last child had gone home with his presents and I was able to change from my Santa suit to my regular clothes. The customs officers were very lenient with me, for I had neither passport nor birth certificate to identify me in a foreign country. After a nominal examination I told them, "Je n'ai rien à déclarer, messieurs," and they allowed me to enter the waiting taxi which was to whisk us around the island.

Soon we arrived at the residence of Monsieur Gui Clech, acting Governor of Saint Pierre and Miquelon. He invited in several of the island's officials and we all sat in his beauti-fully furnished living room, discussing Saint Pierre's past, present and future. After a long talk we decided to visit the important sights of the island. I left several Christmas packages for the lighthouse keepers at Saint Pierre, and we began an auto tour of the island.

The officials were quite anxious that we visit what they referred to as the cabaret. They repeated their invitation several times and we began to wonder whether there was a Saint Pierre rival to the Folies Bergère. Finally, we con-sented to be taken down the hill to the Cabaret Joinville, but any frivolous ideas we might have had were unhappily de-stroyed when we entered the building. The "cabaret" was merely a ballroom where the atmosphere of ancient France still lingered. In the center of the hall at the right was a little raised platform where the mothers of Saint Pierre could watch their daughters as they danced to the tune of a radio from Newfoundland. It was said that very little escaped the hawklike glances of the mothers of Saint Pierre. Somewhat abashed, we went back to the acting Governor's residence.

The island of Saint Pierre is about five miles long, running northeast to southwest. Immediately to the north of Henry Point, the extreme northern tip, is the island of Great Columbier, which rises to a height of 492 feet. Other islands include Massacre, Vainqueur, Pigeon and Chasseurs. The ledges and rocks which abound in the same vicinity are appropriately named as follows: Cat Rock, Enfant Perdu, Les Canailles, Les Grappinots, Marne Shoal, Bonniere Shoal, Hache Rock and Les Cailloux de Terre.

Langlade, or Little Miquelon, lies across a three-mile water passage known as La Baie. Its highest point is 656 feet above the sea, and on the northeastern side stands Cape Percé where there is a natural arch well worth seeing. From Plate Point Lighthouse on the southwestern tip to Cape Percé it is about eight miles.

In the early days it was possible to sail between Langlade and its northern neighbor, Great Miquelon, but for over a century a sand bar has connected the two islands. On that bar score upon score of ships have been wrecked and there are many interesting stories associated with it. But those who can tell the stories speak almost pure Basque which English-speaking adventurers soon discover is very difficult to comprehend.

Try as I could, there were only two of these tales which I was able to write down. The first was about a peculiar ghost, dressed in black and evidently quite similar to Boston Harbor's Fort Warren lady, which roams the beach in an effort to protect her dead husband, drowned in the loss of his full-rigged ship in 1835. They say that she appeared to him at sea and was responsible when he later sailed onto the sand in heavy fog, but there isn't enough of the story available to understand it properly.

The other story is more tragic and undoubtedly true. One of the children aboard a wrecked ship was bitten by a starving, maddened dog after the vessel had crashed at Plate Point on Miquelon. The boy died in horrible convulsions before a doctor from Saint Pierre could cross over and help him.

The bar between the two islands is four miles long. It ends to the north at Great Barachois, or The Lake on Miquelon. From the lake, traveling clockwise around Miquelon, we pass Cheval Point, Carcas Cove, another lake, Bourg de Miquelon, Cape Blanc with its lighthouse, Mount Calvary, The Ladder, Le Bec, La Cormorandiere and the Eagle's Nest at the extreme northern tip. Then we go southward by Cape Miquelon, Otter Point, Virgin Bay, Miquelon Road, Chapeau de Miquelon, Soldier Point, Alouette Point and we are back at Great Barachois, having entirely circumnavigated the island. From the Eagle's Nest to the lake it is about eight miles. The longest distance at the islands is from the Eagle's Nest to Blanche Point at Saint Pierre, twenty-six miles. The three islands have a total area of ninety-three square miles.

The weather is severe during the winter and the Saint Pierrais are often forced to tunnel through great drifts which form in their main streets. It is hard to realize that Saint Pierre, so far to our north, is actually one hundred miles south of Paris. However, the average annual temperature is only ten degrees above freezing. Lilacs usually bloom just after the Fourth of July and the short summer is fairly hot.

Saint Pierre now has town water, an ample reservoir up in the hills, electricity and street lights. This is not the case at Miquelon.

Wood is so scarce at Saint Pierre that many of the children are sent into the hills with their dog carts to bring back branches of the dwarf spruce which grows there.

The population can be divided into three parts: merchants, government officials and fishermen. The fishermen are poor but the merchants and government officials manage to live fairly comfortably.

In 1940, after the collapse of France, thirty trawlers and sailing vessels carrying 1500 sailors, sought refuge from Germany here. For the next few weeks Saint Pierre was bustling with activity as the catch from all these fishing craft were split and dried in the sun.

The money and stamps of Saint Pierre are old-country, but there is a hopeless confusion of Newfoundland, Canadian and United States currency in every storekeeper's till. In spite of other influences, however, it appears that Saint Pierre will always remain loyal to France.

I interviewed the Bishop, Doctor Raymond Martin, Prefect Apostolique de Saint Pierre et Miquelon, who was keeping his flock together in spite of almost overwhelming financial odds. I had a long talk with him about the future of Saint Pierre. "France is keeping us here as part of the old France, for we are just about the only parcel of the Empire left," he said.

No one knows who discovered Saint Pierre, but when Jacques Cartier stopped there in 1536 it had already been named. Undoubtedly it is named after Saint Pierre, or Saint Peter, the protector of fishermen. The early Portuguese navigators called Miquelon "Miguel Island" and Miquelon is a Norman form of Miguel. Voltaire in his *Louis XIV* calls them the Miquelon Isles.

It is said that most of the islanders descend from the Basque, Norman and Breton companions of Champlain who were active in the early days of Canadian colonization. When the Acadians were driven from Grand Pré, many of them sailed to Saint Pierre, where they established residence.

In 1713 the islands were granted to England, along with Newfoundland, but following Wolfe's victory of 1759 at Quebec, they were returned to France as a final outpost in America. After further changes back and forth, the islands were ceded to France in 1815.

In 1884 Saint Pierre was one of the great, and some say the greatest, fishing ports in the world. The commerce in salt and fish alone was over thirty-eight million francs a year and each spring passenger vessels left the French ports of Dieppe, Saint Brieuc and Saint Malo bound for the tiny Miquelon Islands. Breton and Norman crews outfitted fishing craft and sailed for the banks; after their holds were filled to bulging, they sailed back to Saint Pierre, emptied their craft and sailed out again. Meanwhile, their wives and children carried the cod out to the gravel flakes and dried the fish in the sun.

As they do at Newfoundland, many of the fishing vessels carry dogs aboard. They serve three purposes: to go after cod which fall overboard, to warn of coming fog banks and to make rescues at sea.

Going down to the beach where the fishermen land their daily catch, we passed three cannon which constitute the last fortification France has in America. There were formerly four cannon but an enthusiastic celebrator one July 14 blew one up, as well as himself. We may safely say that he is the only casualty suffered by the defenders of this historic fort.

The residents of Saint Pierre still have a seasonal occupation in capturing the tiny caplin which throw themselves ashore every year. In June and July the fish come ashore, are picked up in buckets and carried to long tables on the wharves to be dressed. They are later exported to France where, salted and dried, they bring a substantial price.

In the old days there were many oxen drawing their burdens of fish around the islands, but now the number is small. Dogcarts are often seen, however, drawing wood for the winter season.

For every quintal, or 112 pounds, of fish, the French Government used to grant a bounty of nine francs, or about one-third the value of the catch. There were then about six thousand year-round residents of Saint Pierre and the Miquelons, as compared with 4700 today, and from May to October ten thousand other French fishermen visited the islands. The happy merchants thrived during the season and on their profits they were able to send their children to France for education and culture.

But Newfoundland ruined Saint Pierre almost overnight when its government passed the so-called Bait Bill. The men of Saint Pierre had always sailed into Newfoundland for their bait and the men of Newfoundland had always resented the fact that the French Government helped the Saint Pierrais with a bonus. The Bait Bill, when finally passed, made it illegal for Newfoundland sailors, merchants or fishermen to sell bait to Frenchmen from Miquelon or Saint Pierre.

When the backers of the French fishing enterprises learned that Newfoundland would not sell them bait, they hesitated to hire and pay transportation for sailors from France. Before many years, new methods of fishing prevailed, with vessels outfitting in Brittany, getting periwinkle bait on the Banks and shipping their catch in brine direct to France in large transports. Now the fishermen from France only call at Saint Pierre when they need repairs or provisions.

I talked with an old fisherman who told me about squid fishing. In spite of the revulsion we all naturally feel for the giant octopus, the tiny octopus, or squid, is highly valued as bait for cod and there are many who enjoy it as a table delicacy. The fisherman told me that squid are caught at Saint Pierre with jigs. They are prepared for eating by removing the head and viscera and peeling the grayish-brown skin from the pouch. After this is done the pouch is washed carefully and filled with a mixture of sausage meat, onions, garlic and bread crumbs. Put on ice, the stuffed squid are brought out early the next morning, browned in butter and set to stew in wine sauce. They are declared "rich but good." However, our meals at Saint Pierre did not include this gourmet's delight, so we never knew what we had missed.

Prices are very reasonable at Saint Pierre, especially for

perfumes, watches and rare liquors. The only place in North America where one may buy the best rum at the equivalent of four cents a glass is at Saint Pierre. Champagne sells for eighty-five cents a quart. Cognac and other liqueurs cost only slightly more than a dollar. Here, also, you may purchase fine Swiss watches for $15 which retail in the States for $125. Lovely French lace is as low as eighteen cents a yard, and I bought a flask of exquisite "Christmas Bells" French perfume for one-ninth of what it costs in Boston.

Perhaps the greatest period of prosperity in all Saint Pierre and Miquelon history was during the period of prohibition in the United States. The islanders made fortunes overnight (and most spent them as quickly) by shipping liquor into this country. In 1935 the French Government entered into an agreement with Canada and the United States to stop the smuggling and prosperity in the islands ended abruptly.

Most of the present buildings on Saint Pierre are a bit shabby-looking on the outside but they are seemingly palaces inside. In the lower part of town the buildings are frame, some with a stucco finish, painted red or yellow. Beyond the immediate downtown area, the houses tend to be the clapboard type.

In one period of fifteen years during the last century there were three bad fires, and four blocks in the heart of Saint Pierre were destroyed in 1939. Since that time every house must have a ladder built onto the roof.

With the collapse of France during World War II there were tense moments on the island. For a time it was feared that Saint Pierre would go the way of France. Parisian Baron Gilbert de Bournat, the administrator of the island, was faithful to Vichy and Marshal Petain but finally the Free French movement arranged for "four steatopygous corvettes," according to *Time* Magazine for January 5, 1942, and Vice-Admiral Emile Henri Muselier of the Free French Naval forces landed at Saint Pierre's wharf on December 24, 1941. He quickly captured the amenable force of eleven gendarmes guarding the island.

By this time, a hundred and fifty young Saint Pierrais had already joined the Canadian forces. Most of the islanders favored De Gaulle, but Muselier decided that it was best to hold a plebiscite. The results showed that 783 Saint Pierrais supported De Gaulle, fourteen were for Petain and 215 were voided ballots. When the election results were announced, a band played *La Marseillaise* and there were few dry eyes in the assemblage on the pier. Not a shot had been fired in this particular change of government, though Muselier was ready if the Petainists tried to overrule the people of Saint Pierre.

Throughout our visit we noticed a strong undercurrent of homesickness for Mother France. The people never mention how near they are to the larger island of Newfoundland, but rather how far they are from France itself.

Perhaps nowhere in North America is the atmosphere of a foreign country so in evidence as at Saint Pierre. From the moment we landed in the plane and French gendarmes received us, we could sense the difference. The gendarmes might as easily have stood on the Champs Elysées as on a wind-swept airport at Saint Pierre, North America.

I fell in love with one of the island children and when I left Saint Pierre's town for the airport, this little ten-year-old daughter of France was sitting in my lap, joyously singing *La Marseillaise*. She whispered a secret before I flew away but cautioned me not to tell her younger sister; at her advanced age she was able to recognize me as the Santa Claus of the airplane. She wouldn't say anything, of course, because of the effect it might have on her seven-year-old sister.

Late that same afternoon we landed at Sydney, Cape Breton Island, where a plane of the Trans-Canada Air Lines was waiting to take me to Boston. That same night, as I landed at Boston Airport, I became aware of my pleasant but strange experience of having been in France, Canada and the United States all in one five-hour period.

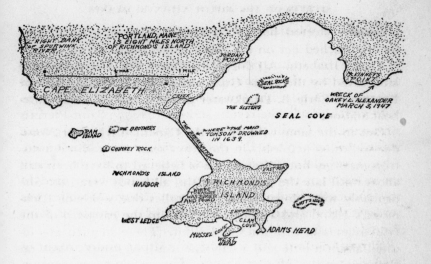

XII. RICHMOND'S ISLAND

RICHMOND'S ISLAND, Maine, is connected by a sandy breakwater to the mainland at Cape Elizabeth. When seen from the air it looks like a feathered turkey scratching in the dirt.

In the old days Richmond Island Harbor was a favorite haven for coasting schooners when an easterly blow hit Cape Elizabeth, and around 1900 the government reinforced the sandy bar with granite blocks.

Off to sea, two miles to the eastward, is Old Anthony, or Vapor Rock, and another mile to the northeast is treacherous Alden's Rock, where the ill-fated steamer *Bohemian* crashed on February 22, 1864, with the loss of thirty-two persons.

A more recent disaster off Richmond's Island was that of the *Oakey L. Alexander,* which snapped in two at the height of the March gale in 1947, said to have been the worst blow on that part of the coast for eighty years. Only by a miracle did Captain Raymond Lewis bring the bowless coal collier to land. He steered her in close to Richmond's Island and finally beached her on the rocky ledges of McKenny's Point at Cape Elizabeth. All thirty-two aboard the *Alexander* were later saved by the Coast Guard in charge of Chief Warrant Boatswain Earle B. Drinkwater of the Cape Elizabeth Lifeboat Station.

Out in the same wild storm the Canadian freighter *Novadoc* wallowed helplessly in the heavy seas. She radioed a distress message, but although she is believed to have been still afloat until late the following night, all hands were lost. She probably went down some three miles due south of Richmond's Island and a similar distance to the eastward of the twin islands of Stratton[1] and Bluff. These in turn are located about a mile and a half due south of Prout's Neck on the mainland.

I journeyed out to Cape Elizabeth with John Light, the seventeen-year-old lad from Newton with whom I had hiked over a hundred miles in 1949. Although it was late spring, the bitter west wind was lashing the beaches as though it were midwinter. We started to cross the natural breakwater toward Richmond's Island, going at first along the western side, where the hard-packed sand made walking easy. But soon we reached the middle of the bar and the angry waves pushed us up onto the huge disordered granite rocks. It was difficult going and our progress was further slowed by the seaweed and barnacles which covered all but the highest boulders.

The breakwater, according to the map, is a trifle more than eight hundred yards long. Before we reached the end of it we were exhausted. I was reminded of a similar granite breakwater which runs from Star Island to Cedar Island in the Isles of Shoals, but this one seemed over three times as long.

---

[1] Named for John Stratton, who lived there before 1631.

Finally, I could see a white sandy beach on the eastern side of the breakwater, and we climbed down to resume our walk under more pleasant circumstances. Soon we were finding large sand dollars by the dozen and put as many as we could into our pockets. Most of them, of course, promptly broke into pieces. Razor clams and quahaugs were also on the bar, and I retrieved a giant quahaug to take back for supper that night.

When we reached the island we headed for the spot where in 1855 a treasure had been found. There we sat down and reviewed the history of this once important island.

Richmond's Island was "the island" in the early years of New England activity. On one of his voyages Champlain visited the island and later he described how the Indians welcomed him with joy. He tells of Sieur De Monts' visit to Richmond's Island, "which is very beautiful in view of what it produces; for it has fine oaks and nut trees, the soil cleared up, and many vineyards bearing beautiful grapes in their season, which were the first we had seen on all these coasts from the Cap de la Heve." He named it Isle de Bacchus.

Champlain pronounced the ripe grapes just as fine as those of his own France and felt sure that they would make excellent wine. But when Samuel Adams Drake visited the island almost three centuries later the location was noted, instead, for its famous cabbages.

Early events at Richmond's Island did much to make the native Indians vindictive and revengeful. Some time around the year 1620, George Richmond of Bandonbridge, Ireland, established himself at the mouth of the Spurwink River on the island which still bears his name. He built a strong trading post and constructed a sloop which he sailed along the coast and up the many rivers in the vicinity. Richmond later fell into the hands of the notorious scoundrel Walter Bagnall, a "dark-visaged man, of scant principle," and that is where the trouble began.

Walter Bagnall had come to America in 1624, probably one of Weston's group of four adventurers mentioned by an early writer as controlling a mysterious house in the vicinity of Cape Elizabeth. Establishing himself at Richmond's Island, he soon showed himself exceedingly ingenious and ruthless in cheating the Indians.

Redmen have been cheated by the white men ever since the first European landed in America, but Bagnall's outrageous conduct was too extreme for the Indians to tolerate long. Bagnall was probably a little better than a land pirate and must have had dealings with pirates of the sea, amassing a sizable amount of gold and silver.

Bagnall, or Great Watt, as the Indians called him, time after time sold the Indians rum to get them drunk and then paid them what he pleased in the trading which followed. When the Indians came to their senses and discovered what Bagnall had done, they decided that revenge was the only way to settle the affair. The leader of the Indians in the region, Sachem Squidrayset, told them to be patient and the time would soon come when revenge could be theirs.

The only white man on the island, aside from Bagnall and his servant, was the notorious Morton of Merrymount fame, whose dances around the Maypole with fur-clad Indian girls are well known. When Morton sailed for England, Squidrayset announced that the time was at hand for revenge against Bagnall and ordered his subjects to take their canoes and paddle out to Richmond's Island at dusk, October 3, 1631.

Bagnall had looked across toward the mainland earlier that day and had seen the signal fires. He realized that he had probably carried out his last crooked transaction and took his crock of gold and silver to the hillside on the northwestern side of the island, where his trading shed stood about eighty feet from the embankment. He dug a hole two feet deep, put the crock of coins in the cavity and covered it over, stamping the fresh earth into place.

By this time he could see the canoes approaching in the gathering dusk. He went down to meet the Indians on the shore. We shall never know what happened then but probably he tried to bargain for his life. Squidrayset decided, however, that death was the only appropriate revenge and the Indians killed Bagnall and his servant, John. Later they burned the trading post to the ground and left the island.

A short time afterwards an Indian who had often visited Richmond's Island in the past went ashore there again. He was Poquanum, the Sachem of Nahant, who had sold Nahant in 1630 to Thomas Dexter for a suit of clothes. He was in legal difficulties because a Swampscott farmer claimed that Poquanum or Black Will, as he was often called, had also sold Nahant to him. Under the circumstances, Poquanum decided to leave the vicinity. He went to Richmond's Island and stayed there for several months.

The Puritans in Boston had heard that Poquanum was at Richmond's Island and that Bagnall had been killed there. John Winthrop, although he knew that Bagnall had been murdered, thought it best "to sit still a while." But in August, 1632, Puritan soldiers arrived at Richmond's Island and found Poquanum. They knew that Squidrayset and his men had killed Bagnall ten months before, but Poquanum was an Indian, too, and, after all, what was the difference between two Indians? Sachem Poquanum was strung up and hanged for a murder which another redman had committed!

Bagnall had occupied the island without title, and so some years later the council at Plymouth, England, granted Richmond's Island and the entire southern section of Cape Elizabeth to Robert Trelawny and Moses Goodyeare, merchants of Plymouth. This patent was sent over to John Winter, agent, to establish a trading post on the island.

Winter soon showed that he was a good trader and a crafty dealer with the Indians. Before long his post at Richmond's Island was the trading center for a hundred miles around.

He built a vessel of thirty tons within a few months, naming it the bark *Richmond*.

Large cargoes of lumber, furs, oils and fish were shipped across to Europe and Winter received in return supplies of wine, liquors, guns, ammunition and trinkets attractive to the Indians. Soon three other ships were necessary in his trading, the *Agnes, Hercules,* and *Margery* and by 1635 another ship of eighty tons and a pinnace of ten tons had arrived at the island.

Three years later Winter had no less than sixty men working in the fishing trade on the island. That same year Trelawny sent a ship of three hundred tons to Richmond's Island with a great cargo of spirits and wine. In the twelve-year period between 1633 and 1645 Richmond's Island became one of the greatest trading centers along the Atlantic coast.

On July 11, 1633, as Winter mentions in a letter to Robert Trelawny, he had loaded 49,000 dried codfish into the hold of the ship *Welcome*. The ship later reached Charlestown, Massachusetts, on another voyage with eighty horses aboard. But the *Welcome* became bewitched, according to no less an authority than John Winthrop. This was shown by the rolling of the ship in calm weather as it was anchored off Charlestown. This strange behavior was attributed to the fact that the husband of a woman recently executed for witchcraft was aboard the ship. Someone suggested that if he were arrested the *Welcome* would stop rolling. When an officer with an arrest warrant boarded the vessel, "she began to stop and after he, the witch's husband, was put in prison, moved no more!"

On August 26, 1635, a certain Naryas Hawkins took inventory at Richmond's Island and a few of the items may give the reader some idea of the magnitude of the trading center:

7 hogsheads & one 3 partts full of Malt

13 barrels and one 3 quarters full of pease of 5 buz; to the barre

2 Bar: of Oatemeale. 4 hogs Meale, 1 hogs flower.

3 Newe Roades 1 hogs pickell Porke

A Maine sayle that belonged to the *James*

3 hogs vinager, one lacking 12 inches.

1 hogs Aquauite. I Crowe of *Iron*

84 lb. of Hoppes. 9 shallopes Oares.

3 paire boats hallyers, the Coasting Boats Maine staye.

4 hogs Indian Corne. 3 *Iron* wedges

6 hogs 1 Butt of Breade. 2 howes

3 higher and 3 Lower plmpe boxes, 3 Irons for the same & a pompe bolt.

2 steel Milles. 1 Iron picke for salt.

17 Saker shott, 2 Chambers and a fidd for a Murderer

415 lb. nett of speekes

2 Hogs pickell pilchards. I puncheon barke.

2 Barrells powder, one of 107 lb. the other 116 in.

1 Saker ladle, 1 Spunge, 1 Worme, 2 peecs *Ordnance* with their carridge.

2 suttes frize, 6 sutes Canuas drawers, 2 ydds spilting cloth 1 trading coate, 16 couerletts, 21 white hatts, 67 paire Irish stockings, 20 trading Shirtts att ½ lb. Beauer per piece, 12 strong shirts att 6s per peace, 6 fine callicoe shirtts, at 1 lb. Beauer per piece or ¾, 9 Munmouth Capps, 17 lb. ½ of sayle twine, 13 lb. beeting twine.

1 Quire papper Riall

Some of the items above need translation. For example, "Roades" are anchor hawsers, "saker" is a cannon, a "murderer" is a ship cannon, "speekes" are spikes, "barke" is a cork float for fishing nets, "frize" is a coarse woolen cloth with a nap on one side, "spilting cloth" is cloth used to bolt meal or strain milk and "munmouth capps" were flat caps worn by common people. This last item was mentioned in Shakespeare's writings.

Of interest to modern hunters and economy-minded house-wives, is the purchase of 32 ducks at 4 pence per duck and 14 geese at 1 shilling per goose.

Excerpts from one of Winter's letters give an idea of the period: [1]

Richmon Iland, the 10th of August, 1634

Mr. Robert Trelawnye:—

Syr: Yt may please you to vnderstand of our pro-seinges. We haue taken at present thre thousand dry fish, & we haue made a C Cor fish by the meanes of the hot season, & we haue not taken aboue 2 C bas, Cor & dry . . . The Hunter departed heare heance the 3 of July. I hope she is saue home by this tyme . . . Since the Hunter departed, we have made a pallastho about our house of 15 foote high, & mounted our odinance in platt formes with in our pallasatho for our defence from those that wish us harm heare. So not hauinge els to write at present, I end and rest,

Your to his power,
John Winter

The bar which has always run out to Richmond's Island from the adjoining shore was the scene of a strange tragedy recorded by John Winter in the summer of 1639.

It was the custom of the islanders to allow their cows,

---

[1] Very little of this remarkable period of Maine history would be known were it not for the unusual find of John Wingate Thornton, after whom Thornton Park in Winthrop, Massachusetts, is named. While looking over an English catalogue he noticed the autograph of Robert Trelawny. On at-tempting to acquire it, he found that it was part of a large collection of docu-ments purchased by the Rev. C. T. Collins Trelawny of Ham, England. After correspondence, Rev. Trelawny presented the papers to the Maine Historical Society. The Society published the collection as *The Trelawny Papers* in 1884 after editing by historian James Phinney Baxter.

guided by milkmaids and farmhands, to cross the sandy bar at low tide. Of course, the cows dallied as long as they could on the bar and would only return when the bar began to be flooded by the incoming tide.

One afternoon the cows were rounded up by the maid "Tomson" and herded across in the face of the rising tide. Halfway across, with the water six inches deep over the bar, the girl's hat blew off and she waded into deep water after it. The men who were watching from shore suddenly observed her floundering over her head. Those nearest ran to help, but the girl drowned before they could reach the scene. Winter's comments were pithy: "I think if she had lived she would have proved a good servant in the house: she would do more worke than 3 such maides as Pryssylla is!" His eulogy ended with the words, "the maid Tomson had a hard fortune."

After the death of Mr. Robert Trelawny, the island passed into possession of his young son, John. Winter continued to run the plantation and trading post for ten-year-old John Trelawny, but, for a series of reasons, commerce began to decline. In 1645 John Winter died, and shortly afterwards Indian troubles around Casco became serious. The vast trade which had made Richmond's Island a miniature London or Paris fell to nothing, and soon the island and the mouth of the Spurwink River became practically deserted.

In 1648 Robert Jordan, the husband of Winter's only daughter, was given a court award of the plantation and all its appurtenances. Jordan's early background is rather sketchy, but we do know that he came from Worcester, England, in 1639. Arriving at Richmond's Island when it was the metropolis of Maine, he "found the charms of Sarah Winters too potent to resist" and, marrying the girl, he later became the sole proprietor of the great Trelawny estate in America.

The decision to award the estate to Jordan was called

hasty and unjust, because it completely ignored young John Trelawny in England. On three different occasions other members of the Trelawny family attempted to recover their possessions, first in 1676, again in 1719 and finally in 1758. As late as 1875 Reverend Charles T. Collins Trelawny was interested in recovering the property, but the Statute of Limitations prevented his doing so.

There had been a dispute between George Cleeve of Casco and John Winter of Richmond's Island beginning in 1631. George Cleeve and another man named Richard Tucker were living at Richmond's Island when John Winter arrived and they were promptly ordered from the island. Cleeve [1] then established residence on Casco Neck. For the next few years the status of property in the area around Cape Elizabeth was uncertain, and Cleeve caused much trouble during the period between 1631 and 1645.

With the death of Winter and Jordan and the decline of trade at Richmond's Island, the dispute faded into insignificance. When Massachusetts finally took over the entire area, the controversy was forgotten.

In the last part of the seventeenth century there was little activity at Richmond's Island. On October 12, 1676, a great Indian force led by Mugg, chief of the Androscoggins, invaded Black Point and then proceeded to Richmond's Island. A vessel belonging to Mr. Fryer of Portsmouth lay offshore and the crew had landed when Walter Gendall on the island had insisted on their help in defending his property. When the Indians attacked, the men fled to their ship but the wind was against them and they were unable to leave the harbor.

---

[1] Later he returned to England and obtained control of Lygonia, an overlapping indefinite region along Casco Bay which had originally been planned for a group of settlers who arrived in Maine. Then the settlers moved away, leaving Lygonia's status decidedly unsettled. Cleeve was a double-dealer, and by playing both Royalists and Puritans against each other, he obtained the position of Deputy of Lygonia. He soon made it very uncomfortable for Winter.

The Indians cut the ship's cable and shot every man who appeared on deck.

Later, the vessel was driven on shore and the eleven men on board were taken prisoners. James Fryer, son of the owner, eventually died of his wounds. Walter Gendall, after being taken prisoner, served the Indians as interpreter and messenger. Both the elder Fryer and Gendall were released after Mugg signed a peace treaty, November 6, 1676.

In the year 1705 a sloop was recaptured at Richmond's Island which the Indians had taken at Kittery, Maine, during a bloody raid on that settlement.

By 1800 Richmond's Island, better known in its day than Portland, Maine, is at the present time, had faded out of the picture as a trading center. Farmers and fishermen had taken over the island.

From year to year various stories were told of treasure buried at Richmond's Island, but they were not given much credence. Then on one spring day in 1855, Mr. Hanscom, tenant farmer on the island, was plowing an uncultivated section with the help of his twelve-year-old son when the boy suddenly stopped his horse and called to his father.

"I've found something." Mr. Hanscom ran to discover an old earth-caked crock which resembled a globe lantern. The boy had noticed it at the side of the furrow, about a foot below the surface.

"Now that you've found it, throw it over the bank," said the farmer. "It's just an old broken rum jug. Come on, let's go!"

"But I'd like to see what's inside," exclaimed the boy. "What harm is there in that?"

"All right, then. Lay it aside and we'll pick it up later."

The boy placed the crock on a pile of stones nearby and they went on with the plowing. A younger son of Mr. Hanscom, who had watched the incident, went over to the stone pile and, turning the pot upside down, shook out the caked dirt. Suddenly there was a cry. "Father, come quickly. Look what I've found!"

When the others joined the younger son, they discovered gold and silver coins at the bottom of the crock. Later, a careful examination of the find revealed not only twenty-one beautiful golden coins, each worth a substantial amount, and thirty-one silver coins of various sizes and rarity, but also a strange-looking ring.

The gold had been placed on one side of the crock, the silver on the other and the ring in the center. Close inspection revealed it to be a wedding signet ring of fine gold, weighing "eighty penny-weights and four grains." A magnifying glass further revealed that the letters G and V were engraved next to each other worked into an ornamental border on the outside surface. A golden cord was entwined around the initials and tied with a love knot. Inside the band of gold the word "United" was engraved with two hearts entwined and then the phrase "Death only Partes." The lettering was evidently done by an expert and the engraving was well cut and beautifully formed.

Perhaps the scoundrel Bagnall purchased the ring by barter from the earliest of all Puritan pirates, Dixy Bull. Certainly Bull knew of the trading post on Richmond's Island. Then it is possible that French pirates, who ravaged the coast earlier, bartered the ring with Bagnall.

The source of the ring would depend on when the coins were minted. The earliest date on any of the coins is 1564. A sixpence is dated 1625. The oldest gold coin is dated 1602. Seven of the twenty-one gold pieces bear the stamp of Charles I, whose reign began in 1625 and ended with his execution in 1649. His coinage may be divided into periods, before and after 1642, and the character of the seven gold coins indicates that they were minted in the earlier period. The personal seal of agent John Winter bears a close resemblance to that on the mysterious ring found at Richmond's Island in 1855. The cross marks and circles on the seal had been for several centuries used by merchants as a hallmark. All these facts surrounding the ring are known, but to whom the initials G and V belonged is still a mystery. The ring with its romantic inscription has become one of the tantalizing unfinished stories of the Maine coast.

Today there are only two houses on Richmond's Island, one of which is a small frame affair. The other was once the main residence of the island, but it has fallen into a neglected condition. Across the meadow stands a great empty barn with two silos. The island is deserted.

As we started toward the grove of trees in the distance, a fat red fox flashed by and leaped over a stone wall into the underbrush. We reached the wall and walked through the opening where four or five muskrat tracks came together. As we walked along we could see a tanker on the horizon pushing her way toward the harbor of Portland.

On the southern shore we found the wreckage of a large vessel, but whether it was a fragment of the *Washington B. Thomas,* wrecked in the vicinity June 12, 1903, or some later wreck, is not known, though it appears to be from the *Thomas.*

The island is now the property of the Sprague Corporation, which also controls much of the land on the Cape Elizabeth shore. Two Jordan "boys," each over eighty years of age, go over to fish every summer and that is about the only activity on this once busy and prosperous island.

As we entered the sandy breakwater to return to the mainland, we glanced back and realized that not one person in a thousand who passes it by has any idea that Richmond's Island, now forlorn and deserted, three centuries ago promised to become a thriving commercial metropolis.

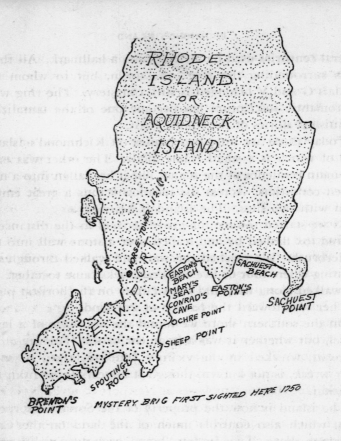

RHODE ISLAND OR AQUIDNECK ISLAND

NEWPORT

HORSE TOWER 1121(?)

EASTON'S BEACH
MARY'S SEAT
CONRAD'S CAVE
OCHRE POINT
EASTON'S POINT
SACHUEST BEACH
SACHUEST POINT
SHEEP POINT
SPOUTING ROCK
BRENTON'S POINT
MYSTERY BRIG FIRST SIGHTED HERE 1750

XIII. NEWPORT

IN 1639 a small group of Massachusetts freedom-lovers, led by William Coddington, William Brenton, Nicholas Easton, Thomas Hazard, William Dyer and John Clarke, founded Newport on Aquidneck Island. They had planned to travel to Delaware in order to find real religious freedom away from the rigid Puritan régime in Massachusetts,[1] but Roger

[1] Newport, alas, also had its witch scare, trial and hanging, that of one Thomas Cornell in 1673.

Williams persuaded them to settle instead on Aquidneck Island. They chose to live at the southern end of the island, and, for a fee of one white man's coat attractively decorated with brass buttons, the native Indians helped them clear their land.

Newport was laid out in streets on May 16, 1639 and each householder received four acres of land. It was in Newport that the first Quaker church in America was built in 1657; it was there that George Fox, who had founded the Society of Friends in England some years before, came in 1672.

Newport was one of the leading colonial towns of the eighteenth century, and by 1730 had a population of over ten thousand, three sugar refineries, twenty-one rum distilleries and seventeen sperm oil factories. It was strategically located for maritime activity and trade with the West Indies and Europe. Before 1700 Newport had became a favored summer resort for West Indian planters who wanted to avoid the sweltering tropical months in their native islands.

Newport, like many other New England seaports, was active in the so-called Triangular Commerce. Yankee skippers would land Jamaica molasses at Newport to make New England rum, which they took to Africa as barter for slaves, which they transported to Jamaica and exchanged for more molasses. African slaves were often brought into Newport Harbor and many New England families owned them in those early days.

It was only to be expected that some ambitious young men carried the idea of profit on the high seas a step further and were attracted to a quicker method of getting rich than the Triangular Commerce. They turned privateers and even pirates. Newport was a hotbed of piracy during many years of its long history and several of its noted buccaneers came from prominent local families.

The story of Thomas Tew is typical. Grandson of Richard Tew, who settled in Newport in 1640, he sailed to Bermuda in the year 1691, eager to purchase a share in the sloop

Amity, which was owned by leading citizens of Bermuda. He succeeded in buying a part-share in the sloop and was promptly made her captain. He then obtained a privateering commission and gathered a crew of volunteers for a voyage to the eastward.

Although his fellow-owners did not know it, Tew had already practiced piracy. In 1699 a sailor named Weaver made the official statement that it was common knowledge that Tew had been a pirate before 1691. Another sailor, long connected with Tew, said that Tew was known to have done much "rambling." Nevertheless, as is often the case, the owners of the *Amity* did not know of the captain's background until too late, and Tew sailed away from Bermuda in company with another privateer sloop.

After capturing almost twenty vessels, Tew sighted another ship off the coast of Africa, and, prompted by dreams of additional booty, he hoisted the Jolly Roger and fired a gun to the windward. The vessel at once hove to and fired to the leeward, a favorite pirate recognition signal. Tew had quite accidentally challenged the famous *Victorie,* belonging to the notorious pirate Captain Mission.

Mission had left France some time before, fitted out for privateering, frequently an intermediate step between merchant sailing and piracy. He had established a pirate kingdom which he called Libertatia on the island of Madagascar. Mission's conduct at Libertatia compels us to admit that freedom, not to say license, was an appropriate name for the settlement.

Tew was royally entertained aboard the *Victorie* and completely won over to the methods and plans of his fascinating host. When he was invited to sail along with the *Victorie* for a visit to the pirate kingdom, he accepted gladly after he had received the approval of his crew, according to pirate custom.

As the *Amity* and the *Victorie* slid in between the outer ledges of the harbor at Libertatia, Tew noticed with amazement that great forts guarded the approaches to Mission's island kingdom. Salute after salute boomed out to them from shore as they ran for the moorings. When he landed on the island, the entire pirate company received Tew with great kindness.

After a pleasant sojourn at Libertatia, Tew set his course for Bermuda. A bad gale smashed his mast and forced him off the course. After a delay of two weeks, he decided to head for Newport. One might imagine that Tew would be afraid to go ashore, suspiciously prosperous as he was, but Newport in those days was generous to pirates and their sins.

Waiting for word from Tew in Bermuda were the five co-owners of the *Amity*, whose number included a member of the Governor's Council. Tew at once sent a dispatch to them, asking for an agent to come to Newport for their shares of the *Amity's* trip. When Captain Starrs, the agent appointed by the Bermuda partners, sailed into Newport Harbor, he discovered that Tew had buried some of the money and that the rest was deposited in Boston. Finally, the profits were suitably divided—and very handsome profits they were! Governor's Councilman William Outerbridge became wealthier by over three thousand pounds from this particular venture and Tew put away around eight thousand pounds of his share. He brought back so much Arabian gold that for a time these sizable coins, worth twice the value of Spanish dollars, were common not only in Newport but in New York as well.

Captain Tew now went to Boston to apply for a new privateering commission but he was emphatically refused. On his return to Newport, with a bribe of five hundred pounds, he obtained a commission. Now legally permitted to capture French ships, Tew went to New York, where he outfitted a ship, the *Frederick*, for a journey to Madagascar. A few weeks later Tew sailed with a full cargo for Libertatia, the pirates' happy land.

Captain Mission welcomed Tew heartily, and his rich cargo

of New England merchandise was brought ashore and traded for Arabian gold. After the welcome had worn off a little, Captain Mission suggested to Tew that a joint cruise to the Red Sea might prove lucrative. For this purpose Mission furnished two large ships, each manned by two hundred and fifty men, and the voyage began.

Off the Arabian coast Tew and Mission fell in with a ship belonging to the Great Mogul which carried 1600 pilgrims on their way to Mecca, the Holy City. Although the Great Mogul's vessel was armed with a hundred guns, when the pirates sailed in against it the crew offered little effective resistance and the ship was captured without the loss of a single buccaneer. The pirates now boarded and examined their prize.

Lack of suitable women at the pirate Utopia was one of its disadvantages. When Tew and Mission saw the hundreds of desirable ladies on the pilgrim vessel, certain ideas at once presented themselves. All women were forced to declare their marital status and the unmarried group was separated from the married group. About one hundred unmarried girls between twelve and eighteen years of age were chosen to become citizens of Libertatia. And despite the pleas of the Mecca-bound Mohammedans, the girls were removed to the pirate vessels and taken to Madagascar. With so much to divert them, Tew and Mission stayed at Libertatia for several months before deciding to sail for America.

Their happy days were over, however. Running into a violent storm on the way to the Cape of Good Hope, Captain Mission's sloop went down a short distance from Tew's. The storm was so fierce that not a single pirate could be saved from the raging seas and Tew sailed off alone after many futile attempts at rescue.

The rest of the journey around the Cape of Good Hope and across the Atlantic to America was more or less uneventful and Tew's sloop arrived safely at Newport Harbor a few weeks later. Here the captain divided gold and diamonds with his crew. The pirates, it has been said, then hied themselves to Boston, where they appeared publicly on the streets.

Tew did not join them but lived quietly in his Newport home. Gradually, however, members of his crew came to see him. As usual among seafaring men, they had squandered their wealth and now they urged Tew to undertake another piratical adventure. Tew was not anxious to go to sea again, but when his entire crew appealed for action, he finally consented.

Sailing from Newport Harbor in the month of November, 1694, Tew was shortly joined by two other vessels, one a sloop commanded by Captain Wake, an old pirate who had been pardoned by King James, and the other a brigantine under Captain Want, Tew's mate on his first trip. Tew's fleet was further augmented by the appearance of Captain Glover in a ship from New York. By June, 1695, the little fleet had reached Liparau Island at the mouth of the Red Sea.

Tew soon sighted a Moorish vessel and opened attack. Perhaps his quiet life ashore had made him soft, for when the Moors offered unexpected resistance the pirate captain realized that this was a battle he would not win. Suddenly a shot struck him in the stomach and disemboweled him. Thomas Tew died a moment later, far from the Rhode Island home where he had hoped to spend his declining years.

Newport's next important association with pirates was the offshore visit of a Boston pirate, the fiendish Captain Low. Arriving off Block Island early in June, 1722, Low overtook and plundered a sloop from New Jersey. Later in the day he captured a Newport sloop commanded by James Cahoon. After disabling the sloop, Low stood away to the southeast in an attempt to flee the vicinity.

Cahoon escaped to Block Island that same midnight and the next morning the terrifying news that Captain Low was in the vicinity had reached Newport. The whole town was aroused. The Governor of Rhode Island ordered drums beaten to summon volunteers for an attack against the pirates.

Two of the best sloops in Newport were outfitted and prepared for battle. Captain John Headlund was chosen master of the first sloop of ten guns and eighty men. Captain John Brown commanded the other sloop, with six guns and sixty men. The sloops were under way before sunset the same day, and they made directly for the pirate ship, still visible from the heights of Block Island. But a sudden wind allowed Low to escape from his pursuers and Captains Headlund and Brown returned to Newport without their prey.

Shortly after this close call, on June 10, 1723, Low and the man he had appointed captain of a captured vessel, Charles Harris, were cruising off Long Island, New York, when Harris sighted a large ship bearing down upon him. As the ship drew nearer, it was seen to be bristling with guns and both Harris and Low prepared their sloops for battle. It was now four-thirty in the morning. When the ship tacked and stood to the south, Low and Harris gave chase and at eight o'clock the pirates opened fire. The strange ship returned shot for shot. The black flags of piracy hoisted on the two sloops were hastily pulled down when Low and Harris realized that they were in combat with a man-of-war, the *Greyhound*, commanded by a man who had sworn to make their capture, Captain Peter Solgard.

The pirates sent a "bloody" flag aloft, signifying that they were not planning to board and then managed to get a mile away. But the man-of-war slowly gained in pursuit, firing as it came. Finally, the wind dropped and then died away completely, giving the pirates an opportunity to escape. Resorting to their sweeps, they rowed steadily away. Captain Solgard soon saw what had happened and ordered eighty-six sailors to man the *Greyhound's* oars. By this method the man-of-war gradually made up the distance lost, and by two-thirty in the afternoon she was close enough to place herself between the sloops.

Captain Solgard now concentrated his fire on the sloop commanded by Harris, allowing Low to escape. Shot after shot raked Harris' craft. The mainsail was first to fall and then the sloop was steadily reduced to a helpless hulk. At four o'clock Captain Harris saw that further fighting was useless and surrendered, asking for quarter. One of Harris' crew suggested that they all blow themselves up. When the pirate captain refused this solution to their problems, he promptly committed suicide. An hour later, all the remaining pirates had been brought aboard the *Greyhound* as prisoners. Now Solgard began pursuit of the other pirate sloop but darkness fell before he could overtake her. Once again the villainous Low had succeeding in making good his escape.

It was a great day in the history of Rhode Island when the *Greyhound* arrived in port carrying forty-eight pirates, both dead and alive. Thirty, some seriously wounded, were brought ashore and escorted under heavy guard to the Newport jail. Eleven had died as a result of their battle, and seven were kept aboard the *Greyhound* as it continued to search for Low and his sloop.

The seven pirates who had been kept aboard the *Greyhound* were brought back to Newport on July 11. They were Captain Charles Harris himself, twenty-five years old, of London; Joseph Libbey, twenty-one, of Marblehead; Thomas Hazell, fifty, John Bright, twenty-five, Patrick Cunningham, twenty-five, John Fletcher, seventeen, and Thomas Child, fifteen, whose homes were unknown.

With thirty-seven pirates in its jail, Newport became the center of all New England's interest. The probability of a mass hanging even attracted attention as far away as New York and Maine.

The Honorable William Dummer arrived from Boston with members of His Majesty's Council and Governor Cranston of Rhode Island, accompanied by several local judges, met with the Boston group at the Newport Town House. The Court of Admiralty was organized on July 10, 1723.

Captain Solgard of the *Greyhound* was among the first to appear against the pirates. His testimony was particularly damning as he told of the fight with the two sloops. One shipmaster, Captain Welland, who had lost an ear in the engagement, then took the stand and by the time he had finished, it was clear what the verdict was going to be.

Every last pirate pleaded not guilty, however. Each claimed that he had been forced into piracy. In summing up the case, the Advocate General said, among other things, that the pirates' plea that they had been forced into service should be ignored. If it were accepted, he warned, every captured pirate would make the same claim and none would ever be convicted. He ended by demanding the death penalty. His demand was granted with two exceptions, John Wilson and Henry Barnes. The others were sentenced to be hanged.

The entire countryside was deeply stirred by the news of the coming execution. The gibbets were erected, in the usual fashion, between the rise and fall of the tide at Gravelly Point, Newport, and the drop was tested for the gruesome occasion. On the morning of July 19, 1723, every person in the vicinity began a pilgrimage across the open fields to Gravelly Point, and those fortunate enough to go by boat were on the scene in time to obtain the best vantage points.

When the pirates arrived at the scaffolding most of them repented of their wrongdoings and cautioned young men in the audience to avoid the sins which lead to a pirate's death on the gallows. From the *New England Courant* of July 22, 1723, we learn that Mr. Bass, the minister, went to pray with those who were about to die on the scaffolding and that the Reverend Mr. Clapp delivered a short exhortation. Then, at high noon, the solemn and terrifying business of executing twenty-six [1] pirates began and within an hour every last one had been hanged. Newport did not follow the Boston and London custom of publicly hanging the bodies in chains after death. The pirates were cut down from the scaffold and unceremoniously buried on Goat Island down the bay. It had been the greatest mass execution in New England history.

Twenty-seven years later, when piracy had gradually died out, Newport had her own *Mary Celeste*.[2]

In the year 1750, Isaac Steele of Newport anxiously awaited the arrival of his brig, the *Beach Bird* which was long overdue on its return from the Bay of Honduras. He had heard that it had been sighted by another vessel two days' journey from Newport and was sure that it must appear at any moment. Steele and his associates scanned the horizon with their spy-glasses but the weeks went by without any sign of the *Beach Bird*. Then one day, when practically all hope had been abandoned, Steele sighted his brig approaching, hull down, sailing toward Newport.

The overjoyed owner rushed back to town with the news and soon the waterfront was crowded with people who were curious to learn the strange story the crew would undoubtedly have to tell when they finally landed. But as the *Beach Bird* drew abeam of Brenton's Reef, instead of entering the harbor, she sailed almost due east, passed Spouting Rock, Sheep Point, Ochre Point and turned in by Conrad's Cave.

"What is wrong with the fools?" shouted Steele. "They'll wreck my vessel."

By now the *Beach Bird* had sailed in toward Easton's Beach, altered her course at the last minute to avoid the rocky ledges near Mary's Seat and slid aground on the sandy northwest corner of the beach. The entire town rushed down

---

[1] Several pirates had died in prison.
[2] Mysteriously abandoned at sea in 1872. The full story appears in my *Mysteries and Adventures Along the Atlantic Coast*.

to the shore, Steele in the lead, and boarded the brig. They rushed aft, but there was no one at the wheel. Darting below, they went from one end of the brig to the other, shouting for members of the crew and exploring every cabin and cupboard. The result of their thorough search produced only a hungry dog and a bewildered cat. The cabin table was set as though for breakfast, a fire was still blazing in the cuddy with a steaming kettle over it, but not a single person could be found aboard ship. No trace of either the captain or the crew was ever discovered!

Newport was a gay town before the Revolution. Many wealthy citizens built beautiful homes, surrounded by magnificent terraces, fine lawns and flower gardens, at which they gave great banquets and balls. They were attended by more slaves per person than were the residents of any other American colony.

The many Quakers of Newport did not and could not indulge in the fashionable social activities of the town. They wore plain clothes and confined themselves to simple festivities such as corn-husking matches and sewing bees. But their lives, though sober, were useful and happy.

All this changed one day in the late summer of 1775 when several British warships anchored at Newport Harbor. Soon thereafter Captain James Wallace of the *Rose,* the fleet commander, ordered the citizens of Newport to send him livestock and food for his sailors. Many frightened people hid their valuables and fled town. The owner of the local newspaper buried his press in the cellar of his house. The streets were clogged with men, women and children trying to leave Newport before the British landed.

When the British commander learned that the people were fleeing the town, he sailed away with his fleet. Immediately, the citizens of Newport returned to their homes as Wallace had believed they would. Wallace came back with the fleet, landed and took possession of Newport. He issued orders that no one would be allowed to leave his home.

The British ruled with severity, burning buildings which were of no use to them, using churches for stables and turning the fine Colony House into a hospital. All trade between Newport and the rest of the world was ended. Even the newspaper press was brought from its hiding place and used to publish a pro-British weekly.

The British did not rule without resistance from the people of Newport, however. Captain Abraham Whipple captured an armed tender belonging to the *Rose* and drove her ashore at Conanicut Island, so enraging Fleet Commander Wallace that he wrote Whipple an arrogant note which contained the threat to hang the insolent Yankee from the yard-arm. Whipple was ready with an answer:

> To Sir James Wallace, Sir:
> Always catch a man before you hang him.
> Abraham Whipple

The first winter of the British occupation of Newport brought intense suffering to the inhabitants. Prices for scarce commodities soared higher and higher. Potatoes were two dollars a bushel, corn twice that and wood twenty dollars a cord. The shortage of fuel became so acute that several ships were hauled up on shore and broken up as firewood.

For four long years the hardships continued until in 1779 it became apparent that the British were planning to leave Newport. By October the evacuation was under way and the tramp of soldiers was heard everywhere. Before leaving, however, the British systematically destroyed whatever they could in the old town, filling wells, cutting down trees, laying waste to beautiful estates and smashing wharves.[1] They crossed over to famous old Beavertail Light and burned it to the ground and then returned to Newport and confiscated

---

[1] In all, they destroyed 480 buildings.

the town records. Their last vindictive act before they sailed was to destroy all the church bells of Newport but one, which had been a present to the town from Queen Anne herself.

Newport never really recovered from its occupation by the British Navy during the Revolution. The following summer, however, when the French fleet arrived in Newport Harbor, the town forgot its misery to give a warm welcome to the allies from overseas. Balls and other gay entertainments were given the French officers and men. Soon the Frenchmen were calling on the young ladies of Newport and it became the rage to scratch the initials of these dashing foreigners into the windowpanes of the homes where they called. Even today several of those windowpanes, still bearing the initials of forgotten Frenchmen, can be seen in Newport.

In April, 1831, an event occurred in Fall River, twenty miles away from Newport, which was to bring to the fore the greatest controversy of Aquidneck Island.

The accidental discovery of a skeleton in a Fall River sandbank began an impassioned discussion which is still raging at Newport. The skeleton in question was found in a seated position, with the legs drawn up under the torso and all around it were a number of brass and copper plates and brass-tipped spearheads. Immediately, the theory was advanced that the skeleton was that of an early Norse explorer and the proponents of this idea cited the so-called Norse Tower in Newport as additional proof. On the other side of the controversy were the ones who maintained that the skeleton was merely that of an Indian warrior.

Those who took sides began writing their arguments to the local newspaper and soon Newport was divided into two belligerent camps. In order to bolster their respective theories, the proponents soon began to use stories and accounts which were pure fabrication.

Longfellow later wrote a poem about the discovery and called it *The Saga of the Skeleton in Armor:*

260

I was a Viking old!
My deeds, though manifold,
No Skald in song has told,
No saga taught thee!

Longfellow goes on to tell how his Viking stole the daughter of another Norseman, putting to sea with her and finally reaching what is now Newport:

There for my lady's bower
Built I the lofty tower
Which, to this very hour,
Stands looking seaward.

Unfortunately for Longfellow's poem and the other adherents of the Norse theory, scientists later proved that the skeleton was actually that of an Indian who had decorated himself with metal given him by the English.[1] But the members of the rival Newport camps never forgave each other and their animosities have continued through the years.

Since I was a child my curiosity has been aroused by a Boston statue of a stately Viking sailor and I have often given thought to a question which probably never will be answered: Did the Norsemen really reach New England before the Puritans?

There are many clues and suppositions which could be gullibly accepted as proof that the Norsemen were the first discoverers of America but when we limit our acceptance to facts—well, that is another story.

There are two indisputable objects which seem to support the Norse theory: The massive Norse Tower at Newport and the famous Kensington Stone, found some years ago on a Minnesota farm.

The Kensington Stone has been proved authentic beyond

---

[1] The decorations are still in the Peabody Museum at Harvard.

any reasonable doubt by eminently qualified experts. But is there any *authentic proof* that the Norsemen built the Newport Tower?

The Norse Tower in Newport, according to the late historian Philip Ainsworth Means, is the most puzzling structure in the entire United States. Most of the residents of Newport have long believed that it was built as a windmill by Governor Benedict Arnold in 1675. But after a careful study of the tower, one must doubt the truth of this supposition. If it had been intended as a windmill, why was it built to rest on eight columns poorly adapted to its purpose? And where could the millstones have possibly been placed? No matter how one figures it, either the rising dust from the grindstone or the open windows would have made the building unsuitable as a mill.

The exponents of the Arnold theory believe that Benedict Arnold built his windmill as a replacement for an earlier and rather flimsy scaffold mill which had blown down in 1675. Ignoring all probability, they claim that Arnold substituted for the usual wooden structure of the time a massive stone building with eight columns, two floors, a fireplace with flues and several double-splayed windows.

The year 1675, in which Arnold's mill is supposed to have been constructed, was the height of King Philip's war. Every able-bodied man, and many women as well, were bearing arms against the Indians. Where would Arnold find masons and carpenters during this desperate struggle? Who would lift the heavy stones, parge the masonry with mortar plaster, hew the floor beams and planks and hoist them into place? How could Governor Benedict Arnold and his workmen so far forget their peril as to undertake such a tremendous construction job?

Isn't it more probable that Benedict Arnold found an old ruin on his property and later utilized it as a windmill, making certain necessary reinforcements?

As Philip Ainsworth Means has said, if Arnold had designed that tower as a windmill, it would have been unique in the history of the world. There is no other windmill like it. Many Newporters have put forth the idea that Arnold copied the tower from one he saw in Chesterton, England. But we know now that Benedict Arnold had never been to Chesterton and could not possibly have built the windmill with such a model in mind. Furthermore, the tower at Chesterton was not built as a windmill but as an observatory. We can only assume that Benedict Arnold had never seen anything but typical early American wooden mills and merely renovated the old stone tower on his property to serve as a windmill. But if Arnold didn't build the mill, who did?

Everything indicates that the early Norse adventurers, men such as Lief Ericson and Thorwald, did not know of such buildings, but it is reasonable to assume that after the Norsemen adopted Christianity and visited the Holy Land, they were inspired to erect towers similar to the one at Newport. In studying a rare book known as the *Deeds of the Pontiffs of the Church of Hamburg,* published in Copenhagen in 1579, we learn that Vinland, as America was called, was still visited by Scandinavians as late as 1362. Acceptance of the authenticity of the famous Kensington Stone further substantiates the theory that Norsemen did build the tower at Newport.

What proof of this exists?

Philip Ainsworth Means, who wrote one of the many books on the subject, believed that either Norsemen of the twelfth century or Portuguese of a later period built the tower. It would seem impossible that the Portuguese, who stayed only a short time, could have constructed such a building. It is known that Gasper Cortereal made the earliest inscription on the Dighton Rock, and it is reasonable to assume that there was another mysterious Portuguese visitor who visited Charlestown, Rhode Island, before 1525. However, to imagine that these travelers would have had either the resources or the inclination to erect such an imposing edifice is fantastic.

After a careful study of all the facts, I believe that the Newport Tower was built in 1121 by one of the early Norse explorers, Eric Gnuppson, who copied it after a round church of the Holy Sepulchre which he had seen in the Holy Land several years before. But there is no authentic proof of this. The tower remains the island's secret. Some day we may discover who built it, when it was constructed and why—but I doubt it.

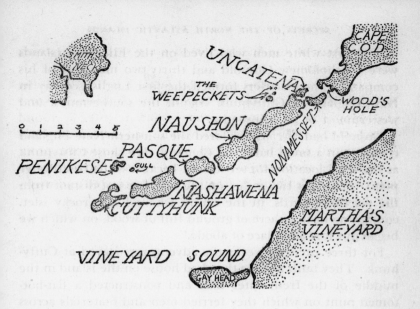

XIV. NAUSHON AND THE
ELIZABETH ISLANDS

THE eight Elizabeth Islands lie almost in a straight line for some fifteen miles off Cape Cod at Wood's Hole in Falmouth, Massachusetts. Alexander Crosby Brown of the Mariners' Museum at Newport News, Virginia, gives us no less than eight different ways of saying a jingle [1] made up of the names of the Elizabeths. I prefer this one, also Mr. Brown's choice, because it gives the islands in a geographical sequence, moving southwest-to-northeast:

> Cuttyhunk, Penikese,
> Nashawena, Pasquanese,
> Naushon, Weepecket,
> Uncatena and Nonamesset.

---

[1] *The American Neptune*, January, 1950, pages 71-78.

The first white men who lived on the Elizabeth Islands were Bartholomew Gosnold and thirty-two members of his company. These settlers formed the first English colony in New England at Cuttyhunk Island, the southernmost and westernmost of all Elizabeths.[1]

Gosnold had already explored the southern New England coastline in a small bark, the *Concord*. He chose Cuttyhunk as the ideal location for settlement because of its fresh water pond "in circuit two miles, on the one side not distant from the sea thirty yards, in the centre whereof is a rocky islet, containing near an acre of ground full of wood, on which we began our fort and place of abode."

For three exciting weeks the adventurers stayed at Cuttyhunk. They built a sedge-thatched house on the island in the middle of the fresh-water lake and constructed a flat-bottomed punt on which they ferried men and materials across the lake. From their headquarters at Cuttyhunk they went on many trips of exploration to the other islands and to the mainland. Crossing over to Martha's Vineyard, they planted wheat, oats and barley and took note that strawberries, raspberries and gooseberries abounded on the island.

"Scollops, Muscles, Cockles, Lobsters, Crabs, Oisters and Wilks exceeding good and very great," were gathered and eaten by the English adventurers. Their greatest discovery was sassafras, however, which was credited with wonderful medicinal powers and in England was considered a cure for such ills as the plague and smallpox. Gabriel Archer wrote that sassafras cured one of the company in twelve hours from a "great surfeit" of dogfish bellies.

On May 25, 1602, Archer mentions that the settlement at Cuttyhunk was visited by an Indian, his squaw and papoose. Five days later the Englishmen stole a canoe from the island of Hills Hap, near the mainland. During the first week in June, fifty Indians in canoes arrived at Cuttyhunk, headed

---

[1] I am indebted to Amelia Forbes Emerson and to her book *Early History of Naushon Island* for much of the background material on the Elizabeths.

by their sachem. In honor of this occasion, the settlers held the first New England fish dinner [1] in history.

After the outdoor banquet, one of the Indians decided to take a shield belonging to the white men and carried it off to the canoes. The Englishmen appealed to the sachem, who ordered the shield returned and the crisis was over. Afterwards, both Indians and Englishmen went back to roasting crabs and red herring, "which were exceedingly great."

On June 10, 1602, several of the settlers were ambushed by the Indians, possibly because they had stolen that canoe a few days earlier, and the Englishmen realized that their little colony was too vulnerable. They made plans to sail away. They loaded their ship, the *Concord,* with sassafras and cedar wood for a return journey to England and the following week they left Cuttyhunk forever. New England's first colony had ended.

In 1641 Lord Stirling's agent granted the island of Cuttyhunk to Thomas Mayhew of Martha's Vineyard. Naushon Island was owned by the Mayhew family from 1641 to 1682, by the Winthrop family from 1682 to 1730, by the Bowdoin family from 1730 to 1843 and by the Forbes family from 1843 until the present time.

In 1671 Governor Lovelace of New York granted feudal rights to Thomas Mayhew and gave him the title "Lord of the Manor," similar to that retained at Gardiner's Island, New York, for many years. It is believed, however, that this grant to Martha's Vineyard and the Elizabeth Islands was the only instance of its kind in all New England.

Naushon Island had the doubtful privilege of a visit from the notorious pirate Captain Thomas Pound in October, 1689. This strange man, who has left us an unusual chart of Boston Harbor and the New England Coast, had been a well-known pilot aboard the King's Frigate *Rose.* Suddenly,

---

[1] The Indians relished everything but the mustard, "wherat they made many a sowre face."

and for mysterious reasons, he became a pirate. Operating with his band of twenty-five cutthroats, he ravaged the area north of Cape Cod and on August 27 chased the brigantine *Merrimack* into Home's Hole.

Soon afterwards he sailed to Virginia, but by October he appeared again off Tarpaulin Cove on Naushon Island, where he soon set up his base. One of his men, Thomas Hawkins, deserted the pirate vessel but was later captured at Cape Cod and brought to Boston.

Shortly afterwards, without the knowledge of Captain Pound, the governor in Boston ordered Pound's former sloop *Mary* to be outfitted for a search for the pirate. Captain Samuel Pease, Lieutenant Benjamin Gallop and twenty sailors left Boston Harbor on the *Mary*, bound for the capture of Thomas Pound.

When he reached Vineyard Sound, Captain Pease learned that Pound was still at Tarpaulin Cove. The *Mary* set sail at once to meet the pirates. Flying the King's Jack, the Boston sloop approached Pound's vessel which promptly hoisted the flag of piracy. The *Mary* immediately released a volley into the pirate vessel, causing severe damage.

Captain Pease now shouted across to the pirate captain, "Surrender in the name of the King of England! Strike your colors!"

Pound stood on the quarter deck of his ship, flourishing his sword through the air, and bellowed, "Come aboard, and I'll strike all right!"

Soon the pirate vessel fired a volley at the *Mary*. The British sloop now ran to leeward of the pirates. The wind was so strong that the weather side of the *Mary* acted as protection for Captain Pease's men and they were able to shoot down onto the decks of the pirate vessel. Blood ran thick on Thomas Pound's vessel, but the surviving pirates kept shouting and shooting.

Suddenly there was a terrific explosion aboard the *Mary*. The pirates were encouraged, but only two of the king's men had been wounded. Captain Pease again offered quarter to the pirates if they would surrender, but Thomas Pound shouted back insolently that it was *they* who would give quarter.

The fight continued, and Captain Pease, in directing the attack, was shot through the body and carried below. He realized that death was at hand and delegated his authority to Lieutenant Gallop.

After maneuvering in Tarpaulin Cove closer and closer to the shore, the two vessels now came together in the lee of a headland and grapnels were thrown across to lock them in mortal combat. Lieutenant Benjamin Gallop took command and, rallying his men, led a boarding party onto the pirate ship. His men fired their muskets and used them as clubs when they ran out of ammunition. This hand-to-hand battle was one of the worst encounters in the entire history of piracy. Pound and his men seemed imbued with that strange fanaticism which overtakes followers of a lost cause.

Gallop's crew attacked the pirates with such fury that six were dead and twelve seriously wounded before the two remaining cutthroats surrendered and the bloodiest combat in the history of Naushon Island was over.

Outside Tarpaulin Cove the weather grew severe. The *Mary* sailed across to the Sakonnet River and anchored between Pocasset and Rhode Island, where doctors could be sent out from Newport. The doctors treated Captain Pease but when the *Mary* set sail for Boston, his wounds began to bleed again. He was taken ashore at a farmhouse where he died October 12, 1689.

Boston's new stone jail awaited the arrival of the fourteen captured pirates, Captain Pound included. The walls of the jail were four feet thick, with a fine, deep dungeon for dangerous lawbreakers. Twelve of the fourteen wounded pirates were badly injured and must have given the doctor called in by the prison a good deal of work, for his bill for their care came to the sizable sum of twenty-one pounds, ten shillings.

Although no gold or silver had been taken by Pound's buccaneers, the appraiser made his usual summary of the pirates' property. He estimated that the value of everything on board the sloop and of the sloop itself amounted to something just over 209 pounds.

Hawkins, who had deserted Pound at Cape Cod, had been taken to Boston before the others. Governor Bradstreet and his magistrates examined him on October 4, 1689, and had him put back into jail. When he was tried again on January 9, 1690, Hawkins was found guilty.

Soon afterwards, Thomas Pound and his crew of thirteen were brought before the court. On January 17, after a trial lasting several days, all the pirates, including Thomas Pound, Thomas Hawkins, Eleazer Buck and Thomas Johnson, the limping privateer, were found guilty of felony, piracy and murder. They were sentenced to be hanged.

As if the end of the trial were the signal for action, Waitstill Winthrop, one of the acting magistrates, changed his mind and declared that the verdict against the pirates was not a fair one. Possibly the fact that he was a brother of Adam Winthrop, who had married Thomas Hawkins' sister, was a contributing cause.

Magistrate Winthrop visited numerous influential citizens of Boston to obtain their signatures on a petition for a pardon. On behalf of the pirates, he himself headed a committee which included Samuel Sewell.[1] The committee appealed to the governor and the old political order, back in power under Governor Bradstreet, gave Hawkins, Buck and Pound a respite.

The respite came almost too late, just as the condemned men had reached the gallows erected out over Boston Harbor. The governor's order did not reach the North End

---

[1] Judge Sewell's ever-active conscience was not satisfied that Hawkins had been freed. In his diary, the jurist says that some of those in the council "thought Hawkins, because he got out of the Combination before Pease was kill'd, might live; so I rashly sign'd, hoping so great an inconvenience would not have followed. Let not God impute Sin."

until Thomas Hawkins was actually standing on the scaffolding with the hangman's noose adjusted around his neck. As the trap was about to be sprung, Bradstreet's messenger reached the execution pier and stopped the hanging.

Thomas Johnson, the limping privateer, seemed to arouse little sympathy among the thousands of persons who came to watch his execution. Although his bad record was well known in Boston, many believed that he was hanged to satisfy the crowd when the others were granted a respite.

Less than a month later, sentence of death was remitted on Thomas Hawkins, William Warren, Daniel Lander, Richard Griffin, John Siccadam, Eleazer Buck and William Dunn on payment of thirteen pounds, six shillings each. Four days later Thomas Pound was reprieved at the request of Epaphus Shrimpton and several women of quality, undoubtedly among them Hawkins' sisters who were then socially prominent. So it proved that Thomas Johnson, the limping privateer, was the only member of Pound's crew to pay with his life on the Boston gallows.

Some years later Captain Thomas Pound, pirate extraordinary and expert cartographer, retired to Ilesworth near London, where his neighbors accepted him as the perfect gentleman. In the year 1703 he died, loved and honored by his acquaintances in and around London. The true story of his experiences as a pirate will probably never be revealed but it seems probable that his activities were somehow outside the piratical tradition.

The last port of call made by Captain William Kidd after he buried his treasure on Gardiner's Island was at Tarpaulin Cove, Naushon Island. He communicated with the island representative at Naushon and "left some small matter at Tarpolin with the man there," according to a letter written by Wait Winthrop on July 12, 1699. The nature of that "small matter" Kidd left at Tarpaulin has never been divulged. Perhaps he met Caleb Ray who lived at Naushon.

Ray was later to be Kidd's jailer at Boston. One day, according to Lord Bellomont, he left the jail door open so that a relative of his, a pirate named Bradish, could escape. For this Caleb lost his job. He returned to Naushon Island and took up residence again at Tarpaulin Cove.

Many tens of thousands of ships have sailed by the Elizabeth Islands since they were first settled by the English. In 1759 a lighthouse was privately erected at Tarpaulin Cove by Zaccheus Lumbert of Nantucket, and in 1817 a Government Light was built there. As early as the middle of the eighteenth century a Tarpaulin Cove Inn- existed for the many weary sailors and passengers who came ashore at Naushon.

Travelers must have enjoyed a brief respite from the wild Atlantic at Tarpaulin Cove. One voyager, Quaker John Woolman, records his visit:

> The wind being slack we only reached Tarpawling Cove the first day; where on going ashore we found a room in a public house, and beds for a few of us; the rest slept on the floor. We went on board again about break of day.

Of the many shipwrecks which have occurred along the shore of the eight Elizabeth Islands, only one, the wreck of the *Perseverance*, seems to have attracted great attention. One hundred and thirty-five days out from Batavia, headed for her home port, Salem, the *Perseverance* was caught in a terrific gale and thrown ashore at Tarpaulin Cove, January 31, 1805.

The *Perseverance* was a famous vessel of her day. She had made the first voyage from Salem to Archangel in October, 1798, running the European blockade during the French Revolution and the Napoleonic Wars. She had also been in a fight with a French privateer during the quasi-war with France in 1799 but escaped from her attacker. Her master,

Captain Wheatland, retired in 1801 and was replaced by James Cook, the captain in command when the *Perseverance* was driven ashore in the great storm at Tarpaulin Cove.

Although there were many dangerous moments as the crew was rescued from the *Perseverance,* not a life was lost. The *Salem Gazette* for February 5, 1805, describes the disaster:

> *The* Telegraph *announces the ship* Perseverance, *Cook, 135 days from Batavia, ashore at Tarpolin Cove, and bilged. We are happy to hear that letters from Captain Cook yesterday announce that all of the coffee is got out of the* Perseverance *dry and in good order; that the sugar is not much wet and that the property is in a far better state than could be expected.*

Three years after the wreck of the *Perseverance,* on September 30, 1808, a Mr. Smith of Martha's Vineyard was on the south side of Naushon Island, when he found a message in a sealed bottle which read:

> *May 12, 1798*
> *I John M...t master of the ship Olive Branch of Philadelphia in Lat. 33.30 long 69.10. I am through the goodness of God lying to under a reef mizzin staysail and expecting nothing but death, at the present moment the sea making its way over us, three men already lost overboard. This I conceal in a bottle & wax seal the same. Whomever who shall be so kind as to pick this up and put it in the prints of the first port that my friends may hear of my sad disaster. Shall be paid by the owners at Phila.*
> *Ship Olive Branch 29 guns.*

Located to the north of the northern part of Naushon, Weepecket Island has two other locations connected with it, Little Weepecket and Weepecket Rock. During the Revolution, a British warship, the *Sphinx,* anchored near Weepecket and landed five hundred men there.

The two islands immediately to the northeast of Naushon, Uncatena and Nonamesset, are connected to Naushon by bridges. James Bowdoin referred to Uncatena as Onkey Tonkey Island when he mentioned it in a letter in 1809.

At Nonamesset is the only eighteenth century house still standing on the Elizabeth Islands. Built in 1769, it has a huge central chimney seven feet square. The historian, Amelia Emerson, tells us that in "the construction of the whole there is a rough perfection."

Pasquenese or Pasque Island is immediately to the southwest of Naushon and separates the two islands of Naushon and Nashawena from each other. Josiah Quincy refers to it as "Pesk" in his account of his journey there in 1801.

During the Revolution, Captain Frederick von der Malsburg rowed over to Pasquenese at the time the British were clearing the Elizabeths of cattle and sheep and the British held a "frolic" for him in John Slocum's house on "Pesque Island."

Nashawena, the second largest of the Elizabeths, is next to the last in the long row of islands which extends across from Wood's Hole to Cuttyhunk. At the time of the first English settlement under Gosnold, Cuttyhunk and Nashawena were possibly one island. In that case, of course, Canapitsit Channel did not exist. Captain von der Malsburg speaks of one of his corporals shooting a deer at "Nashavinna." Josiah Quincy wrote of Nashawena Island in his 1801 Journal, mentioning Quick's Hole as a navigational passage between "Pesk and Nashawenina."

Cuttyhunk has had many shipwrecks because of its position at the western end of the Elizabeth Island group. In 1849 the brig *Spartan* hit on the island, followed three years later by the *Mary Chilton* and the *A. Dunbar.* In 1855 the brig *Saint John* crashed against Cuttyhunk's rocky shore and in

1857 the brig *Vernon* went to her doom nearby. Among the other vessels wrecked there were the *Maria Adilaid* in 1890, the *Rob and Harry* in 1892 and the *Douglas Dearborn* in the following year. The schooner *Monticello* was lost at Cuttyhunk in 1902. The last notable shipwreck there was that of the whaling ship *Wanderer* on August 25, 1924.

Off by itself, immediately to the north of Cuttyhunk Harbor, stands Penikese Island. Josiah Quincy called the island "Penniquees" at the time of his visit in 1801.

In July, 1873, just a few months before he died, Jean Louis Rodolphe Agassiz founded a scientific summer school on Penikese Island. He chose twenty women and thirty men from the hundreds who applied for the privilege of studying under his supervision and listening to his informal daily lectures. Those who were chosen as pupils of Agassiz never forgot the kindly scientist and their studies with him at Penikese.

Amelia Forbes Emerson told me that the great change at the Elizabeths is the drastic reduction in the number of ships which pass through Vineyard Sound. In the old days there were scores and scores of coasters, schooners and other craft visible from the island winter and summer. Now a vessel of any type is a rarity. The absence of the sails is, of course, due to the virtual extinction of the commercial sailing vessel, and the Cape Cod Canal is responsible for the absence of tugs and steamers on the old Vineyard Sound waterway.

Alexander Crosby Brown, in his "Enchanted Voyages," published in the *American Neptune* for July, 1947, tells of his experience as a seven-year-old boy on a visit to Pasque Island, which he calls "the most beautiful island in the world." He says this "advisedly, having since compared at first hand Tahiti, Samoa, Bali, Madeira, Capri and (lest Sam Morison [1] point out a sin of omission) Mount Desert."

---

[1] Samuel Eliot Morison, famous Harvard professor, historian of Harvard College, and chronicler of Columbus' voyages, who is now engaged in writing the United States Naval history of World War II.

Brown's grandfather was an early member of the Pasque Island Fishing Club, founded in the late 1860's, and owned one of the rooms in the "three barrackslike, weather-worn buildings at the east end of the island. By day, the older generation fished for striped bass from stands built over the surf, played tennis or sailed their boats in the Hole. A wagon made the circuit of the island to deposit the fishermen in the morning and to pick them up again in the evening. And there was much ceremony at the fish house in the weighing in and recording of the day's catch. If Father had been lucky, he might give us a taste of his daily 'tipple' of port before supper. This formal meal concluded, the male members of the club drew lots for the choice fishing stand to be used the next day, then withdrew to the smoking room to the stimulating pastime of dominoes, chess or cards, which they played with their hats on until bedtime. Sunday nights we all sang hymns."

Brown tells of his journey to Pasque Island on the towboat *J. T. Sherman* in 1913. He mentions that the *Sherman* "was not famous for her passenger accommodation but canvas camp stools already liberally sprinkled with grit were provided on the upper deck between the lifeboats, and sometimes the captain let us sit on the leather-covered settee in the pilot house and watch him spin his wheel. Fire buckets stowed in a rack around the funnel were available for other purposes in case it got too rough. The power of suggestion being what it was, I avoided looking directly at them as much as possible."

Brown speaks of the spar buoy in the middle of Buzzard's Bay which had an old broom tied to it as a halfway mark. After they had reached this spot, young Brown was able to identify familiar landmarks at Pasque Island. "First the cliffs on the north shore showed up and then the lone cluster of pine trees on the east end detached itself from the surrounding highland.

"Pretty soon Robinson's Hole opened up, and we could

see clean through to the Vineyard beyond and note the small flotilla of island catboats and sailing dories (called 'peanuts') bobbing at their moorings. The tide was low, and as we approached the Hole, the jagged point of Peaked Rock was visible by the eel-grass on the west side of the channel. A minute later we were abreast of the clubhouses and could see the white plume of smoke followed by the sharp crack of the signal cannon. This little brass gun had been salvaged from the wreck of a palatial schooner yacht, the *Tidalwave,* claimed by the Graveyard [1] in 1891 and custom dictated it should salute the approach of visiting craft.

"By this time a knot of people had gathered at the long pier and the wagon was clattering down the road leading to it. With slackened speed the *Sherman* nosed her way in, lines were passed and in another minute we were alongside and scrambling up the gangplank. Utopia was gained."

---

[1] The Graveyard, Amelia Forbes Emerson told me in May, 1950, is along the southern cliffs of Nashawena Island, where the strong currents have caused many wrecks.

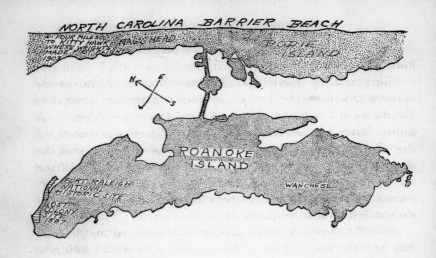

XV. ROANOKE ISLAND AND THE LOST COLONY

IN THE year 1575 Queen Elizabeth of England became deeply interested in colonizing the New World and granted a charter of colonization to one of her ardent followers, Sir Humphrey Gilbert. Gilbert sailed hopefully for America, but the Spaniards crushed his tiny settlement three months later.

Gilbert's venture brought him to Newfoundland, where his men sickened and deserted. A short time later the luck-less colonizer was drowned with all hands when his ship capsized in a great storm.

In 1584 Humphrey Gilbert's half-brother, Walter Raleigh, took over the task of colonizing the New World. Raleigh dispatched an expedition under two men, Amadas and Barlow, who landed on Roanoke Island July 4, 1584. They found the island a paradise, rich in fruit, game and bird life. When they sailed back to England to report their discovery, they took with them two friendly Indians, Manteo and

278

Towaye, and a quantity of tobacco, sassafras, maize, pump-kins, squash, grapes and other fruits.

The report of Amadas and Barlow created such intense interest that Raleigh sent out another expedition, headed by Sir Richard Grenville, with 108 prospective colonists. This group landed at Roanoke on August 17, 1585, naming it Fort Raleigh in honor of their patron. But trouble with the Indians developed so rapidly that the leaders decided to flee the island, leaving fifteen men to hold the fort. Just two weeks before reinforcements would have come to help them, they sailed back to England.

A third expedition was organized as a real colonial venture led by Governor [1] John White. With a hundred and fifty colonists and three ships, White left Plymouth, England, on May 8, 1587. Among the colonists were his daughter Eleanor and her husband, Ananias Dare.

Arriving at Roanoke, they found that the English settlers had completely vanished and the fort was destroyed. Foliage and vines covered the ruined buildings. Later, they dis-covered the skeleton of one man who had evidently been murdered by Indians, but there was no trace of the other fourteen who had been left behind on the island.

Governor White immediately set to work putting the fort in condition and building new houses for the colonists. On August 18, 1587, in the midst of this activity, his daughter, Eleanor Dare, gave birth to a baby girl, Virginia Dare, the first white child born in America!

White now decided to return to England for additional building materials and other supplies. On August 25, 1587, he said good-by to his family and sailed away with his fleet of vessels, leaving 117 men, women and children on the island. Although he promised to return the following spring, he was never to see his colonists again.

Meanwhile, war broke out between England and Spain.

---

[1] The title "Governor" was usually granted to leaders of colonial expeditions.

A new fleet, loaded with desperately needed supplies for the Roanoke settlement, was hastily rushed into service against the threat of the Spanish Armada. In July, 1588, the British launched a series of overwhelming attacks which reduced a mighty armada of 132 galleons to fifty-three mutilated vessels which limped back to Spain at the end of September.

But the English government still feared Spain and was reluctant to allow further help to the colonists for some time. In April two small shallops, considered worthless in the defense of England, had been sent to Roanoke, but they proved inadequate against the mighty Atlantic and returned to port when their captains realized that the journey could never be completed.

Month after month, Spain and England continued to skirmish on the high seas. Governor White, marooned in Britain, had not forgotten his family on Roanoke, stranded without adequate provisions and possibly in deadly combat with the natives. But it was not until March, 1590, that White could sail for America. This time he did not travel with official support for his colony; he was merely a passenger in the West Indian expedition of Captain John Wattes. Wattes had agreed to visit Roanoke but only after touring the West Indies. His ship reached the Indies, spent several months there and finally sailed for Roanoke Island in the late summer of 1590.

White was encouraged to believe that his colony still existed when he noticed smoke rising from the island. As he led a party ashore, he observed another cloud of smoke rising from the southwest and the group changed their course in order to land on the barrier beach, near what is now known as Nag's Head. But they found no sign of human life near the woods fire, which possibly had been set by lightning.

They returned to the ship and planned to come back to Roanoke the next day. As they launched two boats for another visit to the island, one boat capsized and seven sailors were drowned. By the time they were prepared to start again, it was growing dark. Far in the distance, at the northern end of Roanoke Island, they noticed a light. Anchoring offshore near the source of the light, they sang in English and sounded a trumpet time and again, but there was no response from shore. In the morning they landed and found footprints in the sand.

Searching for a landmark to guide them to the fort, they climbed a huge sand dune and saw the camp which had been built three years before. As they neared the settlement, they noticed many changes. The colonists' houses had been torn down and a palisade built around the settlement. As they approached the palings, they found two inscriptions dug into the bark of a tree: CRO and CROATOAN, which White knew as the name of an island. But there wasn't a single colonist anywhere.

Governor White remembered that before leaving the island in 1587, he had secretly buried several chests containing his personal effects. When he found the hiding place, he discovered that Indians had uncovered the chests and stolen most of the goods, leaving only torn books, pictures and maps.

Before he left for England the colonists had told White that if they met with trouble they would carve a cross into a tree near the settlement. There was no cross on the tree which bore the word CROATOAN,[1] nor on any other tree nearby. Therefore, it must be assumed that the colonists left Roanoke willingly for the purpose of finding a better place to live.

Governor White did identify the chests as those he had buried three years before. This fact rules out the theory that he returned to the wrong island to search for his colony. Unquestionably what is known as Roanoke Island today was settled in 1587 by Governor White and his fellow colonists.

Manteo, the Indian who had journeyed to England, was born at Croatoan Island and Governor White knew from

---

[1] Incidentally, I learned that the famous "Croatoan" tree was still standing at Roanoke Island as late as 1778 on the shores of Shalumbus Bay.

him that the Indians there had always been friendly to the whites. This strengthened the supposition that the colonists had gone there.

Captain Wattes agreed to take White to try to find Croatoan but the next day a wild storm hit the coast and Wattes had to order his ship out to sea. The gale continued for days, making further search for Croatoan impossible. Then the winds shifted and the gale came in from the west. Captain Wattes had by now decided to return to the West Indies for fresh water and then come back and attempt a landing at Croatoan. But the storm was of such force that it blew him across to the Azores. From here he went to England, never to return to Croatoan.

By now Governor White's resources were spent. Neither he nor Walter Raleigh could raise funds for a further search for the Lost Colony. White spent his last years regretting, as he said in 1593, that his wealth did not equal his will to find the Lost Colony.

The fate of this little band of colonists remains a mystery to this day, but there are several stories which offer strong probabilities.

In 1864 three young men of the Croatoan tribe of Indians were brutally killed while working on the construction of Fort Fisher. At the inquest which was held afterwards, an old Croatoan Indian named George Lowrie, testified that his tribe had always been friendly to the white people at Roanoke Island. He explained that when the colonists there were in need, his tribe took them to their own island, Croatoan. Eventually, he said, the whites and Indians intermarried. No records were kept and nothing now remained of the Lost Colony but their dark-skinned descendants.

On at least four occasions Englishmen either heard of or met members of the Lost Colony. Captain John Smith, in 1607, heard that they were still alive. Over half a century later, John Lederer met their descendants and observed the long beards of the men. John Lawson saw white people living with the Indians in the vicinity of Roanoke in 1704. Of course, by this time many of those with white blood were almost indistinguishable from their Indian relatives, and blue eyes were often their only sign of white ancestry.

In his fine book, *The Riddle of the Lost Colony,* Melvin Robinson puts forth his opinion that the Lost Colony was originally located at what is now Ocracoke Island, not at Roanoke, as has been believed all these years. I cannot agree with this part of Mr. Robinson's book, but I do believe that the Lost Colony may have gone from Roanoke to Ocracoke in search of better conditions. More than this, I believe that Ocracoke may have been known as Croatoan in those days. This theory was strengthened when in the early 1940's I discovered an ancient map which had been printed over three centuries ago, with what is now Ocracoke Island plainly marked Croatoan. I was so enthused by this discovery that I visited Ocracoke as soon as I could and interviewed several of the older residents, hoping to glean bits of information from their recollections of the distant past. My interviews were successful, not in what these old people said, but in the manner and language with which they said it.

The old people of Ocracoke spoke a pure Elizabethan English, unaffected by time or the infiltration of other groups. As I listened to them talk, I was sure they were the descendants of the sixteenth century's Lost Colony, men and women who had settled on Roanoke Island and later migrated with the help of friendly Indians to Ocracoke Island. I believed that a few of them might have reached the mainland and intermarried with the Indians.

My theory was severely shaken when I later read of an amazing discovery which had taken place in 1937. If this "find" was authentic it completely destroyed my reasoning.

In September, 1937, one Louis E. Hammond of California was driving along a North Carolina causeway when, about three miles from a little town named Edenton, he decided to stop and search for hickory nuts. Several hundred yards from the road he came across a rock slab in the ground. There were what seemed to be hieroglyphics on the stone and so, in spite of its heaviness, he carried it back to the car.

Two months later, he visited Emory University in Atlanta and showed the stone to Hayward Jefferson Pearce, Professor of American History. Professor Pearce was much interested and set out to test the authenticity of the hieroglyphics. After many hours of careful, painstaking work, he had deciphered the markings. One side of the stone bore a short message:

ANANIAS DARE &
VIRGINIA WENT HENCE
VNTO HEAVEN 1591
ANY ENGLISHMAN SHEW
JOHN WHITE GOVR VIA

On the reverse side of the stone was a longer message:

FATHER SOON AFTER YOU GOE FOR ENGLAND WE CAME HITHER
ONLIE MISARIE & WARRETOW YEARE
ABOVE HALFE DEADE ERE TOW YEERE MOORE FROM SICKENES
  BEINE
FOVRE & TWENTIE
SALVAGE WITH MESAGE OF SHIPP VNTO US

SMALL SPACE OF TIME THEY AFFRITE OF REVENGE RANN AL
  ALWAYE
WEE BLEEVE YT NOTT YOU
SOON AFTER YE SALVAGES FAINE SPIRTS ANGRIE
SUDDIANE MVRTHER AL SAVE SEAVEN
MINE CHILDE ANANIAS TO SLAIN WTH MVCH MISARIE—
BURIE AL NEERE FOVRE MYLES EASTE THIS RIVER VPPON SMALL
  HIL
NAMES WRIT AL THER ON ROCKE
PUTT THIS THER ALSOE

284

SALVAGE SHEW THIS VNTO YOV & HITHER WEE PRIMISE YOV TO
GIVE GREATE PLENTIE PRESENTS

E W D [1]

Before announcing that the stone was authentic, Professor
Pearce submitted it to several kinds of experts for analysis.
Botanists testified that the mold in the grooves had been
there for many, many years. The Smithsonian Institution
stated that the rock showed no indication of fraud. Even
professional stonecutters were brought in, and they claimed
that they could never duplicate the inscription by modern
methods.

Professor Pearce was anxious to discover the other "rocks"
mentioned in the first inscription and learn the names of
those seventeen who died. After he advertised a $500 reward
for the stone, in the spring of 1939 a certain William Eber-
hart appeared with a rock bearing the date 1589, which he
said he had found near Greenville, South Carolina. Two
weeks later he returned with two more stones, also marked
"1589." The following week he brought in a fourth stone,
evidently the one which Pearce was anxious to obtain, for it
bore the date 1591 and the names of seventeen persons of
the Lost Colony.

Now Emory College officials developed a suspicion that
Louis E. Hammond, who had found the original stone,
should be questioned further. They asked Hammond to take
them to the scene of his discovery. As a result of their trip
and several other developments which cast suspicion on Hammond's story, the faculty of Emory College decided that they
could not accept the stone as genuine and requested that it
be removed.

Professor Pearce then took the original stone with him to
Brenau College, Georgia, where he had taken the office of
Vice-President, and where his father, Dr. Haywood Jefferson

---

[1] Eleanor White Dare.

Pearce, was President. More and more stones appeared until over forty had been gathered together at Brenau. Historians came from all over the country to examine the stones, and a majority, among them an historian whose famous name I shall be kind enough not to mention, declared them genuine.

In all, forty-eight inscribed stones were found within an area of four hundred miles, extending from North Carolina to the vicinity of Atlanta, Georgia. There were over seven hundred words inscribed on the various stones, and they gave a remarkable account of what had befallen the Lost Colony.

After considerable correspondence, I learned that Pulitzer prize winner George Goodwin of the *Atlantic Journal* had become fascinated with the stones at the time they were discovered and had written a story for his paper, describing them as authentic. Later I learned that the *Saturday Evening Post* had also published an article on the stones written by Boyden Sparks, in which Dr. Samuel Tannenbaum, eminent Elizabethan scholar, was quoted as declaring the stones an obvious forgery. I read these conflicting stories and determined to see the stones for myself and try to get to the bottom of what appeared to be a fantastic hoax.

In the fall of 1949, I asked my brother, Winthrop Snow, who lives in Atlanta, to visit the museum at Brenau College, where the stones are still on exhibition; then in January, 1950, he and I went to the museum together, examined the stones and took pictures of them. We found them piled up without any attempt at classification or identification.

In talking with residents of Georgia, I could see that they had long ago discounted the historical value of the stones. They told me that Eberhardt, who was apparently connected in some way or another with the discovery of nearly every stone, had been previously exposed as having sold fake Indian relics. It seems that Eberhardt also had had experience in stone cutting. On one occasion, for a suitable reward and in the presence of witnesses, he had inscribed, in a comparatively short time, a stone similar to those allegedly left by the Lost Colony.

Several nearby stone cutters had discounted the earlier statement that the inscriptions could not have been made by modern cutting methods. There were many ways, they said, of obtaining an appearance of antiquity. An Atlanta geologist had expressed the opinion that the ancient mold to be seen in the inscriptions had formed in natural crevices which were later used by a forger to appear as part of a letter. All the stone cutter did was to finish the letter suggested by the crevice.

We must, therefore, discard the stones as a deliberate hoax and my own theory that the Lost Colony migrated to Ocracoke Island remains a possible solution.

Each summer the magnificent symphonic drama, Paul Green's *Lost Colony,* is given at Waterside Theater on the site of the first settlement of Roanoke Island. Every year, more and more visitors come from far and wide to see the people of Roanoke portray the heroic colonists, the only persons we can be sure knew the answer to America's greatest mystery—what happened to the Lost Colony?

XVI. EYLAND MANATUS OR MANHATTAN ISLAND

MY LAST island was an easy one to reach, for more trains, planes and ships go to and from Manatus than any other island in the entire world. Eyland Manatus was the early Dutch name. Today it is, of course, better known as Manhattan Island, or New York City.

I had chosen my favorite method and time to arrive at Manatus—by air and at night. There is really nothing which compares to it. Long before we flew over western Connecticut, I could see a beautiful glow in the sky and later, with the city itself only ten miles away, there were tens of thousands of lights stretching off toward the horizon.

My purpose on Manhattan was to discover some of the hidden secrets of this giant island, the central core of the largest city in the world.

The recorded history of our modern world capital began when Verrazano sailed past its shores in 1524, but the island was not really discovered until Henry Hudson landed there on September 11, 1609. On May 6, 1626, Peter Minuit purchased the island from Indians for the equivalent of $24 and the Dutch settlement began. In 1635 Fort Amsterdam was erected where the Custom House stands today.

Named New Amsterdam, the settlement became a city in 1653. In that same year a wall was built along what is now Wall Street to protect the community against attack from the north. Peter Stuyvesant ruled as governor until the English captured the island and renamed it New York, on September 8, 1664. After a brief recapture of the city by the Dutch, who renamed it New Orange, New York fell again to the British in 1674.

During the American Revolution, the British captured the city. They held it for seven years, from September 14, 1776 until November 25, 1783. For a brief period after the war, 1785 to 1790, New York City was the capital of the United States.

But the facts quoted above are too well known by the average American to require more than brief mention here.

What I wished to discover on that first early morning walk around Manhattan were the forgotten episodes in the island's history. All day I trudged the streets, rode in taxis and even took bus tours. But my task was more than I had bargained for. Day after day passed and still new stories and locations lured me on and on.

I first visited the famous Bowery which probably would be known by another name if the city had never had a notorious governor who came to be thoroughly detested by his subjects. Director-General William Kieft was a real Jekyll and Hyde character, an odd combination of good and evil. An expert city administrator and farmer, he was a wanton destroyer in his dealings with the Indians. Soon after he arrived on Manhattan in 1638, Kieft established a strict régime which contrasted sharply with that of the man he succeeded, easy-going Governor Wouter Van Twiller.

Van Twiller had erected several windmills and laid out six *bouweries,* or farms, in the vicinity of what is known as the Bowery today. But he neglected the farms and allowed his subjects to become shiftless and lazy. Eventually he turned to other more profitable and less honest activities. The West India Company discovered his unfaithfulness and appointed William Kieft to take his place.

Governor Kieft soon had the *bouweries* working as well-organized farms, and the people once more became industrious and thrifty, though not without a certain amount of grumbling.

Although his stern domestic policy can be said to have been for the good of his people, Kieft's attitude toward the Indians led to nothing but trouble and grief. Without question, his stupid treatment of the redmen was largely responsible for the long period of hostility between natives and settlers which extended through generations of American colonization.

Indian warfare was always brutal and often unnecessary, but there was no precedent for the inhumanity of Kieft's vindictive behavior. On neighboring Staten Island, Captain De Vries had often had minor differences with the Indians and had been able to settle without resorting to violence. When he learned that Governor Kieft was ordering his troops to cross the Hudson on a mission to murder Indians, he voiced a strong protest. But Kieft was not a man to heed advice.

On the night of February 24, 1643, Kieft's troops crossed over to the New Jersey shore and massacred a hundred Indians asleep at their encampment.

The surviving Indians gained the support of other tribes in wreaking a terrible revenge. Scores of white people were slain up and down the Hudson River, and for the next four months the life of the Dutch community was completely disrupted. In October De Vries gave up the fight and fled the country, telling Kieft as he sailed away that some day he would pay for his cruel and short-sighted treatment of the Indians.

That winter only two hundred men remained to defend

the Manatus colony against a force of Indians seven times their number. The Indians, had they realized it, could have killed every person on the island. Fortunately, they did not make the attempt and by the end of the winter both Indians and whites were ready to smoke the pipe of peace. The terrible warfare came to an end.

When the surviving residents of New Amsterdam complained against Kieft's ruthless policies, a new governor, Peter Stuyvesant, was appointed. Kieft embarked for Hol-

EARLY VIEW OF MANHATTAN ISLAND

land but his ship was wrecked during the voyage and he was drowned. There were those who saw in his death a vindication of De Vries' prophecy. For all his wrong-headedness and arrogance, however, New York's early *bouweries* would have been abandoned if it had not been for Kieft, and his industry has been acknowledged by the retention of the old name, Bowery.

I walked west from the Bowery to Broadway and took that famous street to reach Trinity Church, which stands at the end of the narrow canyon known as Wall Street. It was peaceful and quiet as I reached the cemetery to the south of the church, and I stopped for a moment or two at the impressive tomb of Alexander Hamilton, killed in 1804 in a duel with Aaron Burr. Close at hand was the memorial to Robert Fulton, disputed inventor [1] of the steamboat. He was buried in the Livingston vault at Trinity Churchyard and his remains are still there, although most historians claim that the Fulton memorial is his tomb.

Albert Gallatin, William Bradford, Sir Henry Moore and Marinus Willet are also buried here, as well as Captain James Lawrence of the ill-fated *Chesapeake,* who, mortally wounded in battle off Boston Light, shouted the famous last words, "Don't give up the ship!"

One stone in Trinity Cemetery is something of a mystery. Back in the early 1800's Susannah Haswell Rowson, who had had a very interesting career which included rescue from a shipwreck in Boston Harbor at the age of five, published a novel entitled *Charlotte Temple,* a best seller in its day. It is said that one of the many readers and admirers of the book was a stonecutter at Trinity Churchyard. So deeply touched was he by the story that he attempted to change fiction into fact and placed a slab bearing the name "Charlotte Temple" in the cemetery. Those who stop at the grave are usually told that the lady buried there came to America with a British army officer who later deserted her, leaving her to die in poverty and misery. There are many who visit the tomb of Charlotte Temple, and not a few leave a flower to her memory. But as far as we know, there never was a Charlotte Temple except in the novel of the same name!

The oldest known stone at Trinity is that of a five-year-old boy, Richard Churcher, who died in April, 1681, before the first Trinity Church was erected in 1697. The present building is the third Trinity Church, the first having burned down

---

[1] It is the adherents of Samuel Morey, whose steamboat did more than four knots against the stream in 1790, and not followers of erratic John Fitch, Fulton's supporters must challenge. See *Samuel Morey, the Edison of His Day,* by George Calvin Carter of Manchester, New Hampshire.

in 1776 and the second having been condemned and torn down in the middle of the 18th century.

Not too far from the oldest stone is a curious monument to Sidney Breese:

> Sidney Breese, June 9, 1767
> Made by himself
> Lyest thous here
> I here Lye
> Till time is flow
> To its Eternity

I read the inscription on the tomb of William Bradford who published New York's first newspaper in 1725, only twenty-one years after Boston's *News-Letter* appeared. Bradford's *Gazette* was primarily a government-controlled publication and was instrumental in bringing about the controversial Zenger trial by its suppression of facts.

This affair had its beginning in 1732, when Governor William Cosby took office and demanded that Rip Van Dam, acting president of the city council, turn over half of his salary to the governor. When Van Dam refused, Cosby ordered him brought before the Supreme Court judges, who ruled two to one in the governor's favor. The dissenting judge, Chief Justice Lewis Morris, was promptly removed from office and replaced by James De Lancey.[1]

During Van Dam's scandal the *Gazette* had so one-sidedly championed Cosby's "cause" that Van Dam's friends decided an opposition newspaper would have to be published. John Peter Zenger was chosen as editor of this antigovernment publication, called the *Weekly Journal*. Zenger's brillance as an editorial writer brought him into early disfavor with the administration and when he criticized the governor's act of

---

[1] In 1763, De Lancey forced Governor Danvers Osborne to give him control of the government. Osborne felt so dishonored by this transaction that he then hanged himself from his garden wall.

removing Morris from the judgeship, Zenger was thrown into jail and his newspaper publicly burned.

In those days, any complaint against a public official was automatically libelous. The justice of the complaint was not taken into consideration. Therefore, as Zenger discovered, if there was any criticism of the administration in a newspaper, its editor could be thrown into prison. Peter Zenger was soon tried for libel, both "false and seditious."

Realizing that his hope of winning his case was very slim, he obtained the services of a grand old man, Andrew Hamilton of Philadelphia, who traveled to New York without fee to fight for freedom of the press in the colonies.

Zenger's trial began in August, 1735. An enormous crowd packed the courtroom and listened carefully to the charge of the attorney-general. Then eighty-year-old Hamilton stood up and asked for a chance to prove the truth or falsity of the accusation. The judge refused the request.

Hamilton cited this refusal when he addressed the jury. He emphasized that every free man had a right to complain against the abuses of power and to fight for his own liberty. He made clear that more was at stake than the freedom of a poor printer to speak his mind; that the rights of every citizen of the British Government in America were being threatened.

The jury retired after listening to the admonition of the judge and returned almost immediately with the verdict of "Not Guilty." Pandemonium broke loose and there were many celebrations on old Manatus Island that night. Andrew Hamilton's victory for John Peter Zenger has been called one of the greatest triumphs for the democratic spirit in pre-Revolutionary America.

Before leaving Trinity Churchyard, I paused at the grave of Lady Catherine Cornbury, whose husband was made Governor of New York in 1702. Governor Edward Hyde, or Lord Cornbury, as he was known, was the man for whom Hyde Park is named. The eldest son of the Earl of Clarendon, Hyde was a depraved profligate, completely devoid of morals or decency.

When Lord and Lady Cornbury landed at the Battery, guns boomed from the fort and crowds cheered as they made their way to a waiting carriage. A short time later a banquet was held in Lord Cornbury's honor and he was presented with two thousand pounds to pay his expenses in reaching New York. His High Mightiness, as they called New York governors in those days, had promised to deliver a speech at the end of the feast and those present waited eagerly to hear the new executive's views on city administration.

But the astounded audience was treated instead to an emotional and ecstatic eulogy on a strange subject for a governor's speech—Lady Cornbury's ears! They were, he said, "the most beautiful in Christendom," but what possible bearing they had on affairs of state was more than his hearers could understand.

At the conclusion of his "speech," Cornbury asked every man in the banquet hall to line up for the pleasure of feeling the delicate texture of Lady Cornbury's ears. When all gentlemen present had carried out the governor's strange orders, Lord Cornbury allowed his distinguished audience to go home, considerably bewildered and alarmed.

A short time later Governor Cornbury drove his horse up the steps and into the doorway of the King's Arms Tavern. He demanded whisky for himself and water for his horse and then galloped out of the tavern.

Some nights after this curious event, a watchman near Fort Amsterdam noticed a woman walking slowly along the ramparts. He shouted at her to get down at once. Her response was coy and the outraged watchman decided that he would have to remove her by force. Seizing his cudgel, he climbed the wall and soon overtook the woman.

"Come, now," the watchman cried, "you'll leave the fort." But scarcely had he spoken the words when the woman threw her arms around his neck and began pulling at his ears.

Then the horrified watchman discovered that it was Governor Cornbury, dressed in his wife's best clothes!

When his prey had fled, Lord Cornbury went back into the fort, singing at the top of his voice. From time to time the governor repeated this strange performance, always dressed in the clothes of his wife.

In 1703 Lord Cornbury built a fantastic "pleasure house" on Nutten's Island, according to Cadwallader Cobden. History is sensibly silent as to Cornbury's activities there.

Lady Cornbury was almost as strange as her husband. She decided to create a court around herself, commanding six of the most aristocratic girls in the domain to serve as ladies-in-waiting. When they arrived, the governor's wife discharged her servants and put the girls to work as cooks and chambermaids. After they objected, Lord Cornbury had a guard posted around the mansion, threatening the girls with the lash or even prison if they tried to escape. It wasn't until several weeks later that the girls' parents realized what had happened and descended upon the governor's mansion to remove their outraged offspring.

Later, Lady Cornbury took to visiting the homes of various citizens and commandeering any of their possessions which caught her fancy. Unless the owner offered to buy it back at double its value, the chosen article would then be sold to junk men.

On August 11, 1706, four years after she came to New York, Lady Cornbury died and was buried in the Trinity Churchyard. Her husband was removed from office two years later. But his creditors prevented his departure from the city. They put him in debtors' prison, where he languished for several months, until his father conveniently died, making Cornbury the Earl of Clarendon. Money was now sent from England, most of his debts were paid and this unusual character sailed from New York forever. Over a hundred years later Lady Cornbury's coffin-plate was discovered in the Trinity Church vault and it is copied below to remind a forgetful New York of a strange period in its long and full history:

DEUS NOBIS HAEC OTIA FECIT

Catherine Lady Viscountess Cornbury Baroness of Clifton of Leighton Bromswoold County of Warniek, sole surviving Daughter & Heir of Henry Lord Obrian & the Lady Catherine his wife; who was Sole Sister & heir to the Most Noble Charles Duke of Richmond & Lenox born The 29th day of Jany in the year of 1673 Departed this life att the City of New York
In America the 11th day of August 1706 in the 34 year of her age.

It is a standing joke that slick New Yorkers are wont to sell Brooklyn Bridge and other choice bits of property to unsuspecting visitors from the country. But the boldest of modern city slickers would never attempt a hoax as ingenious as the one I am about to describe.[1] Even Edgar Allan Poe, who duped New York and the rest of the country in 1844 with his famous balloon hoax, could have taken a lesson from two men named Lozier and DeVoe.

In the 1820's the Grand Street Market was a favorite gathering place for those who wanted to sit and pass the time of day. Retired business men and produce dealers came regularly to lounge on the benches in front of the market, to exchange gossip and spin yarns. Two of the more active talkers among the habitués of the place were John DeVoe and his friend, a man who called himself Lozier.

Lozier was a retired contractor and comparatively wealthy. Since he had traveled widely and was a man of some standing, his words and advice were eagerly listened to. He made the most of his authority. No subject was beneath his notice; no

---

[1] We are indebted to Thomas Farrington DeVoe for this story, which he published in his *Market Book* in 1862.

event took place in the political or social world which Lozier couldn't explain in detail. Most of his listeners really believed that Lozier was an intimate of the great people of the day.

One warm week in July, 1823, Lozier disappeared for a few days. The men who congregated in front of the market commented on his unusual absence when Lozier finally returned, but he was silent, an event which, in itself, his friends considered significant. Finally, after much pressure, Lozier admitted that he had been down at the City Hall in secret conference with Mayor Stephen Allen.

Lozier didn't reveal what had taken place at his meeting with the mayor for several days, but gradually his friends extracted the full story from him. Allen had called Lozier in to discuss a terrible calamity which was about to descend on Manhattan Island. Because there were far too many buildings at the southern end of the island, Manhattan was beginning to sink into the water all the way from City Hall to the Battery. Already it had sagged to such an extent that the land went downhill the entire distance from the Commons to the waterfront. There was imminent danger that this section of the island would break off and disappear into the ocean. The mayor appealed to Lozier to use his great knowledge of engineering and construction to find some means of avoiding this catastrophe.

After much discussion, Lozier and the mayor had agreed that the only solution to the problem was to saw off Manhattan at Kingsbridge, turn it around and fit the convex Battery end of the island into the concave northern end! With this heavy piece of land in position at the north, the weight on the island would be balanced and safety would be assured for countless generations of New Yorkers.

However, Lozier explained, he and Mayor Allen did not agree as to the method of solving their problem. Lozier's plan was to float the severed section of Manhattan out into the bay and turn it around; the mayor believed that this could not be done until Long Island had been moved out of the way. Lozier's view eventually won out and he told his associates of the fact several weeks later. For political reasons, Mayor Allen had turned the entire project over to Lozier, authorizing him to supervise the work himself and obtain the necessary labor and equipment.

Lozier's story was made to seem more credible by the fact that the Erie Canal was then in the final stages of construction. Whenever a doubt was raised, he reminded his listeners how many prominent engineers had announced that the Erie Canal was an impossible scheme, only to be proved wrong later. And if a canal could be run through the very heart of a mountain, why couldn't an island be sawed off and moved to another place?

One morning Lozier appeared at the benches in front of the Grand Street Market and announced that he was about to record the names of all who were interested in jobs on the new project. The records were to be kept by "Uncle John" DeVoe, and the name, age and address of each applicant was duly written down. Within a comparatively short time, three hundred men had volunteered for the task of sawing off the southern end of Manhattan Island.

Lozier then told several butchers that in order to feed his huge labor force he would need plenty of chickens, hogs and cattle. For a starter, he ordered 5000 chickens, 1500 cattle and 1000 hogs. Because of the size of this order, prices went up at once in the markets in New York.

Now Lozier engaged several master carpenters to build barracks as housing for the many workmen needed on the project. Over-anxious contractors delivered load after load of lumber to a designated point near Kingsbridge so that construction could begin as soon as Lozier gave the signal.

The following week Lozier appeared with detailed plans for the equipment needed to accomplish his project. Eighty gigantic saws were to be manufactured, each more than 150 feet long and with teeth four feet apart. Each one would require fifty men to work it.

To bring the sawed-off section to its new location, Lozier had drawn plans for twenty-four oars no less than 250 feet long and twenty-four rowlock towers to hold the giant oars in place. Twelve were to be mounted on the East River and twelve on the Hudson, and for each oar one hundred men would be needed. In case of a storm during the moving process, giant chains and anchors were designed to prevent southern Manhattan from blowing out to sea.

Laborers who manipulated the under-water ends of the saws were to receive three times the regular pay. Volunteers were many for this particular job, and trials were held in which each applicant demonstrated his breath-holding abilities.

As the weeks went by and the prospective work force grew, Lozier kept delaying actual execution of the project. First, there were not enough laborers and then estimates on the towers and oars were not satisfactory. But finally he could delay no longer. He announced that all the workers should report the following Monday at Number 1 Bowery, on the corner of Spring Street. Lozier himself would head the march to Kingsbridge, accompanied by a fife and drum corps.

Almost five thousand workmen presented themselves at the time and place set by Lozier. The fife and drum corps, laborers, contractors, butchers, cattle, hogs and chickens milled around the street in hopeless confusion. Everyone was there—with two important exceptions: Superintendent Lozier and his assistant, Uncle John DeVoe. After several hours a group walked over to the Grand Street Market to find their leaders, believing that some last-minute oversight had caused a delay. But neither Lozier nor DeVoe could be found at the market and gradually the would-be saviors of Manhattan Island realized that they had been hoaxed.

The unhappy emissaries went back to Spring Street and the Bowery to find the fife and drum corps listlessly performing to the accompaniment of moos from the cattle and grunts from the hogs. The men gathered there were in no frame of mind for the announcement which followed, and if either Lozier or DeVoe had come in sight, there is little doubt that they would have been strung up and hanged on the spot. But with no way of expressing their fury, the victims gradually drifted off, telling each other that it had been a wild plan at best.

Two weeks later Lozier and DeVoe reappeared at the well-worn benches outside the Grand Street Market, but even they could not have called their reception a cordial one.

Salem, Massachusetts, has long been known, and falsely so, as the center of witch-burning in America. Actually, the records show that no one was ever burned at the stake in Salem, although nineteen men and women were hanged and a twentieth pressed to death, all because of a wicked rumor spread by an eleven-year-old girl.

It is a well-kept secret that in 1741, on Manhattan Island, a series of events took place which outdid anything that ever occurred in Salem for brutality and fiendishness. New York was so thoroughly ashamed of itself afterwards that it is no wonder that modern Manhattanites know little of this disgraceful chapter in their city's history.

During the winter of 1740-1741 a Spanish pirate vessel was captured and brought into New York harbor. As was often the custom in those days, the members of the crew were sold into slavery and became servants in many of the prosperous homes on the island. As might be expected, they were surly and unwilling and were often heard to utter threats against their masters. Still, their grumbling had not assumed dangerous proportions and everything seemed normal on the island until the early spring of 1741.

Suddenly, in the middle of March, within a period of about a week, a series of fires broke out on the island. There was no alarm at the first two or three, but as more fires sprang up, there were whispers that this was the work of the Devil, in league with human witches.

All of the fires except one or two were probably accidental and at most there were not more than two firebugs at work, but rumors spread and took hold that witches were planning to destroy the city. It was not long before the entire island was engulfed by an hysterical fear like that which had so disrupted the city of Salem half a century earlier. This hysteria was to prove far more disastrous than New England's reign of terror.

In the middle of the panic a certain Mrs. Earle announced that on the preceding Sunday she had watched three servants swaggering along Broadway when suddenly she heard one of them exclaim: "Fire, fire, scorch, scorch, a little damn by and by!" Then, she said, the men fell to laughing strangely and the speaker threw up his hands in a peculiar way, as though he might be pledging obeisance to the Evil One.

Mrs. Earle believed that this episode might have had some connection with the mysterious fires and she decided to report the incident to an alderman. The alderman, in turn, informed the justices, and from that day on there was no stopping the idea that the Devil had authorized his human representatives to destroy New York and its population.

The very next day another fire broke out and the crowd which gathered saw a servant leave the blazing house at the last minute. "Catch him, catch him!" came a cry, and the mob ran to corner the miserable servant in an orchard. He was carried to the jail and imprisoned.

The city government now took steps to prevent further fires. All suspicious persons carrying bundles were stopped and searched, though nothing of an incriminating nature was found. When no one was caught setting fires, the officials were more than ever convinced that the Devil himself was responsible.

By the middle of April excitement was reaching greater and greater heights and the government ordered the militia out. Scores of ordinary citizens believed that Manhattan was already doomed to destruction and, packing whatever they could carry, they fled the island. Those who lived along the highways, especially the farmers, were panicked in turn. Soon there were hordes of families clogging the roads in their efforts to escape the evil power which they believed was in control of the island.

Many servants of both sexes were arrested and hurried off to jail. The Supreme Court was not to sit until late in April and the officials decided they would have to act at once to stop the occasional "mysterious" fires which still occurred. They offered a reward of one hundred pounds to any prisoner who would confess or implicate others in the wicked attempts to destroy New York. Not one prisoner volunteered information in order to obtain the tempting sum.

On April 21 the Supreme Court met, with Judges Adolphus Philipse and Daniel Horsmanden [1] presiding. By this time one Mary Burton, imprisoned servant of John Hughson, had been threatened with death and when the officials appealed to her conscience she decided to confess, though the crimes of which she knew had no bearing on the fire-setting. It seemed that Mary's master, Mr. Hughson, had allowed stolen goods to be accepted in trade by one of his tenants, a prostitute named Peggy Carey, alias Margaret Sorubiero, the "Newfoundland Beauty." When the men of Peggy's acquaintance, mostly servants, wished to visit her and were short of money, they brought her stolen household furniture as substitute for cash.

Two servants, Caesar and Prince, were specifically accused by Mary Burton of stealing goods from their masters to bring to Peggy Carey. As the stealing was presumably done with

---

[1] Horsmanden wrote a summary of the affair, *The New York Conspiracy*, but his efforts were published "before the delusion had passed away." So his remarks were influenced by the spell of the Evil One, which had not then abated.

the sanction of the Hughsons, husband and wife, all five persons implicated were soon lodged in jail. It did not seem to occur to the authorities that these sordid and petty transactions had no connection with the fires. They were sure that if only they probed deeper, they would get to the heart of the matter. They prodded Mary Burton for fresh revelations until the girl realized that she would get no peace unless she invented the sort of evidence they wanted to hear. She now made up an entirely new series of accusations which more than satisfied the worried officials. There were a great many servants and slaves, white and black, she said, who had joined in a conspiracy for the complete destruction of New York by fire and the massacre of all the inhabitants. She claimed that Hughson planned to become the new governor and that a servant named Cuff, in the employ of the Philipse family, was plotting to reign as King of Manhattan.

Peggy Carey was brought onto the witness stand. At first she denied all of Mary Burton's accusations. But when she was sentenced to death, she decided that if she could implicate others in a series of false charges, she herself might go free. She now confessed to plotting destruction with a certain John Romme who lived in a miserable little shanty down near the Battery. Romme was the ringleader, she said, and his plans were complete. After stealing many articles from various homes on the island, he would order the servants and slaves at his command to burn all the houses and kill the inhabitants. He would then arrange passage for his followers overseas, where they could start life anew as free people.

The New York militia rushed down to Romme's shanty with a warrant for his arrest but, warned of Peggy Carey's falsehoods, Romme had fled the island. His wife, who had not thought it necessary to escape, was apprehended and placed in jail.

On May 11, 1741, after a brief and wholly unfair trial, the servants, Caesar and Prince, were taken out to a little island in a fresh water pond [1] and hanged. Many of those who had fled Manhattan returned when they heard that two of the Devil's agents had been sentenced to die and hundreds of New Yorkers were on hand for the executions.

By now, all of Mary Burton's early reluctance to give false testimony had completely vanished. She had already claimed that the authorities would find guns and ammunition in the attic of Hughson's tavern. The fact that the militia found nothing of the sort should have made the officials doubt her word, but all reason had long since vanished in the face of hysteria.

The city fathers now turned their attention to the leading actor in one of Mary Burton's more imaginative stories, the servant Cuff, who planned to be King of Manhattan. When Cuff was brought to trial, he decided to prolong the proceedings by implicating another servant named Quack, who, according to Cuff, had attempted to force him into setting the fort on fire. Others testified against the pair and it was agreed that the real perpetrators of the series of fires were Cuff and Quack. They were sentenced to die and, for what is believed to be the first time in the history of America, the chosen method of execution was burning at the stake.

On May 30, 1741, the residents of Manhattan arose early and flocked to the place where Cuff and Quack were to be executed. Before an excited mob the two terrified and trembling men were chained to stakes set up twenty yards apart. Faggots were piled high around them and soon all was in readiness for the executioner to light the torch. But both men, desperately grasping at a final respite, shouted out that they had additional information to reveal. The executioner then ordered Cuff and Quack unchained until it was decided whether their last-minute testimony would be heard.

The executioner and the sheriff debated at length as to whether the condemned men should be returned to prison

---

[1] The Tombs and the Criminal Courts Building now stand where this pond used to be.

and given further hearing, but the sheriff prevailed with the decision that the men had been sentenced to die and die they must then and there.

Cuff and Quack were chained to the stakes again and this time the torch was applied to the fagots. As the flames began to reach the two men smoke concealed them from view but their cries were heard even above the roar of the huge fire, and the little valley where they burned grew hotter and hotter. The heat became so intense that the crowd was forced to retreat as the shrieks of anguish from the men in the flames grew fainter and fainter and at last stopped altogether. Two hours later two wretched bodies, burned to a crisp, remained as mute evidence of man's inhumanity to man.

Soon another servant named Curaçao Jack, who had been accused of setting several of the fires, was given a quick trial and, with three others, sentenced to be burned at the stake on June 7. Within a few days of this multiple execution two more men met their death by the same horrible method and three were hanged, all near the site of City Hall.

Mary Burton, who had by now grown fond of publicity, had vaguely accused a Catholic priest named John Ury, a school teacher in the city, of being a party to the plot. The authorities who had already sentenced to death Hughson and his wife, allowed their daughter Sarah to remain alive when she promised to testify further against Father Ury. The girl swore that the priest was a witch. As proof she said that she had watched him take a piece of chalk and, in the presence of an audience, kneel down on her father's spacious tavern-room floor and draw a large ring of white. Then, according to the imaginative girl, Father Ury stepped across into the ring, uttering strange words in a language which had been furnished him for the occasion by the Devil. As she watched, Father Ury had sworn every person present to secrecy before he took certain mysterious liquids and scattered them over the faces of his audience. Then he had conducted another witchlike ritual.

THE EXECUTION OF CUFF

Others, eager to save their own necks, stepped forward to further incriminate the helpless priest. In vain Father Ury repeated that he had no part in any plot against the people of New York. His words were unheard and he was sentenced to be hanged.

Fresh from her triumph over the priest, Mary Burton began a new series of wholesale accusations. Scores of persons were so frightened that they began to accuse their neighbors before their neighbors could accuse them.

One servant, to escape execution himself, implicated fourteen others, all of whom were executed except for still another confessor, who in turn implicated another large group who were likewise sent to their death. And so it went through that terrible Summer of Suspicion, 1741.

On June 12, Hughson, his wife and the Newfoundland Beauty, Peggy Carey, were conducted to the gallows. As the hangman's cart drove them to the scene of execution, Hughson dramatically pointed to heaven, as though to indicate that help would soon come to him from that direction. The authorities had tried every means possible to make him confess that he had set the fires in league with the Devil, but Hughson admitted to nothing but the truth: he was aware of the petty thievery to which Peggy Carey was a willing accomplice. Even Peggy herself recanted on the gallow steps. She said that since she was to be hanged anyway, she might as well admit that her accusation against Romme was a lie and that her only crimes were prostitution and thievery.

After the Hughsons and Peggy Carey had been hanged, John Hughson's body was cut down and taken with that of the previously executed Caesar to a high gibbet where their remains were encircled with iron bands and chains and exhibited for many hot summer weeks to the terrified populace.

The city jails grew so crowded that the judges were forced to choose quickly between executing and pardoning in order to make room for new victims.

But Mary Burton, the hysterical heroine of the Summer

of Suspicion, gradually became overconfident of her own powers. She began to accuse persons of wealth and position. They remembered certain glaring irregularities in her testimony and put a stop to the executions—excepting one.

On August 29, 1741, Father John Ury was driven to the gallows in the hangman's cart and the noose fastened around his neck. Then in the presence of a large crowd of more than a thousand sadistic watchers, his hands, holding the cross, were tied together in front of him and the horse was started up, pulling the wagon from under the priest. Father Ury then stepped out to his death.

There was a certain awesome feeling in the air the August day that Father Ury was hanged and those who had convicted him decided that his would be the last execution.

Mary Burton was given her one hundred pounds and departed the city. September 24 was proclaimed a Day of Thanksgiving for those who escaped destruction. But for those whose friends or relatives had been burned at the stake, hanged or deported, there was little to be thankful for that day.

We shall never know whether the persons actually responsible for some of the fires were punished along with the innocent. After saner heads took control of the ghastly situation and stopped the executions, there were no more fires and there was no more talk of the Evil One for many years.

But from May 11 to August 29, 1741, one hundred and fifty-four persons had been crowded into the little Manhattan prison. Of these seventy-one were deported to a foreign land, never to return; twenty-two were hanged; and to New York's everlasting shame, fourteen victims were chained to the stake and burned alive.

As in the case of the Salem witchcraft trials, the court proceedings on Manhattan Island were dignified and orderly but they were so dominated by the unspoken hysteria in the crowded courtroom that not one person dared to defend a single prisoner, and those executed perished without a word of testimony in their favor.

Man's treatment of man is often beyond comprehension. During that terrible Summer of Suspicion, fear so gripped the people of Manhattan that they became wild and inhuman, like the imaginary representatives of the Devil they sought to destroy.

At Tompkins Square I paused at the memorial to those more than one thousand persons who lost their lives on the *General Slocum* in the worst peacetime marine disaster ever to occur in the United States.

The *General Slocum* was launched on April 18, 1891, and at the time was considered the queen of pleasure crafts. She was a four-decked paddle-wheeler, 250 feet long, with a beam of seventy feet, and could do sixteen knots for fifty miles. Named for Major-General Henry W. Slocum of Civil War fame, she was owned by the Knickerbocker Steamship Company of New York.

In her first twelve years, the *Slocum* encountered a series of minor accidents, each of which might have led to real disaster. One night, with 4700 people aboard, the vessel hit a sandbar and panic was narrowly averted. On another occasion, during a squall, she hit bottom off Coney Island, and the captain and crew fought the panicked passengers until they could be transferred to another ship. Again, on June 16, 1902, the *Slocum* ran aground briefly in Jamaica Bay with two thousand aboard.

On the morning of June 15, 1904, St. Mark's Evangelical Lutheran Church had chartered the *General Slocum* to take some 1800 of their parishioners to a Sunday-school picnic at Forest Grove, Long Island. About one hundred men accompanied their families on the trip, but most of the passengers were women and children.

There was a holiday atmosphere on board as the *Slocum* left her pier near the Brooklyn Bridge and made her way toward Hell Gate. Although there was a slight wind, the weather was sunny and the sea was calm. A band which had been hired for the day merrily played the old favorite tunes.

Then as the *General Slocum,* guided by the skillful hands of her master, Captain Van Schaick, drew abeam of the 138th Street shore slip, smoke began to pour from the woodwork near the cook's galley. The fire which caused it had started in a nearby storeroom filled with paint, oil and rope. These inflammable materials quickly burst into flames and in a matter of minutes the fire began to spread to the rest of the ship.

Captain Van Schaick's first instinct was to beach the *Slocum* near the 138th Street slip, but when he considered what a blazing ship might do to the gigantic oil tanks on the Harlem shore, he steered for North Brother Island, half a mile away.

Now, in what was a matter of seconds, not minutes, the flames spread from stem to stern of the wooden vessel and hundreds of screaming women and children were caught in the holocaust.

The trapped passengers stampeded in their efforts to escape, and, where the pressure was greatest, scores of women and children were trampled to death. The deck-rail gave way in several places and many shrieking victims were pushed into the river to their death. Others, who were packed together in the path of the fire, were burned where they stood, the flames spreading from one person's clothing to another's in a split second.

Meanwhile, although not ten minutes had elapsed since the smoke was first noticed, the crew was manning the pumps and the hose. Efficient as they were, their efforts were ineffective. They found most of the hoses rotted and the pumps rusted. There were more than enough lifebelts for the passengers aboard, but most of them were lashed with wire to the ceilings beyond the reach of all but the tallest women. The few lifebelts which were put to use were found to be worthless, for they had been filled with a cork and glue mixture which sent their wearers straight to the bottom of the bay.

Most of the one hundred men aboard the *Slocum* snatched one or two children and leaped into the sea, saving scores of helpless boys and girls.

From all up and down the water front, rescuers were on their way, but they were too late to accomplish very much. The dry wooden decks of the *General Slocum* had ignited so rapidly that within nineteen minutes after the fire was discovered, the upper decks had collapsed, carrying scores of dead and dying into the furnacelike hull below. No rescuing vessel could get within twenty feet of the burning ship because of the intense heat, and only a few who leaped into the sea were rescued. Later the heat went down a trifle.

One tug steamed up close to the windward side of the *Slocum* and lashed onto the paddle wheel where two hundred persons were clinging. After over fifty passengers had been rescued from the wheel, the tug itself burst into flames. A quick-thinking Negro deckhand proved to be the hero of the situation. He flung a tarpaulin over the blaze, rushed for the hose and soon had the fire extinguished. The entire party on the tug reached shore in safety.

Other craft weaved in and out through the flames, pulling the living and the dead from the surrounding waters. Through it all, the *Slocum* continued on her mad dash for North Brother Island. When she finally grounded in the shallow water off the island, many women and children leaped into the harbor, believing that they could wade ashore, but the water was over their heads and most of them drowned before crews from the rescue tugs could reach them.

By this time, the New York Harbor fireboats had reached the *Slocum* and were pouring tons and tons of water into her smouldering hull. Other craft continued to circle the death ship, rescuing an occasional mother or a child from the debris before it was too late. Finally, there were none left on board the *Slocum* but the dead.

No one will ever know exactly how many people lost their lives in the disaster, but various estimates run from 1031 to 1200 men, women and children. Every member of the crew escaped except the steward, to whom money was more important than life. When he leaped into the sea he was so loaded down with silver coins that he never rose to the surface.

There were many heroes of the catastrophe. Eighteen-year-old Charles Schwartz, Jr., was one. He swam back and forth from the burning vessel until he had saved the lives of twenty-two women and children. Many of the nurses at the hospital on North Brother Island plunged into the harbor and swam out again and again to rescue scores of passengers.

Policeman Hubert C. Farrell and Special Officer James Collins went out from shore in a yawl and found several persons hanging to the paddle wheel. "I will never forget that sight," said Farrell later. "Above us was a fiery furnace. Clinging to one of the paddles was an old man, and on either shoulder was a child. I got out on the paddle wheel and grabbed first one and then the other child. But the old man fought with me, for I think he believed I was going to drown him. But I finally got him into the yawl with the others. It was hotter around that wreck than I ever believed it possible."

James L. Wade, owner of the tug *Wade,* in which he had invested his life's savings, ran his boat ashore close to the *Slocum* in order that it could be used as a bridge for the struggling passengers. Soon the *Wade* itself caught fire and was burning briskly by the time the fireboats arrived. Wade felt that his only possession was of no importance when compared to the human lives it had saved.

One of the marvelous escapes of the holocaust was that of Clara Hartman, fifteen years of age, whose body was picked up in the harbor and placed in a row of twenty-nine dead at the Alexander Avenue Station. Three hours later a woman who was searching for her missing relatives came to Clara Hartman's body and saw that she was alive. She shouted to the doctors nearby who ran to the girl and found that she was still breathing faintly.

Clara Hartman was rushed to the Lincoln Hospital where she eventually recovered. Some time later one of the doctors noticed a tag tied to her clothing and cut it off with his knife. "She doesn't need this any more," he said, and threw it into the waste-basket. It was the identification number the morgue attendants had attached to her apparently life-less body.

Blame for the *Slocum's* catastrophe was later placed on Captain Van Schaick, Captain Pease of the Knickerbocker Steamship Company and the steamboat inspection service. It is said that very little actual punishment was ever enforced, though at the time of the disaster the aroused citizens of New York were assured that the guilty would suffer in proportion to their negligence. Many such disasters are forgotten in a few years and the public is easily lulled into a feeling of security with a minimum of effort.

To obtain my last story I went to a busy corner on New York's east side. Here one of America's great heroes, Nathan Hale, was executed during the Revolution. The words he spoke just before he was hanged have been repeated thousands of times, but there are few who know where those words were spoken.

Born in South Coventry, Connecticut, in 1752, Nathan Hale was interested at an early age in becoming a teacher, but his father, a deacon, sent him to Yale to study for the ministry. Young Hale's interest in the ministry did not increase at college, but he did show great prowess both as a student and as an athlete. At his commencement in 1773 he debated in Latin on the advantages of female education and won for his side, the affirmative.

Young Hale and his step-sister, Alice Adams, fell madly in love about this time, but stern Deacon Hale forbad the courtship and finally forced his step-daughter into a marriage with one Elijah Ripley. There was no other girl for Nathan Hale, however, and when Ripley died a year after his marriage, Alice revealed that she still loved him, too. But they never met again.

After his graduation Nathan Hale still wanted to teach school. His first position was at Haddam, Connecticut, and within a year he had received an offer of a better post at the Union Grammar School in New London. His plans for a quiet and useful life were disrupted, however, when news of the battle of Lexington and Concord reached New Haven. A mass meeting was held in Miner's tavern the night the news arrived and Nathan Hale was the last person to speak. He warmly advocated the formation of a Connecticut regiment and ended by saying, "Let us not lay down our arms until we have gained independence!"

The next day Nathan Hale returned to the school and debated his next step. He wrote a letter to his classmate, Benjamin Talmadge, asking for advice. Talmadge suggested that Hale give up teaching and fight for the independence of his country.

Hale resigned from his teaching position within a short time and on September 1, 1775, was commissioned a captain in Colonel Knowlton's Connecticut regiment. That regiment was quartered in New York City when the Declaration of Independence was read there on July 9, 1776, and Hale watched with delight as the citizens of Manhattan overturned the statue of the king at Bowling Green.

A month later Hale mounted the redoubts during the battle which took place on Long Island after the British fleet landed on the Brooklyn shore. Gradually, the Yankees were forced to withdraw on their right flank, with the enemy pressing them hard. Then, by a great stroke of good fortune, a severe rainstorm sent the British back to their tents, and when the rain ended, one of the best-timed fogs in history set in to shelter the Americans from the sight of the enemy. In that fog, the Yankees under George Washington fled to the north end of Manhattan.

Washington's army was still in danger, however, and he desperately needed information as to the Britishers' next move. He appealed to Colonel Knowlton to find him an officer who would go behind enemy lines and report on British activities. When the colonel called volunteers, Nathan Hale, recently discharged from the hospital after being wounded on Long Island, was the only man who offered himself for this dangerous mission.

A fellow officer and classmate at Yale drew Nathan Hale aside. "Don't be a fool, Nathan," he said. "Let someone else volunteer. There are plenty of others."

"Who?" Hale asked pointedly.

There was no reply to this question. Hale accepted the assignment and was sent at once to George Washington for instructions.

"Captain Hale," the great general began, "your task is to spy. You are to rid yourself of your uniform and land secretly on the Long Island shore. You will gather detailed information as to what the British are doing, and when you have a complete report, you will return to me here. Report to no one else!"

Three nights later, Nathan Hale was landed at Huntington Bay, Long Island. For the following week he wandered unmolested over Long Island. By the end of it, he had a complete record of all British activities and plans. He knew how many troops were on Long Island, how many more were coming and when and where they would go next. Finally, he shipped aboard an oyster schooner and landed in Manhattan, where he learned that Lord Howe, the British supreme commander, had just set himself up in new head-quarters.

Now his mission had been accomplished and he could simply walk along the East River and hail a passing boatman to take him across to the area on the mainland under the control of the Continental forces. The river was patrolled by guards, but they were known to be lax; in fact, at Harlem Creek, where American and British sentries were in sight of each other, the enemies often exchanged tobacco and other commodities across the so-called lines.

Hale noticed the British brig *Niger* anchored offshore near Montressor's Island. He hailed it and asked for a small boat to row him across. When he was taken out to the *Niger,* he introduced himself as Nathan Hale, a Yankee schoolteacher who was tired of war and wished to go back to his old profession. The captain of the *Niger,* Talbot by name, agreed to have him taken across.

Then an amazing coincidence took place, one so strange that no author would dare include it in a work of fiction. Just as Hale was about to step into the skiff, a Lieutenant Quarme came aboard the *Niger* and was introduced to Hale and told his story. "That is very strange," Quarme said. "Did you say *Hale?* It sounds impossible, but we have just taken aboard our ship, the *Halifax,* another Yankee named Hale." Quarme went on to explain that the man aboard his ship had been discovered in a tavern, and, although opposed to the rebels, refused to join the British Army. He was brought aboard the *Halifax,* where it was thought he might be useful in a civilian capacity.

This curious coincidence mystified Captain Talbot, as it has mystified every historian who learned of it later. Why were two men named Hale so close together behind the British lines and under identical conditions? That question has never been answered.

The two Hales were brought together. Quarme had told Talbot that the man aboard the *Halifax* called himself John

Strong Hale, but when Nathan confronted the other, he exclaimed: "Your name is not John Strong Hale. You are my first cousin, Samuel Hale."

"That's right, Nathan, I am. But what are you doing aboard this brig? When I last heard from you, you were with Washington's army. Aren't you in the Continental Army any longer?"

The game was up. Nathan Hale finally had to admit that he was a Yankee officer, spying for General Washington. Captain Talbot immediately called a detail of men and ordered Hale taken to the brig and carefully searched. His coat, breeches, shirt, the lining of his hat and even his hose were searched in vain. But when a sailor ran his knife between the soles of Hale's shoes, a thin paper fluttered onto the deck. On that paper were Hale's notes, written in Latin. They were soon deciphered, revealing the extent of the Yankee spy's information.

Two days later, Nathan Hale was ushered into the presence of Lord Howe himself. Lieutenant Quarme was with him and explained in detail the various charges against the American. When the lieutenant had finished his recital, Howe threw up his hands in disgust and asked Hale, "Why did you do all this?"

"To serve my country, sir!" Nathan Hale answered.

"How would you like to serve *my* country?" asked the general.

"That can never be."

Howe crashed his fist against the table. "Then, by God, sir, you may die for yours!"

Three days later, just before Nathan Hale was due to be executed, he sat in a small tent near what is now the corner of First Avenue and Forty-Sixth Street, New York, composing a farewell letter to his superior officer, Colonel Knowlton. He did not know that the colonel had been killed a week before in battle, but the letter would never have reached its destination anyway. As Hale finished writing, the provost marshal entered the tent, snatched the sheet of paper, read it and tore it to shreds, saying: "That letter will never be delivered. We cannot let the rebels know that they had a man in their army who faced death with such firmness."

A tree was to serve as a gallows for Hale and an open grave beneath it awaited him. The British arranged themselves in a circle around the tree as Hale mounted his coffin. Then the hangman threw a rope over a branch and tightened the noose around the condemned man's neck. "Well, young fellow," the provost said, "what have you to say for yourself?"

Nathan Hale's answer was low, but it was heard distinctly by every person present:

"I only regret that I have but one life to lose for my country."

"Swing him off!" came the cry, and Nathan Hale stepped from the coffin into eternity.

When the old houses at the corner of Forty-Sixth Street and First Avenue were torn down to make way for the United Nations, the plaque which commemorated Nathan Hale's execution near that site was removed. But as I stood on the busy corner, I thought how fitting it was that the buildings for this world organization should be erected where the peace-loving schoolteacher from Connecticut made the greatest sacrifice of the American Revolution.

The End

ISLANDS INCLUDED IN THIS VOLUME

INDEX

335